CW01025134

Ompteda of the King's German Legion

Ompteda of the King's German Legion
A Hanoverian Officer on Campaign Against Napoleon

Based on the letters and diaries of

Christian von Ompteda

edited and with a commentary
by his grandson
Louis von Ompteda

LEONAUR

Ompteda of the King's German Legion: a Hanoverian Officer
on Campaign Against Napoleon
Based on the letters and diaries of Christian von Ompteda
edited and with a commentary by his grandson
Louis von Ompteda

Published by Leonaur Ltd

ISBN: 978-1-84677-418-8 (hardcover)
ISBN: 978-1-84677-417-1 (softcover)

http://www.leonaur.com

Publisher's Notes

The views expressed in this book are not necessarily
those of the publisher.

Contents

Preface

The following Memoirs of Christian von Ompteda have been edited by his grandnephew, Baron Louis von Ompteda, who has made use, for that purpose, primarily of the letters and diaries of his grand-uncle, and the personal literary remains of the late Baron Louis, Christian's brother, secondarily of the following works: *History of the King's German Legion*, by L. Beamish, translated by Major Heise. Hanover 1832: The Service Journals of the Infantry Battalions of the King's German Legion, 1803 to 1815; *History of the Royal Hanoverian Army*, by L. von Sichart, 1631 to 1803. Hanover 1866-70; *Life of Field Marshal Count Neithardt von Gneisenau*, by G. H. Pertz and Professor H. Delbrück. Berlin 1864-80; *Scharnhorst*, by Max Lehmann. Leipzig 1886. *German History from the Death of Frederick the Great to the Founding of the German Confederation*, by L. Häusser. Berlin 1861-3.; *German History in the Nineteenth Century*, by H. von Treitschke. Leipzig 1886-9.

It is thought that the publication of this work in English will be found to be justified by its contents, both as regards the wider historic interest of the momentous period of Ompteda's life and death, and the narrower personal interest of the forms of human character, incident, and vicissitude set forth. The hero who now lies at the gate of La Haye Sainte deserves to be remembered by English people certainly not less than by other people for whom he died.

7

The English reader of the later nineteenth century, habitually shy of ceremony and suspicious of sentiment, may not unnaturally think Christian Ompteda's language affected or over-sensitive, unless reminded that such copious and unreserved expression of feeling belonged to the place and time in which he grew up, a period when the cultivated world of Germany and elsewhere was as wildly Wertherist as it subsequently became gloomily Byronic.

Christian Ompteda is really quite genuine and natural when he repeatedly assures his brothers of his lasting affection, and his friends of his profound esteem—feelings modern brothers and friends would perhaps take for granted. The man's natural simplicity and nobility of character are to be discerned behind the veil of the style, now almost archaic, of only *a hundred years ago*.

J. H.

CHAPTER 1

Youth and Early Training
1765—1792

Christian Frederick William, Baron Ompteda, derived his descent from an ancient race of Frisian nobles and chieftains, which had its seat from time immemorial, ascertainably from 1317, at Ompta in Fivelgo, on the western side of the Dollart, in what is now the province of Gröningen. His ancestor, Henry Ompteda, being a patriot and a Protestant, was obliged to fly from the Catholic Spanish authorities into the neighbouring and allied province of East Friesland, in the year 1580. From thence he migrated to the principality of Lüneburg, and was, at the time of his death, privy councillor and steward of Scharnbeck, at that time a territorial lordship near the city of Lüneburg. His sons inherited property in the county of Hoya, near Thedinghausen, and in the Würden country, a part of Oldenburg, on the right bank of the Weser, and above the present Bremerhaven.

There the family abode, and there, on November 26th, 1765, on the paternal estate of Wulmstorf, Christian was born, the eldest child of his parents. His mother belonged to the originally Scottish family of Von Bonar de Rossie. One of her ancestors had fought in the Swedish and Danish armies during the Thirty Years' War, and afterwards settled in the Duchy of Bremen.

When Christian's father, High Bailiff John Henry Ompteda, was driven by undeserved losses of property to alienate his inherited allodial estate and take an official situation at Ahlden, the boy, then six years old (1771), entered the family of his uncle, Court-Councillor Theodoric Henry Louis von Ompteda, *where* (according to the record of his next brother, Louis) "he received that refined education the impression of which he bore all his life."

This foster-father or guardian, both a man of the world and an accomplished jurist, became twenty years later electoral Hanoverian Deputy to the Reichstag at Regensburg, and there became one of the leading members of that illustrious body (though perchance that distinction is not by itself particularly striking), as well as a publicist and writer prominent above his contemporaries.

In the year 1777 Christian (then barely twelve) entered the Royal Corps of Pages at Hanover, and in that capacity began his military career. In 1781 the sixteen-year-old page received his appointment as ensign *(Fähndrich)* in the Foot Guards, it being at that time ten years since the loss of his father.

As regards his general progress up to this time, and further till 1785, information is lacking. But, taking into consideration the ripeness of education which the young officer displays when we meet him a few years later, we are bound to conclude that the training of the page was good, and that both capacity and tendency became markedly effective in him at an early age.

In 1787, at Easter, the brother Louis (born 1767) entered the University of Göttingen. There begins from that time a correspondence, which continued for twenty-eight years, whenever the brothers were separated.

The end of the year and the beginning of the next Christian spent in the house of his friend Court-councillor von Vrints, president of the local Taxis [1] Postal Department.

There he heard, on January 10th, 1781, of his promotion to Lieutenant *{Premier-Lieutenant).*

In the summer of 1789 Christian was again with his friends at Rheden. From Hanover, September 7th, 1789, he expresses to his brother Louis the warmest desire to live with him as much as possible in the future.

You know how often I have made known my wish to spend a good long while studying with you in Göttingen. A combination of difficulties which mar my life here, doubles and trebles

---

1. The princely House of Thurn and Taxis had for a long time the monopoly of the postal arrangements in a large part of Germany.

my desire to be with you where you are. You are further aware what sort of a position I have striven (?) for two years to get, how for its sake I gave up the great project of travelling to the south of France with Court-councillor Böhmer, and how I have been given some hopes here. These seem inclined to dissolve. I got a competitor, who opened for himself channels of which I neither may nor will avail myself. You know my unspeakable disinclination for all intrigue, cabal, and solicitation. I have gone a simple way to attain my purposes—purposes more suggested by others than my own. I disdain the patronage of our lady aunt (or cousin); it would not perhaps be very difficult for me to get hold of something of the kind. What with these opinions, this dilatory uncertainty, and the embarrassment which I seem to occasion in various people, I should like to get out of the whole business, and seek my consolation and joy more surely with you and the Muses than in all this pitiful place-hunting here. I can readily see that half a year would be an inconsiderable time to spend at a University, and that one would only be able to enjoy a few drops out of the ocean. But as I do not contemplate studying for a livelihood, but merely philosophic and literary matters, and as I want to acquire a certain systematic order for these studies in order to make better progress, and rearrange (as I know very well already) in a better and more useful way the fragments I have collected, it seems to me that even so short a time could be of substantial utility, especially as I should have you to give me guidance in so many matters.

Then followed negotiations with the guardian, the captain in the 11th Infantry regiment, John Frederick Ompteda, at Lüneburg, to obtain his financial consent. From this we learn that the income of the young lieutenant in the Guards came to eighty marks a month, so that for a half year in Göttingen he would require about five hundred marks more.

The faithful servant, Hegener, would be taken too, and would save the expense of the barber (in those days a daily necessity), of the boot-cleaner, tailor's man, and housekeeper (probably housemaid).

The brothers spent the following winter of 1789-90 in Göttingen, in the most intimate intellectual association, if not actually under the same roof. Christian was an inmate in the house of Alexander Humboldt, who lived separately from his retiring brother William. Social intercourse, properly speaking, only took place with Alexander. Besides him there joined the very limited circle a son of Vrints from Bremen, who had left the French military service on the outbreak of the Revolution, and was preparing himself in Göttingen for his subsequent position in the Taxis Postal Department at Frank-fort-on-the-Maine. To these was added another French officer, the Marquis de Cepoy, with whose fortunes the brothers were later concerned.

At Easter 1790 both went back to Hanover, and shared a home with the youngest brother Ferdinand, then in the Foot Guards, wherefore there were no letters between them. Still we know that they were in intimate association with the circle of high officials then known as the Second Rank, with Brandes, Rehberg, the author of *On the German Nobility, The Art of Education Examined*, and other then recognised works. Among others the brothers knew very well the Court-councillor Küstner, and his wife, born Charlotte Buff, the original of Werther's Lotte.

In the autumn of the year 1791 the brother Louis was sent to Dresden as Secretary to the Legation. Hereupon Christian's letters begin again. Louis appears to have been sorry to leave his home for the, to him, strange, and at that time very far-off world of Dresden. Fie describes himself in his Memoirs as having been awkward and shy in society.

With reference to this, his elder brother Christian (still far ahead of him in ripeness of manhood), says:

November 3rd, 1791: I hope, as a result of your journey, that agreeable impressions have been able to obliterate the very natural grief you felt at leaving a place where there are so many persons and relationships which you should and do most properly value.

I myself might have much to say on this subject if I had not continually before my eyes the truth, confirmed by many a sorrowful experience, that this flinging about to cast and west and north and south is part of the destiny of us men, and that we have no right to complain when we, or those dear to us, are sent away into some position, whatever it may be, which will not only be advantageous to them for the whole of their remaining life, but also, in many respects, an extremely pleasant situation for them. I tell you, I know that when I see you here again in a couple of years' time, you will again begin to carry on the most prosperous existence, all on account of your present post. Many of your friends have said to me very nice things about you. I will only mention, without naming, a person much valued by me, from whom I have the greatest pleasure in sending you a greeting, which I take it you will not receive with indifference. She thinks a great deal of you, and that is worth much, very much, coming from her.

The next letter contains the news—soon afterwards discovered to be untrue—

Hanover, November 27th, 1791: . . . . that the King of France has taken to flight, and more successfully than the first time, out of the country. As soon as he got across the frontier he put himself at the head of twelve thousand Imperial troops, and seized Valenciennes. I assure you that this news, setting on one side the trouble I see ahead for poor France in consequence of it, is a source of real satisfaction to me. You know whether any one hates despotism and a corrupt aristocracy worse than I do. But an ochlocracy[2] I dread still more, and that, with its sister anarchy, was all that a people was led to by its sublime metaphysical theories, a people seemingly incapable of legal and rational liberty, or a constitution which will adapt itself to circumstances, and not circumstances to it (that of 1789). In the end, it is to be hoped, after the present tumult, that order will again prevail, and I hope that the spirit of the century will prevent its being a peace like that of Charles V. in Spain, or towards the end of Philip II.—viz., peace of the grave. If I could only help, instead of looking on! I feel more than ever like Shakespeare's Hotspur—*that life demands action.*

But God knows how. I am not decided myself. But if I could clash into the most raging part of the storm I think it would do me good. Then again, when I reflect that rest and peace are the best things for our good Fatherland, which deserves so much devotion, I don't know my way out of the dilemma.

---

2. Gr. a mob.

A great part of the contents of the letters of this and following years consists of information about personalities and social
occurrences, which are here omitted.

Hanover, December 1st, 1791: I cannot tell you, my dear Louis,
what pleasure your letters give me. There are people who think
me cold. I am not; but it is often true that the disquiet which
stirs almost perpetually within me renders me impervious to
many impressions from without. But the happiness of those near
to me in spirit is not one of the things I am insensible to, and I
am convinced that I love you sincerely by the lively joy which
every intelligence of your happiness and contentment brings
me. I am always more firmly established in the belief that your
life at Dresden will be full of pleasant features, and the description of your house where you live, and the installation on both
floors, is an extra confirmation of that belief.

The brother lived with his ambassador, the Count Hardenberg, at the house of the Countess Schall, who also received
him very kindly.

He who is drawn by his calling into the great world, or into
life in large cities, must find his pleasure chiefly in larger or
smaller social relationships, and you seem to have both kinds
most favourably to hand without the trouble of crossing your
threshold. In order to heighten my joy by seeking the fullest
and most feeling sympathy, I took it into my head to show your
last letter to the lady, who, possessing the noblest and tenderest
qualities of feminine nature, always unfolding themselves more
gloriously, becomes daily more dear to me. She is a true friend
to you. Were she even less so, she still possesses, in all matters to
which she is a third party, a discretion rare among women. She
told me she would shortly give me a letter' for you, but you
know how, and on whose account, she lives in perpetual anxiety, and in consequence has to be very cautious in choosing her
time for writing.

Concerning the future Duke, then Prince Frederick William of Brunswick, who remained on the field of Quatre Bras,
June 16th, 1815, Christian observes:

We have just now got here the youngest prince of Brunswick, William, who is passing through on his way to a tour in the Netherlands. You must know that he is his father's favourite, and according to general opinion seems to deserve it. His demeanour is polite and kind, and his intellect seems naturally good, and not uncultivated. This gave me an opportunity of hearing a moving *trait* of the Duke" (Charles William Ferdinand, who afterwards died of his wounds, received at the battle of Auerstadt). "You know how imbecile nearly all the other princes are; well, as he presented this his favourite young son to the King of Prussia, he said, with tears in his eyes, '*Sire, void le dernier des Bronsvics*' The prince is major in the regiment of Kalkstein, and has already, as a distinction from the other brothers, the Order of the Black Eagle.

Hanover, December 4th, 1791: I write to you again already, dear Louis, because I cannot let the slightest postponement deprive you of the pleasure the enclosed must give you. Yes, must give you! For if even a different interest on your part does not permit the degree of joy which lines traced by this dear hand have often brought me, nevertheless there is so much amiability and friendship in the way she thinks of you, and in the obliging kindness manifested by the enclosed, and I know you so well, that I can safely imagine your pleasure. I need not ask you to send the answer to me, but rather, if your correspondence with *him* progresses, to let it pass through me.

The brother had in the meantime very soon accommodated himself to Dresden life.

Hanover, December 8th, 1791: I have looked after your letter to Brandes, and read it. I would not willingly have been deprived of the news contained in it. It is extremely interesting. I am glad, as a Hanoverian, of the favourable comparison of Hanover in view of the ideas circulating in the larger state, the freedom of speech and writing, and its many intellectual and material advantages. But I think it is none the less a pleasing thing for you to find a kind of compensation in the arts of music and painting, at Dresden, both as material in Hardenberg for conversation, and for their own sake, and also suitable to your intellectual pursuits.

Hanover, December 22nd, 1791: I have seen to your letter, but not yet spoken to the dear person to whom it is directed since she can have had time to read it. This will serve you, by the way, as guide how often I have the happiness to see her.

In the meantime Christian's position and mental anxiety had awakened the sympathy of his friends. His trusty old patron, Court-councillor von Vrints, in Bremen, had opened a prospect to the young man of becoming tutor to the Hereditary Prince of Oldenburg (a position which had been honourably filled by an Ompteda one hundred and fifty years before). But Christian declined. He said, "I am not made for the post, and I should be very sorry to cast myself permanently adrift from Hanover, had I no weightier and worthier grounds for wishing to remain where I am." The brother advised him to take it. In support of his refusal Christian writes:

Hanover, January 8th, 1792: You are really too partial, dear L., if you believe me to be endowed with all the qualities demanded of one following the calling of tutor. Could I reckon on the necessary amount of calmness and self-control, could I even answer for their success on my own self, I might perhaps come to the determination to sacrifice all my own concerns for the sake of such an important and useful thing as the education of a future reigning prince certainly is in this world. But what would have come of it, and of me, if, with all the dubious uncertainty which surrounds in a general way all that can be called educating youth, I could not reckon with certainty on myself? If I could free myself from my own embarrassments! So it is evidently better for me to have refused.

Hanover, January 22nd, 1792: The reason I did not mention to you Wallmoden's death" (a mutual friend, eldest son of the future Field Marshal Wallmoden-Gimborn) "may have been that I find myself in a condition in which I have no perception of the strongest impressions, in which what immediately concerns me is a matter of indifference, in which I could smile when others weep, and weep when others laugh. From which you may deduce, dear L., that I am in a condition which it would be as well for me to alter. Also I have new projects, *for a change of scene.* For your consolation I may add that I am speaking, not only according to my own feeling, but with the knowledge of others, so that you need not fear anything extravagant.

A project was on foot to accompany the son of the Duke of Ursel, a Netherlander, to Göttingen, and subsequently to go on a tour. While negotiations were still going on, Christian wrote (He had at first suggested other persons to his friend Vrints, at the proposal of the latter.):

Hanover, February 5th, 1792: In the meantime the fretting storm of inward strife had increased, as I need not describe to you, with the solitary, rare, and lovely moments which the most noble and amiable lady vouchsafed to me, in her celestial character and disposition. Sunk in bitter melancholy, enfeebled in my forces, lost to all but her, to whom I might not be that which alone could raise me again to good and noble altitudes, limited and constrained by my insufficient circumstances, progressing downwards in all the phases of my being, moments must necessarily arrive in which it seemed evident to me that to grasp at any useful occupation, even an unpleasant one, were for me the only issue possible. Brandes advised it with all his might. She would not decide, but approved of this project as much superior to any Oldenburg one. And I had at least the consolation that I need not look forward to any permanent separation. So I wrote to Vrints and offered myself. But shall I be suitable for the post? God forgive me if the poor Ursel is deceived in me. But I hope to pull what remains of my forces together so as to do what good I can,—and thereby to redeem many errors and reproaches of my storm-driven career.

The project broke down because the Duke of Ursel *could not abandon the stipulation of the Catholic religion.*

The next letters are calmer. The distant prospect of warlike activity begins to arise. Christian went again to his friends at Rheden, and the lady who was the friend of his heart travelled to South Germany with her husband. Regarding the deliberations then proceeding over the partition of Poland, Christian writes:

June 3rd, 1792: Although I take less interest than aforetime in worldly affairs, I am still sorry with you that the great lady of the North (Catherine II) is about to crush poor Poland out of pure benevolence. If this sad event should come to pass, may it so happen as Rousseau advised, in his *Sur le Gouvernement de Pologne,* the brave Poles *'Si les Rursses parviennent à vous engloutir, faites au moins qu'ils ne puissent vous digérer!* If you have not done so, I advise you to read this treatise of Rousseau, because it—besides the observations on the Polish situation—contains more practical sense than his speculations on the *Contrat social.*

Rheden, July 13th: I go back to Hanover the day after tomorrow, very much against my will. What I shall do there for my salvation and benefit, I do not for my part know. I can hardly calculate on going on guard very frequently. But here also I am driven by the evil demons of anxiety, and the feeling of not being the agreeable associate which I otherwise might be and would be increases the pain of such a state of mind. My bodily health has gained greatly by the Pyrmont waters, although not completely rehabilitated. That is certainly what I hoped. But *complete* and *gratification of wishes* are demands too large for this sublunary world.

In the meantime the brother Louis' chief in Dresden, Count Hardenberg, was changed to Vienna, and the War-councillor Bremer (younger brother of the future minister and Count Bremer) nominated ambassador to Dresden. He invited Christian, who was a friend of his, to make the journey with him, and spend the winter with him and Christian's brother in Dresden. Christian eagerly accepted the proposal in order to get out of Hanover for a considerable time.

The route lay through Berlin, where they arrived on October 18th, proposing to stay about a fortnight. The joyful anticipation of both brothers was great, but a few days afterwards all these fair projects came to grief. They became involved in the world's history. In the course of the month of October the Austrian-Prussian army started its retreat from Champagne. On October 21st the fortress of Mainz capitulated to Custine. In Hanover those on leave were summoned back to their regiments.

In the Reichstag at Regensburg it was resolved to raise an army *in triplo* (= 120,000 men). According to the Act of 1681, the Hanoverian contingent to this should consist of:

	Cavalry	Infantry
Hanover	1053	2375
Osnabrück	78	237
Müulhausen		100
Nordhausen		30
	1131	2742
Total		3873 men

Field Marshal Freytag undertook to form this contingent forthwith.

Christian now saw the fulfilling of his old longing for active service. In any case his duty called him back to his corps. He writes from Berlin in the greatest haste and excitement:

Man proposes, God disposes. Instead of me, dear L., you will receive these lines. Bremer will tell you the rest. My regret at being so near, and yet not seeing you, is softened by the hope of folding you in my arms before the end of the year. I do not believe that we shall have anything serious to do. If we do, I hope it will be done most honourably, and that exalts me.

Hanover, November 8th, 1792: I was sure, knowing your love for me, that the disappointment would make you ill. Still no other course was open to me than to go back from Berlin, in spite of the fact that my presence here is superfluous. (The Foot Guards did not form part of the contingent.) But I hope we shall meet again. Only a little patience, and all will settle down again, and really there has been a great deal of unnecessary fuss made here.

Hanover, November 18th, 1792: In your expressions about our so near and yet abandoned prospect of meeting again, I recognise all your brotherly love. It is superfluous to say that this disappointment has also affected me. And yet, pardon me for saying it, Hanover contains something too precious to me to make the idea of my coming back repugnant to me. You understand this, and will not misinterpret my candour. Nevertheless I do really wish to follow out Bremer's friendly plan for the Dresden journey to be undertaken after all. On the probability of it, I can at present say nothing, for up to now, even the officers of the regiment who wanted their usual leave in the country here cannot get away. Under the circumstances you will see that I cannot very well make my request more pressing to (Field Marshal) Freytag at such a time. But there is a crisis going on, which must soon decide both great and small fortunes.

The journey never took place, owing to the mobilisation of the whole of the Hanoverian troops. The rapidity of this mobilisation is a remarkable feat for the War Office of the period.

The French had, in the meantime, at the close of the year 1792, advanced on Holland. George III determined therefore to place an English army there, and to add to this an *Auxiliary Corps* of from 12,000 to 13,000 men of his Hanoverian troops in English pay. The contingent was in eluded in this. Prussia made vigorous efforts to have the latter left to push to the Rhine. But King George replied, that—

> .... he would only let his contingent advance with a national army, to which all states contributed ; moreover, that he did not recognise the *protective* policy of the Allied Powers (Austria and Prussia) in their operations.

In the meantime, the Prince Josiah von Coburg-Saalfeld had been nominated Field Marshal Commanding-in-Chief (for Germany). When he found, after the lapse of months, that no Hanoverian contingent arrived, he sent to the Hanoverian Ministry to invite them to set the contingent on the march. He received the reply that:

> That His Majesty had already placed his contingent in marching order, but seeing the incredible dilatoriness of formation of the national army, thought he had the best reasons for making use of his own army corps, which His Majesty had ordered to march to defend the United Netherlands from the danger which threatens them, whereby in the holding and repelling of the common enemy, it (the army corps) would do the greatest immediate service to the German fatherland.

And there it rested. Meanwhile the Auxiliary Corps had travelled a long way, and in May 1793 Christian stood, with his regiment, in the Netherlands.

Here ends, properly speaking, the youth of the man to whom these pages are devoted. From the *Lehrjahre* of his life we now come to that *Wanderjahre*, which only ended with his glorious death. It will be therefore fitting to insert here a sketch of his personality, derived from the testimony of his relatives, as well as of his elder and younger comrades. In putting together the features of this portrait, a few will be omitted, which only made themselves conspicuous in later years, and after his final departure were given over to his family, through the loving recollection of some of his younger subordinates. To this let the reader be good enough to add what he has gathered from the preceding pages, from the inner spiritual life, so hidden from the world, of the young man in the days of his development. We shall call him throughout these pages, through all his military grades, by the simple untitled human name of Christian Ompteda.

He was of unusual height, with a slender, but symmetrically proportioned build. In the army and at home he went by the nickname of *the long gentleman*. I remember in my youth a chair he had had made for him, of extraordinary depth of seat, and on such high legs, that the feet of people, of average build, sitting on it barely touched the ground. A good miniature of the date 1793 shows us Christian as a young man of twenty-seven years. A remarkably high and broad forehead, half-long blonde hair combed backward, and slightly powdered. Under finely curved brows, two mighty big blue eyes, earnest and deep, with an unmistakable tinge of melancholy. The nose curved with a fine bridge, thin, silent, shut lips, and the beardless fashion of the period. The civil costume consists of a single-breasted green coat, high white *batiste* cravat with a large knot, and under it a wide folded *jabot*.

His appearance was very attractive, and supported by a lofty and cultivated tone. His character was noble and morally pure, sustained by a strict sense of honour. His behaviour to others betokened a sympathetic goodwill, and his treatment of his brothers and relatives always testifies the greatest love, devotion, and care for their best interests. The education of younger members of his family he looked after with untiring-zeal.

His own scientific attainments were of great range. Principally through private study, he had fully mastered the English, French, and Italian languages, and read the Latin writers fluently. His favourite study was history, of which he possessed an extensive and grounded knowledge. Already at an early age his rare aptitude had manifested itself, and developed under the tuition of his extremely clever, learned, and cultivated uncle. Even King George III., who looked into all that concerned Hanover in detail, like a true *Landesvater*, got to know of his attainments when Christian was a page. Furthermore, in 1786, when the young princes were to be sent to Germany, he was repeatedly recommended to the king as one of their suite, and only refused on account of his youth.

As a handsome, entertaining, and accomplished man—he played the violin very well—he had the most favourable reception in society, which was readily open to him on account of his position and connections. But the activity and tendency of his mind soon led him to associate with riper, more imposing personages, such as Brandes, Böhmer, Rehberg, Küstner and his wife Charlotte, who did not frequent the so-called Court society. There he made close and lasting friendships. His critical faculty was keen and severe, but he applied it to others with mildness and toleration, unless he thought he had before him an actually dishonourable nature.

In his military career, to which he was heart and soul devoted, he gave the most zealous attention with all his forces, both to his own training and that of his subordinates. He exercised severe discipline, but with great justice. At the same time he sought unceasingly the welfare of those under his command, more particularly those of the lower classes, by which he earned the lasting love, attention, and respect of all.

The young man, whom we have accompanied hitherto through his early years, has exhibited to us, in his confidential letters to his brother, an unusually excitable temperament, and frequently, behind an externally calm demeanour, an inner life of strong passions. We learn at the same time to perceive the straining of a mighty and deed-hungering soul to escape from the trammels of narrow, perpetual, and deteriorating influences. An inward trouble hovers evidently over the otherwise bright spirit.

He had caught badly that complaint, that morbid, often stormy and fermenting state, later known, half-ironically, as *Weltschmerz*. He was, however, a highly gifted child of the *Werther* period. *The Sorrows of Werther* were not yet twenty years old (published 1774), and Christian Ompteda's mind was full of Albert and Lotte.

Wherefore it is extremely natural that his style of feeling, thinking, and writing, vivid, picturesque and objective as it was, should often contain traces of the celebrated romance which had seized on the German world with a greater magic force than its predecessor *Götz*. And his own conflicts were not unlike those of Werther. Two springs of conduct together moved the gifted youth—unsatisfied ambition, and an unhappy, hopeless passion for a lady who could not be his. This inclination was not un-responded to, but the contemporaries of this pair were strongly convinced that there was nothing impure in their relations, and that they both kept strictly within the bounds of duty. To this relation the clement of a *soul's friendship* was not wanting, which, to our latter-day minds, appears somewhat sentimental. The lady to whom Christian devoted a reverence so warm, so youthful, so creditable to himself, was at this time of his life already a mother, therefore more mature, and she outlived him more than twenty years. She enjoyed the warmest sympathy and most unlimited respect among all who knew her, both in her youth and her age. Her children lived with the older and younger relatives of Christian in great friendship, which received a mournful consecration in the common memory of the two distinguished people. May, therefore, those who come after that excellent lady, consider it a desire on my part to erect a memorial of pious respect, if I mention her name.

Henrietta von Wurmb, born 1766, married at seventeen (1783) the War-councillor von Reden (born 1754), and lived a married life dutiful rather than really affectionate. Reden had, both in the course of his duty as a diplomatist, and through restless strivings for things beyond his powers of attainment, roamed about the world a good deal (Rastadt, Mainz, Berlin,

Regensburg, Rome). He likewise involved himself in unsuccessful speculations, and in learned but futile literary efforts.

His talented, tender-hearted, and not inexperienced wife did not find in his company the satisfaction of the higher and more refined longings of her heart and mind. So, after several years of chilly wedlock, she returned with a warm, friendly affection the pure and tender passion of the warm-hearted and intellectual young officer, whom she frequently met in Hanover society, intentionally or accidentally.

The danger of the situation was not ignored by either of them. Henrietta desired and urged, as we know, the permanent absence of Christian from Hanover.

He himself struggled between renunciation and the attractive charm, and was inwardly delighted when circumstances repeatedly enabled him to postpone the parting.

So with its fullness of sorrow and joy closed the year 1792.

CHAPTER 2

The Campaign in the Low Countries
1793—1803

For the more ready insertion of the following events in the life of Christian Ompteda in their proper framework of time and place, in the expedition to the Netherlands, it will be desirable to briefly allude to the following historical facts.

After long negotiations, protracted through the jealousy of divided interests, and mutual mistrust of the Powers, after the lamentable issue of the campaign of 1792, the great coalition against the French Republic was called into existence in the early part of 1793. An army composed of Imperial, Prussian, and English-Hanoverian troops was collected on the Belgian frontier, roughly speaking along the line from Valenciennes to Dunkirk. Its nominal Commander-in-chief was the Imperial general, Field-Marshal Prince Josiah of Coburg-Saalfeld. The Austrians were under Generals Clairfait and the young Archduke Charles, the Prussians under Knobelsdorf. The Duke of York, twenty-eight years old, second son of King George III., commanded the English-Hanoverian army. The Hanoverians in particular, about 13,000 strong, were led by the seventy-three-year-old Field Marshal von Freytag; under him was the nineteen-year-old Prince Adolphus, Duke of Cambridge. Against this multiplicity of commanders the French were led by a single will, that of the Convention, and its Committee of Public Safety.

At the outset even the expectations of success in the approaching campaign were not great. The Duke Charles William Ferdinand of Brunswick writes about it from Frankfurt:

25

February 20th, 1793: If this chaos of political and military combinations leads to a prosperous outcome except by accident, I congratulate the leaders at the head of it. If one is not master of the needful resources, if one must request instead of commanding, if one has to negotiate for troops instead of leading them against the enemy, if, in point of fact, each of the Allied Powers seeks its own private ends, and the leading strings do not lie in one hand, one must either shut one's eyes, or hope that the same disunited policy will not lead to the same disadvantageous results which were at one time our good luck in the Seven Years' War.

These general shortcomings, and the consequent mistakes and failures in the conduct of the war, are reflected in the personal experiences of the young Hanoverian officer.

In the beginning of March the order was received in Hanover, from London, to have the Foot Guards in marching order by the 15th of the month. The regiment was wholly on its peace footing. The companies were strengthened from 150 to 170, a minority being taken from regiments that were not marching, but the majority freshly recruited peasant lads.

According to the organisation of that period, every infantry battalion had a Grenadier company in time of peace, while on a war footing four such companies were drawn from every four battalions, and combined into an additional Grenadier battalion. In this way the two battalions of the Foot Guards and the two battalions of the 10th Regiment of Foot had given up their Grenadier companies to form the 1st Grenadier battalion. This was brought into an unusual organic connection with two Light Dragoon regiments for the purposes of outpost duty.

In one of the Grenadier companies, from the Guards the author of the diary was senior lieutenant.

The formation of the 1st Grenadier battalion, to the command of which Major von der Wense of the 3rd Infantry was appointed, took place in Hanover on March 10th, and the march began on March 20th. On March 31st the battalion held its first out-door Divine service in the market-place of Rheine, in the Diocese of Minister. On April 2nd it was engaged for English service at Bentheim by Major Gun. On the same day it marched to Gildehaus in the county of Bentheim, the last place on German soil. Here begins the first entry in the diary.

Gildehaus, April 2nd: We have arrived here at the first place of assembly of our troops. The weather has been most favourable to their march. The successes quickly following on one another in Brabant, the confirmation of the news that Breda is taken, and so forth, make us feel with regret that we shall only have to follow in the train of the victorious army, without ever getting a glimpse of the enemy.

Enschede, April 6th, evening: We are here in a little town which presents a very Dutch appearance. Several factories give it a prosperous look. Externally it is clean, well-kept, and has a pleasant effect to the eye.

Our Grenadiers, who, without the least idea why, are deadly foes to the patriotic party, asked every casual passer-by or gazer as they marched, 'Syn ji Patriot?' ('Be'st patriot?'), and the answer always was, 'Alltyt Prinzisch!' ('On Prince's side for ever!'). There really is in this province, and particularly in Enschede, a large number of patriots who conceal their real convictions sullenly. I could not help smiling at the blind following of human party spirit. What can our soldier know of the difference between a patriot and an adherent of the Stadtholder? And yet, blindly, and without provocation, he is ready to go and break the neck of any one who dares to call himself a patriot. In such wise the excitable as well as the phlegmatic nations are ruled by sounds, the meaning of which they do not in the least understand.

I am quartered in the house of a former burgomaster, who was a colonel of patriots in one of the last disturbances. Since then he has, however, entirely changed his views. He is a regular Dutchman, and his whole appearance, including his costume, is suggestive of the kind of butterfly heroes whom the Prussians found it so easy to scatter.

Neighbourhood of Grave, April 15th, morning: On the 12th and 13th we made two marches through the Cleves country, a charming and fertile district, improved by cultivation, and by the benevolent hand of a Stadtholder of the province, who in former days had fine avenues made in every direction. Towards the border of the Duchy of Cleves the ground becomes unfruitful and the landscape less pleasing, until one gets over some rising ground into another district, that of Dutch Guelderland. On the right bank of the Maas one descries smiling meadows and pretty country houses scattered about, in the midst of which is the castle of Huen. From here I was sent to the Governor of Grave, the Dutch fortress on the other side of the Maas, to request a passage for our troops. He was Prince Christian of Darmstadt, a general in the service of the Republic, and received me very kindly.

As our Prince Ernest (Duke of Cumberland, afterwards King Ernest Augustus of Hanover) had come into the town yesterday, the Prince of Darmstadt showed us over the works himself. They had expected a siege, as at Breda, so had made ready for it, and traces of the inundation were still to be seen. The place is very strong, and the prince would not have failed to make a brave defence of it. Our quarters are in the neighbourhood of the fortress, but we leave to-day in order to reach Antwerp by the 19th. There we shall halt for a while, to assemble the whole army of Hanoverians, English, and Dutch.

Hoogstraaten in Brabant, April 19th: I took advantage of a day of rest spent at Tilburg to visit the celebrated Breda, which is about three (German) miles from Tilburg. Who would have believed six weeks ago, when all was amazement and confusion at the capture of Breda, that we, so short a time after, should drive in a simple *vergout* (kind of Dutch caléche) into a fortress whose re-capture, but for the revolt of Dumouriez, and the spontaneous evacuation of the place, would have been a tough undertaking for an army of 50,000 men!

When we were in the fortress and observed the works and the tremendous defensive appliances, we thanked Heaven for a blessing the magnitude of which only those who saw the place can grasp. The town is very fine, and the damage done by a few twenty-inch bombs not extensive. The fortifications have not suffered. The castle of the Prince of Orange, in which the French had quartered themselves, exhibits some traces of these savages, conspicuously in the case of a work of art, a monument to the honour of a prince of Nassau, by the hand of the famous Michael Angelo, for which large sums have several times been offered, now mutilated by these maniacs. The damage is irreparable. The arms of the hereditary Prince-Stadtholder, which have been knocked down everywhere, can be more easily replaced.

Here I saw for the first time (happily cast on a midden) the notorious Tree of Liberty. According to their practice, the French had stuck it up before the town-hall on entering the place. In its immediate proximity they erected a gallows for their enemies. Truly an excellent gathering of emblems of freedom ! The gallows was left standing, but the French knocked over the Tree before they retreated from Breda.

Tournay, May 3rd: During the last marches a spirit of insubordination[1] has been noticeable in a few companies of the infantry, engendered by too hasty promises and consequent misunderstandings, which threatened to become an open outbreak at Mechlin and Vilvorde. This phenomenon, hitherto unknown among Hanoverian troops, was the more bewildering because the greater part of the men demonstrated the greatest respect and attachment to their officers, and offered all to go to the front whenever volunteers might be required to attack the enemy.

I was sent with a written report to the Duke of York, whose headquarters were in Tournay, to acquaint His Royal Highness with the condition of affairs. On April 24th, at eight in the evening, I mounted my horse. As I crossed the market-place, just as tattoo was being beaten, and rode through the crowd, several soldiers reached their hands out to me, while others looked at me suspiciously.

From Brussels I proceeded by post-horses to Tournay, and was introduced to the cabinet of the Duke of York at eight in the morning of April 25th. His Royal Highness at once realised the importance of the matter. The Duke's first words were: 'I shall go there myself.' Shortly His Royal Highness added: 'What has been promised to the men must be fulfilled.'

---

1. It appears that disturbances took place in the 10th Regiment, because they complained that their English pay was not forthcoming, and that Grenadiers of that regiment were called upon to join in the complaints. About 150 Grenadiers out of all the four companies assembled in the market-place, and refused to march till their alleged rights were obtained.

An hour later the Duke started off, accompanied by an adjutant. I went some distance ahead with post-horses. Two hours from Brussels I learnt that our battalion had marched, despite the ill-will of a large portion of the men, and was quartered at Hall, a town between Brussels and Tournay. The unexpected arrival of the Duke made a great impression. His Royal Highness at once assembled several companies out of the nearest cantonments, proceeded in front of the line, and made known to the troops, through General von der Bussche: 'That their conduct had brought him thither; that the said conduct was highly criminal; that all promises made to them should be kept; that he would dispatch a courier forthwith for that purpose to His Majesty the King; but that His Royal Highness hoped, on the other hand, that the men would conduct themselves like good soldiers and brave fellows.'

This treatment, and the measure we took the next day, of reading aloud to the troops the *Articles of War* with the utmost military solemnity, brought everything back into its previous order. Each company sent its senior man as a deputation to their majors and captains to ask pardon and express their repentance for what had occurred. So this matter went into oblivion. The other regiments, especially the cavalry, blamed them loudly.

On April 26th we marched to Enghien. Thence I was again sent here (Tournay) in advance of the battalion. They wanted to put the infantry in barracks, which would again have caused great dissatisfaction, and I had great trouble in convincing the magistrate of Tournay that the men must be quartered in the burghers' houses.

On April 30th our battalion came in, in capital condition, and in spite of nearly six weeks' marching, looking as neat and set up as on parade, and made an evident impression on all the spectators. Even our recruits were sufficiently trained during the march. We hoped to get a few days' rest here, but the following day, May 1st, Captain von Löw, and two other officers, with one hundred and thirty men from the Grenadiers and 10th, were ordered to occupy the advanced post of Rüme, which lies on the French frontier.

On that same May-day was fought the important battle of Condé, between the French, and the Prince of Coburg and General Clairfait. This victory was decided by the bravery of the Austrians and Prussians, particularly the 2nd battalion of the Prussian Kalckstein regiment, and will, it is to be hoped, contribute largely to the general success of .the campaign. On the following day the French made a fresh attempt on our side, and so it happened that Captain von Löw and his detachment were the first of us to come in actual contact with the enemy.

I was orderly officer to the Duke of York that day. I reported myself at headquarters at the usual time—*i.e.,* between eight and nine. The Duke had already ridden out, at half-past four, I believe, towards the Prussian camp at St. Amand, which lies to our left. At headquarters I only found the orderly officers, and among them one from the Austrian cavalry, which, several divisions strong, was under the command of the Duke, and encamped in front of Tournay. The Imperial officer explained to me the perplexing position in which he found himself placed. He had just been sent by his colonel, the Count von Hohenzollern, commanding the Imperial cavalry, to inform the Duke that the French were advancing against the outposts, adding that it would be a good thing if some infantry were sent in support. The Duke and all his adjutants were absent. I went after the Field Marshal and General von der Bussche, but neither was to be found. We afterwards ascertained that they had themselves ridden to the outposts.

In this dilemma, I met the Duke coming back into the town, and reported to him what had occurred. He asked for the Field Marshal, and hearing that he was absent, went back to headquarters, made out some orders, and got on his horse again, accompanied by St. Leger, the above Imperial officer, and three Hanoverian orderly officers, among them myself. We galloped to the camp of the 10th, which had been near the Imperial cavalry since the day before, and the Duke ordered one battalion, under Colonel von Diepenbroick, to advance to the support of the post at Rüme. At the same time I was sent to order eight squadrons, of our cavalry, cantoned on the other side of Tournay,

31

to advance. This took some time, but I soon got back to the Duke, who had in the meantime gone to Rüme.

The state of things was as follows: A detachment of about one hundred and fifty French, with two guns, wanted to seize the post occupied by Captain von Löw. After being harassed for a while by French chasseurs, he opened fire on them. At the same time, about ten men of the Imperial cavalry, with a lieutenant, charged and took one gun from the enemy before it had been discharged six times. Shortly before this I had joined the Duke, and we hastened to meet the victorious Austrians as they brought in the captured cannon. The French fled hurriedly, leaving two killed, and fourteen prisoners, of whom five were wounded. Our generals, Freytag and Bussche, were both present. The battalion of von Diepenbroick and a squadron of Imperial cavalry were sent in pursuit of the enemy. The latter took refuge in a wood, which we could not sufficiently reconnoitre. We sent in a few cannon balls, which accelerated the flight, and spread such alarm among the inhabitants of a French village, against which we advanced, that they followed the example of the troops, and fled too. The French did not return our fire, though they had taken away with them one of their two guns. We pursued for a considerable distance into French territory, and it was not till four in the afternoon that the troops came back, as we did not wish to expose them further in a country much cut up by woods, with which we were insufficiently acquainted.

This first success, unimportant as it was, made a very favourable impression on our men. On our side there was only one man wounded, in the Imperial cavalry. The Imperial cavalry, like all the troops of which our army is composed, rightly, and in a high degree, deserve their reputation for bravery, of which they have given, and still give, such brilliant proofs. Particularly satisfactory, however, is the harmony which prevails between all these different troops under the Duke's command, Imperial, English, and Hanoverian. It is only between the Prussians and the Imperial forces that traces of the old animosity may be still detected.

The Guards quitted Hanover on March 20th, and arrived at Tournay on April 30th. From thence Christian writes to Louis in Dresden:

May 7th, 1793: Do not suppose, best and always sincerely beloved brother, that my long, long, unpardonable silence implies want of consideration or decrease of love for you. I have, since the time when I was so near you, and yet had to withdraw again (Berlin, October 1792), really been in a constant, and often very active state of movement and anxiety. In the first place, there was my expedition with General Wallmoden to Osnabrück, where it was certainly more peaceful than here, although a good deal of instructive work was done.

When the French, after the victory of Gemappe over the Austrians under Clairfait (November 6th, 1792), advanced far into Holland, the Hanoverian Government established a military *cordon* under General Count Wallmoden-Gimborn on the Dutch frontier at the end of January 1793. The troops, however, returned in a short time to the garrisons, in order to be mobilised for the auxiliary corps. Christian served on Wallmoden's staff.

Then came the untiring exertions which I, like all the other officers, had to devote to the mobilisation of the small military circle in which I worked, on my return to Hanover.

Our march, from March 20th to April 30th, when we arrived here; in the meantime the training of recruits; and, in the early days of the month, commissions of our generals, which I had to carry out. May 2nd, an engagement with outposts at Rüme, where I served as orderly officer to the Duke of York, and where we were fortunate enough, with the help of the brave Austrian cavalry, to take one gun, and fourteen prisoners, and could therefore thank Providence for a first success. All that can excuse me to some extent.

The relations of the seventy-three-year-old Field Marshal Freytag with the twenty-eight-year-old princely superior were from the outset seriously strained. Signs of this appeared even in this small first action. According to Sichart,[2] the proceedings were as follows:

---

2. Sichart's *History of the Royal Hanoverian Army*, 4., p. 207.

The Duke rode out in the morning to reconnoitre, and informed the Field Marshal to that effect. On his return he learnt that the French were attacking, and sought the Field Marshal and General von der Bussche, but found neither at home, because they too had ridden out to reconnoitre, which annoyed the Duke very much, because he had expected to find them in their quarters. The Duke then went to Rüme, but first ordered the Light Dragoons to advance. The Field Marshal, however forbade their marching, and it was only after fresh orders that they set out, but arrived too late. The Austrian Colonel, Count von Hohenzollern, who commanded the outposts, wanted to take the five guns, with which the French appeared, in the Duke's presence, but this *coup* could not be carried out because the Dragoons came too late, and only one gun was taken, to the great regret of the Duke. The Field Marshal declined to sit by the Duke at his table that day, and left before the joints were served.

The young orderly officer naturally does not confide this personal difference of his high superiors to paper.

Still I could, and should have written to you, and would have, had not the consciousness of my debt, and my perhaps exaggerated alarm at the quantity of the matter which I had to communicate, made me delay from post-day to post-day, from week to week, from month to month. I also assure you that in all my correspondence, the whole time I have only begun and continued one letter. My history during the last few months I can only give you very briefly. The fact that General Wallmoden made me adjutant of the Osnabrück *cordon*, of his own free choice, without seeking on my part, was a most flattering distinction for me. It did not last long. I came back because we *all* had to march. Prince Adolphus placed me in an embarrassing position by inviting me to accompany him on the campaign. Now I knew that I was already so appointed by the King himself. With your knowledge of the persons, you will understand that I declined the proffered honour, and requested to be allowed to remain with my regiment. Diepenbroick and Hammerstein, both generals, proposed to me to be their adjutant. I had only the one reply.

My present prospect is Charles Alten's place as captain, and chief adjutant, when it is vacant. I gain nothing by that except what is always first in my mind, the possibility of being useful. So I am first among the marching Hanoverians, and will quietly await the decision of fate in store for us all in general, and for my small individuality in particular, without troubling myself for my own interest except by being always ready for action. My regular—

Here the letter breaks off, and is continued:

Monceau (Outpost near Cambray), July 7th: On the night of May 7th—8th I had just written as far as ' regular' in the main guard-house at Tournay, when once more something much the reverse of regular occurred. It was the night of one of the hottest attacks of the French against the several armies—that of Prince Coburg at Quiéverain, that of General Clairfait at Vicogne, and the Prussians under Knobelsdorf at St. Amand. The latter were rather near our army-corps at Tournay, and our outposts were in close touch. Had the attacks extended to us, and energetically, we might have found it a very dangerous game. Our good genius averted this, and we only heard in the distance, yet very distinctly, the ceaseless thunder of a tremendous cannonade, which even experienced Prussian officers in Tournay did not altogether like. Just as I had written the word at which I broke off, there galloped in *a reeking messenger stewed in haste*, as Shakespeare says, a non-commissioned officer sent by General Knobelsdorf. He asked for the Prussian ammunition stores in Tournay, saying, 'Good heavens! our fellows have been under fire for forty-eight hours, and fired off all their ammunition!'

I did not know my way much about this extensive town of Tournay, my Grenadiers still less, and it was pitch dark. Fortunately I had (though unwillingly) given shelter to a Prussian ordered to Tournay in the guard-room, and with his help, and a little planning, I was able to accelerate this extremely urgent transport. Immediately afterwards the Duke of York marched with the English Guards and a couple of our battalions to the assistance of the Prussians. The above episode merely by the way. To go through the details of all the occurrences since then, even if I confined myself to what I personally saw would be impossible. If Custine should contemplate breaking through (our position) now, he would run his head against a proper stone wall.

But the French are very quiet, and since Famars (victory of the allies under Coburg, May 24th) nothing has happened in these parts except a few skirmishes, in which the French have invariably been driven back with broken heads.

My greatest pleasure is in concerning myself about the dear ones I have left behind. But I intend to be passive with regard to my own fate, but always ready for action.

Froidmont, village near Tournay, May 11th: At 8 a.m. a great battle began, but it was only against the Austrians and Prussians that the French directed the violence of their despair.

Since the French were driven out of the Austrian Netherlands by the bravery of the Imperial army, under Coburg and Clairfait, and since the Prussians united with the latter, under General von Knobelsdorf, and the English and Hanoverians under the Duke of York, and the Dutch under the Prince of Orange, advanced to the French frontier, the long line between France and Belgium from the sea, to beyond Valenciennes, has been occupied by the Allies.

On our arrival, at the beginning of this month, the positions of our armies were as follows:

The left wing, the most important, and the strongest of the whole position, was formed by the Prince of Coburg's army placed on the right bank of the Scheldt, so as to so far enclose Condé, that all connection between that fortress and the French army was cut off. Moreover, Coburg's army threatened Valenciennes on its eastward side. On the left bank of the Scheldt the army of Count von Clairfait completed the enclosure of Condé, and observed Valenciennes on the other side. The army of Clairfait was in close connection with the Prussians under General von Knobelsdorf, who had taken over the command on the withdrawal of the Duke Frederick of Brunswick, whose departure was generally regretted.

The Prussians made the communication in the camps of St. Amand and Maulde between the Austrians and us—*i.e.,* the army under the Duke of York which lay before Tournay, and one or two leagues further to the front towards Orchies.

On our right wing were the Dutch, whose main position was at Courtray.

Since the 7th inst. our battalion has been cantoned at Froidmont. The Light Dragoons, with whom we act, lie in two neighbouring villages. The rest of our troops, who have arrived up to the present, among whom, to our great joy, are the Horse Artillery, are encamped on the rising ground of Tournay. There are stationed there also a few thousand English, and three divisions of Imperial cavalry, whose experience instructs us, whose courage whets our ambition, and whose presence is altogether very important to us.

The two columns of our troops, among which are the Guards, might be with us now, but for a halt they had to make for a considerable time on the other side of Brussels. The reason of this delay was that the English commissariat had not been able to complete the stores. But in this particular General von Freytag took the most forcible and practical measures, and we hope to have the majority of our force collected here in about eight days' time.

In the meantime, the French have made desperate, but fruitless efforts to get back Condé, and drive back the Austrians and Prussians. Their attacks were extremely fierce.

We Hanoverians have taken part neither in the action of May 8th nor in any other important affair, while yesterday, before daybreak, the Austrians and Prussians surprised the French, killed many, captured several very troublesome entrenchments, and drove the enemy from a position in which they impeded the advance of the Allies, and delayed the taking of Condé, which probably will now soon fall.

Yesterday's butchery must have been fearful, for the Prussians and Hungarians gave the French no quarter, catching them asleep in their entrenchments, drunk from the previous day, and putting them to the bayonet.

The action of the 8th can have been in no way decisive, though wonders of courage were performed, particularly on the part of the English Guards, whom the Duke led to the support of the Prussians, who were greatly outnumbered by the French.

37

Froidmont, May 18th: A change is to take place in our position. Our army corps is to move tomorrow, and most likely join the army of the Prince of Coburg. This union with a victorious army of incomparable troops, under tried leaders, cannot fail to be very pleasant for us.

With the considerable reinforcement which we shall bring him, the Prince of Coburg will be in a position to advance further into the enemy's country, where, according to our information, disorder, dissatisfaction, depression, and civil war will facilitate our operations. It appears that the first ten lively days of this month have seen the last efforts of the French. For since then, with the exception of a few insignificant attacks on outposts, we have been entirely left in peace.

In our position in the neighbourhood of Tournay we shall be relieved by the Dutch troops. All that is required here is to protect the frontier from invasion. The true point of attack is the one which the Prince of Coburg has already successfully approached.

Wicheries, village one hour from Quiévrain, headquarters of the Prince of Coburg, May 21st: Our union with the Imperial army has taken place. The English and Hanoverians, forming the army corps of the Duke of York, have got here in two marches. Our battalion is in cantonment on the extreme left wing of this army, while the rest are encamped between here and Quiévrain.

This union is of the greatest importance, both for the Austrians and for us. Since the internal disturbances in France, particularly in Paris, have moved the National Convention to send for detachments from every company, with guns, from the army opposed to us, to be forwarded by post-horses, we expect our task to be all the lighter."

Famars Camp[3] May 24th, Afternoon: We have been so fortunate yesterday as to have fought a victorious battle, and now occupy the strong position on the heights where the French were

---

3. In the earliest antiquity a place sacred to the God of War, on D'Anville's map of ancient Gaul *Fanum Martis,* in the province of *Belgica Secunda.* Valenciennes, *Valentini-anae,* dating probably from the time when the Roman Emperors resided at Treves, is not to be found on that map, and Busching says (2. 801): "Famars, a village formerly called *Fanomarte, Fanum Martis,* had a district to which Valenciennes belonged."

yesterday, surrounded by several entrenchments, on which they reposed their last hopes.

Our troops fought with their old courage, which has attracted fresh attention on the part of the Austrians and English. The *Garde du Corps* distinguished itself extremely. Being unexpectedly brought into contact with several squadrons of French cavalry of greatly superior strength, a fierce encounter took place in which the hostile cavalry were completely repulsed. But this victory has cost us dear. Adelepsen was killed; Lieutenant-Colonel von Bülow, Captains (of cavalry) von Bülow and von Zedwitz are wounded. Bock has got two sabre-cuts on the arm, which are, however, not of importance.

The most unfortunate thing is that, as far as we can ascertain, Scheither, William Bülow, and the youngest Kielmansegge must be prisoners. It is stated that the French prisoners say they saw two of these officers being taken to Valenciennes.

Our battalion has been exposed only to an artillery fire, which did it no harm. The general loss, in comparison with the great importance of the success, has been but slight.

The *Garde du Corps,* the Life Guards, and the Light Dragoons and the 4th and 10th infantry, have found excellent occasion to distinguish themselves.

The advantages of yesterday's work are generally apparent. Clairfait and the Prussians have occupied the heights of Ancin. Valenciennes, lying between the two points, Famars and Ancin, will be under fire from both, and must probably soon fall into our hands.

There follows here a description of the battle of Famars, so far as the left wing of the Allied army under the Duke of York is concerned, to which the 1st Grenadier battalion belonged. It sets forth, and criticises what particularly was done or lost there. The report of Field Marshal Freytag to the King, of which we have the original, says little or nothing on these points. And the other reports, and the historical narratives which followed them, concern themselves exclusively with the storming of the French trenches and the cavalry engagement of the *Garde du Corps* in the centre, when Count Wallmoden commanded the Hanoverians under the Imperial

Master of Ordnance, Count Ferraris. And yet the left wing, if ably used at the right time, could have made the victory much more decisive. The description is entitled: *An account of what I saw and experienced in the Battle of Famars.*

Our army corps, which came from Tournay on May 21st, to which several more Hanoverian regiments, notably the two of Guards, had been added, quitted its position between Wicheries on the left and Quiévrain on the right to march up to Seeburg, where the main body of the Imperial army, under the Prince of Coburg, was encamped, exactly opposite to the French army. The latter, behind the tremendous entrenchments of Famars, their left supported by Valenciennes, and the Ronelle before their front (a small river, but owing to the steepness of its banks difficult to cross in presence of the enemy), took for granted a safety which afterwards became fatal to them.

Our army corps was at first marched to the left, which would ultimately have brought us into an extended line on the right flank of the enemy's army. This disposition, and a few hints I had picked up in Tournay, convinced me that a movement was intended with the object of turning the enemy's flank. This form of attack is one which attracts by its simplicity and its advantages, and is the manoeuvre by which Frederick II won the majority of his battles. I was extremely pleased to see it, and put great confidence in the successful outcome of our undertaking, which the happy result has since justified. As we, however, were not hitherto acquainted with the precise positions of the opposed armies, we were, as it were, thunderstruck when we met the Imperials at Seeburg. This was especially the case with our battalion, which was lodged in a corner of hollow ground by a village, from whence we could only see a small bit of the Imperial camp, and only those of our own regiments to the left of the Imperials and *in front* of us, though by rights and always observed custom *we* ought to have been in front. That little cause of dissatisfaction, however, was soon removed.

That day it was my turn for so-called fatigue-duty. As soon as the battalion had arrived, between 3 and 4 p.m., I got orders to fetch the battalion straw from the Imperial stores at Couroube, a good hour from Seeburg. This was annoying on the eve of a battle, but I had to go, and I went, and got back to the battalion with my convoy about 7 p.m. Nothing further, however, happened to us of the kind on that or the following day. But just at the moment when they were going to pitch tents, the order came to move at once, and on my arrival I found the tents ready struck. I had scarcely time to take some refreshments before I had to take post in the battalion again, which was already under arms. We went through the line in front of us, and four battalions, viz.—ours, the 2nd Grenadier battalion, and both the Guards—were formed at the distance of some hundred paces to the front of the camp, so that if the infantry should march to the left, these battalions would be leading. All the minor precautions usual before a battle with regard to arms, etc., were taken, and we remained bivouacking several hours till midnight. The night was cold and damp. The fires were left burning in order to deceive the enemy—a great and glorious sight! I went over for a minute to see my friends of the Guards, while the Grenadiers and most of the officers were sleeping by their arms, which I soon after did also. Shortly afterwards Marschalk came to see me. He explained to me something of the plan of attack. It was thought at our headquarters that the position of the enemy, on account of the river, could only be attacked by means of a few bridges defended by cannon, and it was contemplated to give us the honour of forcing these. With impatience we awaited the hour of dawn. At last we heard: 'Slope arms! By platoons, left wheel! March!' It was the Count Merveldt, one of the most distinguished of the Prince of Coburg's adjutants, who, being acquainted with the *terrain,* led our column. At the head of it were our generals, Freytag and Bussche, and we led. It was too dark to see what road we were traversing. If the eyes could not see, the ears were all the keener, and we marched in the strictest silence. The incessant 'Werda!' echoed in the distance from the hoarse throats of German and Hungarian soldiers, sentries at the outposts, not withdrawn in order to deceive the enemy. At first we heard the 'Werda!' before us—we were approaching the outposts line—and soon behind us as we marched through, and

41

echoing ever fainter in our rear. Soon we were halted for a time, then made to leave the road and march in the corn alongside, probably because the road itself was exposed to the hostile cannon. But on their side all was quiet, although I was expecting every minute to hear '*Qui vive!*' in place of 'Werda!'

We continued to advance. From the knowledge I subsequently obtained of the battle-field, which I went all over and got up thoroughly, I conclude that our column must have passed close to Jalain. Every one marched in the greatest order and silence. After we had marched for some time, but before daybreak, we came on a column of several regiments of Imperial cavalry, which were halted in perfect order in half-squadrons on our right. We also halted, the two columns being about two hundred paces asunder. The two regiments nearest to us were the Nassau-Usingen (which so distinguished itself in the action of March 18th) and the Karaczay. While our men were resting, several officers of the Imperial cavalry came over to us, and we soon struck up a very friendly chat–They were forbidden to smoke their pipes, but we had received no such prohibition. A few of them lit their pipes at ours, and we spoke of the attack about to take place, of the probability of its success, of our forces, and the resistance we might have to expect. One of the Imperial officers, whom I presumed from his stoutness and age to be a captain at least, expressed a general opinion on this war which I have found more and more confirmed as experience continued. 'Comrade,' he said, 'I think you'll find this a special sort of war. Usually it is only the cavalry and artillery that open the fight. Since their defeat in Brabant the enemy have lost the staying power to let an attack come on, and I don't believe it will come to small-arm fire at all. What happens is that the French do a cannonade, and then our cavalry go and take their guns.'

And such, indeed, was the fact, for, as far as I have been able to learn, with the exception of a Hungarian Grenadier battalion, which stormed an entrenchment before the centre of the position, near the part where our *Garde du Corps* delivered its attack, not a single infantry corps had a chance of distinguishing itself other than by steadiness under fire of opposing cannon, to which it was more or less exposed. Of our troops the 1st battalion 4th Regiment under Drechsel, and the two Grenadier companies of the same, were principally noticeable for firmness and coolness, being exposed to the strongest and longest fire.

Gradually it began to get light. The mist lasted a long time, and thickened. In the meantime another column of cavalry arrived, consisting of English and Hanoverian Light Dragoons, and placed itself on our left flank, at about the same distance as the Austrians were from our left.

Finally, there was a general advance. During this fresh march of a good half hour the sun at last came out, and scattered the mist which hid distant objects. When we got on the rising ground at the foot of which the Ronelle winds in a deep cut, we began to hear a few single shots, and then a continuous fire of skirmishers. That was our extreme advanced guard, consisting of Austrian Hussars, who had come into contact with the French outposts. The latter, placed on the left bank of the Ronelle, occupied the villages between Valenciennes and Quesnoy, namely, Artre, Sapmeries, Maresche, and Villerspol, which this little river ran through.

This was on our side the signal for a general attack. Our battalion deployed and went to the front. It was the first on the left flank, and the only one in the first line, as the cavalry on both flanks left no room for more (infantry) to deploy. The second battalion of our Grenadiers adopted the same formation fifty paces behind us, and I suppose that behind them the Guards did the same. By this manoeuvre there were several lines of infantry, one behind the other, which perhaps accounts for the French calling out as they broke and fled in excessive confusion: '*Sauve qui peut, Us sont dix contre un!*'

When we had advanced a few hundred paces, we got on the downward slope of the hill. In front of our right flank was the village of Maresche, in front of our left that of Villerspol, and straight beyond them, barely an hour's distance, the fortress of Quesnoy, which we saw distinctly. As the outpost skirmish in front and below us continued, our Captain Bremer with-his company was detached to go to the support of the Hussars.

But he was too late. When he got there he found that the Hussars had already driven the enemy out. The rest of the battalion halted, as did the other deployed troops.

On the opposite heights, on the other side of the Ronelle, we saw a considerable body of infantry and some cavalry making different hasty movements to one side and the other, as if doubtful whom to attack. Finally, they took to their favourite arm, which, it may be remarked, does not speak much for their personal courage. On the slope of their rising ground they placed several howitzers and cannon, and opened fire with that battery.

The first cannon-shot I saw fired at us made a quite different impression on me to that which it made on older soldiers, according to their admissions to me. It was a misapprehension on my part. I thought the range was too great, and laughed at it, and I was wrong. The balls went right and left over our heads, and inflicted some losses on the Prince of Wales' Light Dragoons. They even carried as far as the second line, where the Grenadier companies of the 5th and 6th, who had served in Gibraltar, and were *au fait* at that sort of thing, clucked their heads, and let the projectiles pass. Our Grenadiers stood very steadily, and as nearly all the lower classes, particularly the peasantry, have surprisingly long sight, they all regarded what was going on before us with the greatest attention, and my neighbours often helped me to verify observations I despaired on making, though my own eyesight is not bad.

In the meantime our horse-artillery under Captain Braun in this column was not idle, and replied very successfully to the enemy's fire. A howitzer of this battery set the village of Villerspol on fire.

But the cannonade did not last long. We soon perceived a swarm of light cavalry which suddenly opened out, and dashed at full speed at the (French) battery. We did not recognise them at first, but soon discovered them to be a detachment of one hundred to two hundred Austrian Hussars, who had worked their way through the difficult valley of the Ronelle, and charged with lightning speed on the hostile guns. The troops near them fell into the greatest confusion, and fled towards Quesnoy, while the Hussars cut down everything they could reach.

This attack was the finest thing possible to see, apart from the service it rendered to us. Had we at once taken advantage of that moment to detach a corps to the front, we might have taken the place (Quesnoy) by a *coup de main*.

As the ground was clear in front of us, several of our officers were of the opinion that our left wing ought to cross the Ronelle now at Maresche, and so throw ourselves by a *détour* round the right flank of the camp at Famars. But this did not yet happen, for they sent us off to the right to defile towards Préseau, whence the attack on the enemy's centre was directed. In this neighbourhood a fire of heavy guns had begun on several points, but we were sufficiently protected by the undulating ground, which stretches through the fertile land of southern Brabant, and Imperial and French Hainault. We halted in column. Several Imperial infantry regiments were in the same position. It seemed as if we were waiting for the extinction of the cannonade. As we had nothing to do, our men grounded their arms, and many stretched their wearied limbs on the ground. Most of the officers were at the head of the column, where with General Bussche and his staff we observed what was going on this side of Préseau. We saw several squadrons of our cavalry making various movements, and some in blue were advancing at full speed. Probably this was the attack of our *Garde du Corps*, who wore their blue capotes over their red uniform that day.

But as it was all too far off to discriminate properly, as I had no knowledge of the ground, and could form no clear idea of what was going on, as the excellent entrenchments of Famars straight in front of us were masked by an avenue of big trees, as I only take an interest in things I understand and have something to do with, and as I was beyond all things tired, I came to the conclusion to go back to my post, and lie down off the turf with my Grenadiers. And I fell into a soft slumber, only to be awakened again by the words 'Slope arms!'

It was Victor Alten who brought us an order from the Duke of York to carry out exactly the manoeuvre we contemplated at the time when the French corps retreated on Quesnoy. Our four battalions—namely, two of Grenadiers and two of Guards—

went back again, therefore, only in the reverse order; that is to say, the Guards leading instead of us, and led by Prince Adolphus, Duke of Cambridge, as was expressly prescribed in the order. We marched back to above Maresche, where we crossed the Ronelle. We did not go through the village, although it would have been the shortest way. It is very desirable to avoid defiles on such occasions, where there may be concealed enemies, or, as in this particular war, fanatical peasants, who could do us mischief. For this simple reason I always impressed on the men in my small sphere of activity not to fall out of their ranks or straggle. In spite of this clear and evident necessity, I witnessed the force of a certain human impulse which is stronger than any authority. It was thirst It will not be denied that eating and drinking are prime articles of faith to the Hanoverian soldier. Our men had fasted for twenty-four hours. So as soon as we approached the Ronelle they broke out like mad people to the bank of the little river to slake their thirst. It was impossible to control them, and some wretched hostile patrol might have made short work of the whole battalion. Fortunately the field was sufficiently clear of enemies to spare us such a disaster. Order was restored again gradually, and we marched on till after an hour and a half we reached Quérimain, which is a long cannon-shot in front of the right flank of the Famars camp.

This manoeuvre was excellent, and would have had the most complete success if only it had been fully carried out. I expected nothing else, and was congratulating myself beforehand on the pleasure of being among those who, in such brilliant style, would decide the fortune of the day on May 23rd, and perhaps sweep away a large portion of the French army. But that was not the only thing. The heights and clumps of wood behind which we had marched had hidden us so effectually from the enemy, that we were at Quérimain some time before they discovered us.

This happened from the following reasons: the battery situated on the extreme right wing of the position of Famars, which was likewise one of the most important, directed its fire unceasingly on the central attack, consequently in a direction quite different from ours. This continued for a considerable time, and at last, when they became aware of our presence, they fired on Quérimain, and we saw the shot *ricochet* without reaching us. Our amazement can, therefore, be imagined when we were rendered powerless by a 'Halt!' once more. And this at the happiest moment, and under the most favourable circumstances, just when I expected we should go round the village, get into line, and take the enemy's position by a rapid attack on the flank and rear, their defeat having had the way already prepared by the brave efforts of those troops who had overcome so many difficulties in the centre, more particularly by the attack of our *Garde du Corps*.

But we were condemned to inaction, so much so that our battalions went to sleep while the midday heat passed by.

Since then much has been said about the effect an attack from us might have had, *at the first moment of our arrival at Quérimain,* in spreading confusion among the enemy, who would have found themselves unexpectedly engaged on their flank.

Two reasons have been adduced for this attack not taking place. First, because General Bussche had no definite orders to that effect; second, because the French were so strongly entrenched that we should have had to sacrifice too many men in order to drive them out.

To these I reply: First, although the word *attack* was not literally contained in the Duke's orders, the whole disposition of the manoeuvre was such that they could bear no other meaning. Further, the commander-in-chief cannot be everywhere at once; and if those commanding under him cannot, make use of favourable moments when they occur (the general disposition of things not making the contrary their duty), I must say very few complete successes will ever be obtained.

But with regard to the second excuse, I readily admit, that after a subsequent careful inspection of the entrenchments we should have had to attack, I found them much stronger in reality than I had estimated them, but think that they would not have been so formidable as was supposed, *because they would not have been defended to the last with extreme obstinacy.* The approach to them consists of uneven ground, by which heavy gun fire would be rendered very uncertain in its direction. The last part of it is a deep dry ravine hindering an attack by cavalry, but not that of good infantry, whom, on the contrary, it would have sheltered from the enemy's fire as they crossed it.

If we add to these advantages of *terrain* the fact that the French were beginning to lose their heads, and were firing to a certain extent at random to cover their retreat, it is more than probable that an attack on the trenches would have cost us relatively few men, while we should have set against that the credit of taking a considerable number of guns, part of the enemy's camp, and their baggage.

But the sequel confirmed our views in an incontrovertible manner, for towards evening a considerable number of troops defiled into the part of the country where we were, nearly all the English, some Hungarian infantry, and some artillery, and the Duke of York started us off to attack the trenches, to which the French, in the meantime, had despatched a strong reinforcement of artillery. It was only on the representations of the Prince of Hohenlohe that the Duke then desisted from his purpose, and the next morning we were to advance to take them by storm. Indeed there was no choice. The trenches had got to be taken somehow, and if the French had made a better stand, we should never have found our favourable moment again.[4]

We bivouacked for the night in the neighbourhood of Quérimain, and as the different corps mostly camped out just in the order of their arrival, they presented a highly variegated spectacle. On our immediate right was the Hungarian regiment Sztaray, one of the most distinguished in this war. Their appearance, and their half-savage customs (for the Hungarian soldier, although brave and well disciplined, has a tincture of wildness), made a striking contrast to the elegance of the English Guards thirty paces behind them. But among these various nations, united by a mighty, just, and honourable cause in common brotherhood in arms, cordial union of exertions, hardships, and alas! also excesses (for there were some, this and the next day), there was

---

4. This description of the battle corrects those of von Witzleben, Prince Frederick Joseph of Coburg, 2., 181, *et seq.*, especially the incorrect statement about the Hanoverian artillery, p. 202.

48

one feature common to all—viz., fatigue and gnawing hunger. The baggage was two or three hours in the rear, and although we sent for it, General Wallmoden, who accidentally became aware of it, distinctly forbade it to advance. In truth our position, as well as that of the enemy, was not sufficiently established and known to make it safe to expose our effects to so many possible accidents. Instead of tents we had bushes to shelter us from the strong wind of a cold night. Nevertheless I do not remember to have often slept better than under this shelter, rolled in my cloak, a fire at my feet, and a soldier's knapsack under my head, among the other officers of the company. My faithful servant brought bread and beer to the relief of my hunger, which of course he had got from the nearest village, like the other marauders, but I enjoyed them a great deal too much to seriously rebuke him. On the 23rd, at sunset, the enemy's guns, which our artillery had briskly replied to, ceased firing, and ours did the like. It was nearly night when Captain von Marschalk came to see me again. We were both very glad to see each other well and sound, and he, noticing our deficiency of provisions, brought me a bottle of red wine from headquarters, which was real nectar to me and some of my friends.

Uncertain what further awaited us this day, we continued our march very early in the morning, and advanced along the flank of the entrenchments with the view of attacking them in the rear. We could not possibly imagine that the French had evacuated them. I first obtained the certainty of this when an English Dragoon, belonging to a patrol sent out to reconnoitre, said to Field Marshal Freytag, who was just halting in front of our battalion: 'Sir, there is nobody!' with all the coolness and indifference peculiar to his nation.

And so indeed it was. There was nothing left for us to do except march into the camp, which we did along the same road by which a part of the enemy's army had hastily quitted it the evening before.

Camp at Famars, May 26th, 6 a.m: In two hours our battalion will leave the camp in order to advance towards Bouchain. We shall be cantoned in a village by the Scheldt, and on the Bouchain road. I went to visit the brave *Garde du Corps* yesterday. Bock was wounded on the head, but was on his horse again a quarter of an hour later. Adelepsen and Wilhelm Bülow were killed. All gave proofs of splendid courage. Lieutenant-Colonel Bülow and Zedwitz are gone to Mons, the former slightly, the latter severely wounded. Scheither and Kielmansegge are probably prisoners. Nearly all the officers bear the marks of the enemy's sabres.

This morning I was awakened at three by the opening of the siege of Valenciennes. The bombardment is so lively that I hope we shall soon be masters of this fortress.

Outpost at Monceau, village between Valenciennes and Cambray, May 27th: We are the furthest outpost here on the military road from Valenciennes to Paris, supported by our Light Dragoons, and the Hussars of Esterhazy.

Before we marched out of the camp at Famars we were eyewitnesses of the beginning of the siege of Valenciennes. At daybreak a numerous siege artillery opened fire. This spectacle I saw from the highest part of the ground at Famars, at the foot of which our battalion had been encamped. On the summit of this rising ground the French have erected a memorial to their General Dampierre, who was killed in one of the fierce combats at the beginning of the month. It is a triangular pyramid, decorated with trophies, and with a medallion portrait of the general. On the three sides of this pyramid are three inscriptions. On the side next France one reads: *Il aima sa patrie.* On the side obliquely towards Belgium: *Il détesta les traîtres.* This is an allusion to Dumouriez, who would not follow Dampierre. On the side bearing the medallion is written over it: *Ses vertus, lui assurent l'immortalité.* Lower underneath: *Soldats de la liberté Francois Républicains! Il fut pour Vous un bel exemple de valeur et de civisme.*

This immortal monument was made of painted canvas, supported by wooden stakes. The word *civisme* was in tatters. But the position of the monument was unique—on an eminence from which one would see the camp of Famars with its formidable defences, the rich city of Valenciennes with its fortifications, the hill of Ancin on the opposite side, and the fair and fertile plains surrounding. From this point I noticed Valenciennes at three o'clock in the morning, in a thick mist, which was every moment lit up with the flash of heavy guns.

On the right one of the suburbs was in flames. At six fire broke out in the middle of the city, and spread more and more as we marched hither.

The Duke of York has taken direction of the siege, but the Prince of Coburg has taken the command of the army which is to protect the siege.

Quérimain, June 3rd: Everything has been calm in this neighbourhood for several days. Our battalion has changed its position, and we are at present posted in the direction of Quesnoy, of which, however, the garrison is very weak and not likely to annoy us much. In the meantime, the preparations for the siege of Valenciennes are making rapid progress, and we expect it will formally open to-morrow. As our function will be to protect the rear of the besieging army, we shall only see the spectacle from a distance.

Quérimain, June 4th: Contrary to our expectations, the siege has not yet been opened. Our workers are now only five hundred paces from the *glacis,* and yet they are scarcely fired at. They say that within the fortress are two parties in lively dispute, as everywhere in France. Scheither and Kielmansegge are wounded, and prisoners in the fortress, whence they have written to General Wallmoden.

Quérimain, June 11th: The French on the Cambray side are quite quiet, likewise in Valenciennes. It is said that the siege of the latter place will be opened today.

Custine, who arrived at the beginning of this month to take command of the army, sent to inform Prince Coburg with a certain pomposity that *he was there.* A detachment of Prussian cavalry, stationed as an outpost in the neighbourhood of Marchiennes, very nearly returned the compliment a few days later by taking him prisoner. It happened that Custine, accompanied by a body of officers, made a reconnaissance, when the Prussians fell upon them like a storm, cut down a colonel and a lieutenant-colonel, and killed and wounded several other officers, while the remainder took to flight at full speed. Their chief unfortunately escaped with them.

Quérimain, June 17th: The parallels (trenches) have been open for some days, and the commandant of Valenciennes summoned to surrender. He had the impertinence to address his reply to 'Frederick York,' sending him at the same time his oath and a French national *cocarde.* Moreover, they have been trying to send despatches to the National Convention by means of small air-balloons, which fortunately fell into our hands. The fire of our batteries began to play on the place, and parts of the city were set on fire, which were, however, extinguished by the besieged. A brisk fire was returned by the fortress, by which, as yet, very few soldiers are wounded.

The day before yesterday a horde of Carmagnoles made a sortie on us from the fortress, shouting: '*Vive la nation!*' But they were boldly received, and although I was unable to observe anything closely, I gather that Colonel von Bothmer with a detachment of our Guards gave them some heavy volleys. They left twenty-four dead on the field without having killed any of our men.

Our battalion is still in the same station, with the Light Dragoons, forming the chain of posts between the army of Prince Coburg and the army corps placed between Quesnoy and Maubeuge, for the protection of the besiegers.

Custine has made some marches and counter-marches which disturbed nobody.

Quérimain, June 24th: For a few days the fire of the besieged has diminished markedly. Deserters inform us that they lack ammunition, particularly shot and shell. In the meantime ours drop plentifully into the unfortunate town. Our fire is much the hottest at night-time. Nearly every night there are more or less serious conflagrations, which fill the city with loud lamentations clearly audible in our trenches. Two nights ago I saw from my picket the notable church tower of Valenciennes in flames. An officer and some men were placed in the tower for the purpose of making observations. These unfortunate persons are said to have all perished in the flames, or by a hazardous leap. It is further stated that the women of the city besought the commandant on their knees to give up the fortress, or they would not have a roof left, but that Ferrand replied that in that case he would pitch tents for them. It is especially Ferrand, and Cochon, a commissioner from the National Convention, who persist in this obstinacy, of which, in the general opinion, they will have to become the victims in a short time, if they will not give in. Our losses are very unimportant, especially in comparison with those of the Austrians and English, although our regiments have similar duties to perform during the siege.

It seems as if the besieged built their hopes of deliverance on a relief by Custine's army. But General Custine, according to a not very trustworthy rumour, finding our position too strong and his force too weak to drive us out of it, has sent an explanatory despatch to the Convention, and started on the march towards Paris with 10,000 men to meet the counter-revolutionary army.

In the meantime Prince Coburg, with the covering army, to which our battalions and the Light Dragoons belong, remains immovable in his position.

A few days ago we were set in motion because two or three hostile cavalry regiments, weak in themselves, but relatively much stronger than our advanced posts of Light Dragoons, attacked the latter, who were at first obliged to fall back, but, hastily supported by Colonel von Linsingen, re-occupied their positions, and the enemy did not wait to encounter a less unequal force. The Dragoons had only a slight loss, and brought in a severely wounded *Chasseur à cheval* as prisoner, who belonged to the best troops in cavalry and line the French possessed. Another *Chasseur* came in next day as a deserter, after twenty-two years' service. He stated that the troops were perpetually growing more dissatisfied, and scattering in all directions.

Werchin, June 28th: I have been detached for forty-eight hours to this village, half an hour from Quérimain. Although the unhappy city of Valenciennes has been in great part destroyed by our bombardment, the chiefs of the predominant party are still obstinate. In the meantime the siege operations are regularly proceeding, and we shall soon be in a position to make a breach, unless the besieged prefer not to let things come to extremes.

The month of July was spent in uneventful movements on the part of the Allies against the French frontier fortresses. On one solitary occasion(Häusser, *German History*, 1., p. 492), the allied forces made up their minds to advance in force against the enemy, with most favourable results. On July 28th the fortress of Valenciennes fell. From August 6th—8th there was an attack on the French positions, which compelled the enemy, being far inferior in strength, to quit them, and fall back on the line Arras, Bapaume, Peronne. It was generally expected that the Allies would at once cross the Somme and make a dash for the French capital, which was separated from them now by a distance of only twenty (German) miles. But the contrary happened. The English, Hanoverians, and 15,000 Austrians marched northwards against Dunkirk, and the Prussians to the Rhine. Coburg employed the remainder in a fruitless siege of Le Quesnoy. The two fortresses are seventeen German miles asunder.

The Hanoverians were advanced against Dunkirk in August, where the English wanted to get a permanent footing advantageous to their commerce. On the 5th, and to the 8th of September, Field Marshal Freytag, who commanded the corps of observation covering the besiegers, was attacked at Mont Cassel by a superior French force, and driven back with great loss on Hondschoot, south of the fortress, after the Hanoverians and Hessians had fought most bravely in a disadvantageous *terrain* for four whole days. Prince Adolphus, Duke of Cambridge, was wounded, and the Field Marshal taken prisoner. The entire loss of the Hanoverian corps was 95 officers and 2,236 men. Lieutenant Ompteda of the Grenadier battalion of the Guards was among the wounded. Sichart, 4., p. 290:

> Although the Hanoverian troops were indisputably made the victims of a mistaken plan of campaign, in which the Duke of York separated himself from Prince Coburg in order to besiege Dunkirk with resources wholly insufficient for the purpose, they nevertheless won un-fading though blood-stained laurels by the ex-

traordinary courage they displayed on those fateful four days (5 th, 6th, 7th, 8th) of September.

Moreover, the old Field Marshal had pointed out beforehand, both to the Duke of York and to the King himself, the certain failure of such an undertaking. Also in Scharnhorst's opinion, who distinguished himself on this occasion as a captain of artillery, the dispositions ordered by the Duke of York (and still more by his incapable English staff) were 'incredibly inefficient.'

Monceau, July 5th, Morning: Here we are back again at the post we occupied two days after the battle, and whither we only sent pickets since we were at Quérimain. Count Colloredo arrived yesterday with 4,000 men and more, among them the famous and brave Latour Dragoons, to go into camp at Quérimain.

Our position here is now very strong, both by reason of the Escallion, and the troops who defend that river. Should it occur to Custine to try and force it, I think he would run his head against a wall. But the French are very quiet, and nothing has happened here since Famars except a couple of skirmishes, from which the French were sent home with broken heads.

And we are more fortunate than our other countrymen, in so far as our duty is lighter, and the country not so barren as that near Valenciennes.

Monceau, July 15th: The siege of Valenciennes is still prolonged. Yesterday we celebrated the birthday of French Anarchy with a *feu de joie,* ordered on account of the taking of Condé. Besides that, the day was further *fêted* by an attack on an advanced corps of Custine, of whom a great part were cut down and taken prisoners. At least so says report

Monceau, July 18th: General von Hammerstein, who came from the besieging army, ordered me to accompany him on an inspection of our advanced posts on this side. This involved me in a ride of several hours, which, however, I found very useful in giving me information from two different and sure sources on the events of the day before yesterday, which are not without importance.

A report spread yesterday morning through the whole army, evoking great curiosity, that Valenciennes had surrendered, or at least capitulated.

I did not place confidence in this rumour. It originated in the following manner. General Custine sent to the Prince of Coburg to ask his permission to deliver a letter to General Ferrand, and to allow the latter to send a certain Madame de Mettière out of the fortress. Our general had the politeness to accede to this request. Then, after the latter had been taken to General Ferrand by a trumpeter, Ferrand sent out two officers with a trumpeter in front of them towards the trenches, while at the same time a white flag was planted on the ramparts to signify an armistice. Both sides at once ceased firing, and Frank Alten, who happened to be in the trenches that day, was sent to the Duke of York with a bundle of despatches which the two French officers had given over. He went to the Duke, who asked, after going through the documents, if firing had ceased. When he heard that such was really the case, he sent Frank Alten back with orders to begin it again, which happened as soon as the two officers were back in the town.

The whole *pour parler* had been about Madame de Mettière, a lady of rank, who was known among others to General Ferraris. She is shortly expecting her confinement, and is fortunately now removed from the shocking scenes of a beleaguered city. She left the day before yesterday at midday, by a gate on the side of the city remote from the trenches, which was not fired at at the time. Two trumpeters, a French, and a Hanoverian officer, her servants, and a wagon load of effects accompanied her. She walked to a certain distance away from the town, where one of the Duke of York's carriages awaited her. She was driven to the neighbouring village of Beuverage, where an Austrian colonel offered her hospitality for the first night. Afterwards she went to Brussels. Custine wanted her to be allowed to go to Paris, but of course such a dangerous favour could not be conferred.

Madame de Mettière also brought letters from our two prisoners, Scheither and Kielmansegge, both for General Wallmoden, and for their families. These letters naturally passed through the hands of Ferrand, who wrote a postscript himself, and put the Arms of Liberty on the cover of Scheither's letter.

The letters state that the writers are better in health, and getting on tolerably well under the circumstances.

During the interval, while the cessation of fire lasted, the ramparts of Valenciennes became crowded with people. On our side every one left the trenches, and mounted the parapets to look at this spectacle. Several of our officers even went as far as the palisades of the covered way of the fortress, to talk to the French officers and soldiers. Marschalk tells me that the latter are nearly all agreed in desiring a surrender. A French deserter who came over in the night confirms this statement, especially with regard to the troops of the line.

From another source, my brother writes me that during the armistice, the French outposts approached some of ours, and brought wine with them, which everybody drank together in a very friendly way.

I wish I could think that all this was a sign of an approaching capitulation. Some go so far as to state that during the negotiations about Madame de Mettière, far-fetched allusions thereto were made on the part of the French general.

Furthermore, it is certain that during the last few days a powder magazine has blown up in the city, and all our information confirms the fact that our fire has cost the besieged many dead and wounded, and that the hospitals are crowded with the latter. In the meantime we on our side remain undisturbed in our position. The same is the case with the army of Custine, which the latest intelligence gives at only 20,000 men. Our duties are slight, as they have been very much relieved since the arrival of Colloredo's army corps. As this now takes up two-thirds of the ground which previously we alone had to defend by our battalion, and four squadrons of Light Dragoons, naturally our comfort is much increased. Moreover, we find ourselves much better off in this village than we were at Quérimain. I am quartered in a mill, which I should, as usual, have had to share with Low, and the two other officers, had I not had my tent pitched in an orchard, in spite of the attractions of the miller's charming young daughter, Mdlle. Reine. I prefer this rural solitude to the ruined elegance of the castle of Quérimain, and while a few apple trees shade my tent, an old but well-preserved barn affords me a more agreeable view than the beautiful architecture and ruined shrubberies of the poor Marquis de Vignacourt.

Monceau, July 27th: Yesterday evening we took three of the most important outworks of Valenciennes by storm, after the covered way of the place had been blown up by three mines.

This enterprise made so great an impression on the enemy, that an armistice has now been established, for the purpose of treating about capitulation.

At this moment, 11 p.m., an Austrian trooper is passing through to Prince Ernest, who assures us that Valenciennes is ours. I was fortunate in being an eye-witness of these great events. General von Hammerstein, to whom I had expressed the wish to visit the trenches, took me there on Wednesday, 24th inst, when he had the command. His command should have lasted for twenty-four hours, but through a misunderstanding no one came to relieve him, so we remained there fifty-five hours instead of twenty-four. This small difference afforded me the advantage of being present at the final efforts which delivered Valenciennes into our hands. I saw the explosion of the three mines which spread the first alarm among the enemy. Half an hour later, the enemy's own mines would have blown up a principal part of our third parallel with a battery of sixteen 24-pounders.

Then when the attack had begun, and General von Hammerstein was uncertain about the extent of its success, I was fortunate enough, on Thursday evening, to convince myself with my own eyes that this important part of the works of Valenciennes had fallen into our hands, by going into the dry ditch of the main hornwork which we had taken, at the moment when the Hungarians, who had made the attack, were cheering vigorously.

All the troops engaged in the storming distinguished themselves by great courage. The different columns were led as follows: The Austrians by Generals Count Erbach and Wenkheim; the English by General Abercrombie; the Hessians by Colonel von Lengerke; and the Hanoverians by Lieutenant-Colonel Offeney. Before 6 a.m. I was speaking with young Tollemache, an officer in the English Guards. As he understood German, which he had learnt in Brunswick (where about two years ago he was wounded in a duel), he was put under the command of Count Erbach during the storm. Between 9 and 10 a.m. I found the same young man shockingly wounded with a piece of a shell, so that he died in a quarter of an hour's time. Nevertheless he bore it with such fortitude, that the expression of his features was in no way altered. I looked for some water for him, which he wanted badly, but it was, unfortunately, impossible to obtain any in the trenches. 'You are very good,' he said, as they carried him away. This young man, son of one of the first ladies in England, Lady Bridget Tollemache, who had the prospect of a very fine property, and was engaged to Miss Manners, one of the most beautiful girls in England, had only joined this campaign out of military ambition. By another extraordinary coincidence Colonel Pennington, commanding the 2nd Guards, happened to have the command of the English in the trenches that day. This man had the misfortune to kill the father of our unlucky Tollemache in a duel in America.

A fine *trait* on the part of an Englishman is equally deserving of mention. In the night, during the storm, a soldier of the English Guards was wounded by a musket-ball. He fell, and was not noticed in the confusion. When daylight came, and every one had got behind the parapets again, it was found that this unfortunate fellow lay in a place where he was fully exposed to the small-arm fire of the enemy. Nobody dared for his own life's sake to go and carry him away. It was only in the following afternoon that a young man, by the name of Murray, an officer in the Guards, who had been ordered to make a lodgement with some workmen for us in the works taken from the enemy, learnt the situation of his wounded countryman. He persuaded two men of the Guards to follow him, and in spite of the enemy's fire they brought the wounded man safely in. The simple way in which he told this story bore witness to the nobility of his character, to which all his comrades rendered full justice.

English soldiers' wives, among whom I noticed one of the

greatest beauty, came into the trenches to bring their husbands' dinners. The one just referred to remained there with the greatest coolness, and even went to sleep with her head on her husband's knees.

Monceau, July 29th: Yesterday the gates of Valenciennes were taken possession of by our troops. The garrison, which has dwindled from 10,000 men to half that number, will lay down their arms, and be sent home under the condition that they do not bear arms again for two years.

It was Cochon, and not Ferrand (who must be a man of limited capacity), who really had the command. A French prisoner, who was asked how they got on in Valenciennes during the siege, replied pointedly: '*Que voulez-vous qu'on devienne quand on est commandé par un Cochon!*' But the garrison must be given the credit of having made an extremely courageous defence.

During the armistice the fair ladies of Valenciennes showed themselves on the ramparts, and made a number of polite and inviting signs to the English and Hanoverian officers, but not to the Austrians, against whom the French display a deadly hatred.

Monceau, August 3rd: The day before yesterday I witnessed the most splendid spectacle which a man can see.

The evacuation of Valenciennes by the French garrison was fixed for August 1st, a worthy celebration of the anniversary of the glorious battle of Minden, which was fought on that day thirty-four years ago.

According to the conditions of the capitulation, the 6,000 men, composing what remained of the garrison, were to march out through the Cambray gate, and pass before us with all military honours and the pomp of a parade, and were then, at a little distance further from the city, to lay down their arms and be escorted by two divisions of Imperial cavalry to the nearest French post, which was the village of Avesne-le-sec, a good hour's distance.

At the appointed time I placed myself, with Captain von Low, by the Cambray gate. The greater part of the besieging army, amounting all together to 20,000 men, was drawn up in two lines on both sides of the road. It seemed as if the corps of the different nations were vying with one another in splendour of appearance.

The astonished lookers-on paid the first tribute of admiration to the Hungarian Grenadiers; but when they glanced at the fine English cavalry, at our brave and imposing *Garde du Corps*, then at the elegant and easy bearing of several detachments of English infantry, of which those who were engaged in the storm had the foremost positions, they did not know to whom the palm was due, and came to the conclusion that it was impossible to see a more admirable army.

Midway between the two lines stood all the generals of the different army corps employed in this part of France, and they, with their numerous staff, as well as a number of officers from every European army, formed a most brilliant and interesting gathering round the distinguished personages who had played so conspicuous a part in this war. What a sight! to see together at one spot Coburg, Ferraris, Clairfait, so many young serene princes who burned with eagerness to tread in the footsteps of those mighty commanders, particularly our three royal princes, the Archduke Charles, and Prince William of Brunswick.

Among several other persons who have become known in more recent history, my attention was especially directed to Prince Poniatowsky, a nephew of the noble and unfortunate King of Poland. He commanded for some time with credit an army of his own nation, which was unfortunately overcome by the superior forces of the Russians. This Poniatowsky is a man in the prime of life, finely built, with a noble, manly, agreeable, and resolute countenance. By his side was the only too-well-known favourite of the unhappy Marie Antoinette of France, the handsome Fersen, a Swede. Of his former beauty only traces are visible. He looks worn now, and is a sad contrast to Prince Poniatowsky, who, in a simple blue frock, with his physically and morally powerful appearance, put the pompous and Oriental-looking costume of Fersen to shame. The latter could apparently only with difficulty keep his seat on his fine, beautifully caparisoned horse. Among others was also the Prince Lambesk, celebrated for his fruitless exertions at the beginning of the Revolution. He wore now an Austrian general's uniform. The regiment Royal Allemand, distinguished for its loyalty, which nothing could shake, and its exemplary military discipline, was also with the army under his command. But he does not please me over-much; he recently played a foolish trick, which at least is not creditable to the high position he occupies. The matter was as follows:

During the armistice, while negotiations were going on, the Prince went into the town accompanied by some officers and troopers of the regiment Royal Allemand. He had formerly been Governor of Valenciennes, and was therefore well known there. Regardless of his rank and birth, he lowered himself with his small following to brag against the French garrison. Two parties arose. The democrats insulted him, while others took his part, and they were on the point of coming to blows, which would have brought about a very disagreeable *intermezzo*, had not the Prince avoided it by leaving the city, after this useless bravado. But Prince Coburg sent for him, and gave him a severe and well-deserved reprimand.

Concerning the *Emigrés* generally, the letter of October 25th from Bruges speaks.

Romain, near Orchies, August 13th: Since the 6th we have been in motion. On that and the two following days we marched in a wide circuit to the other side of Cambray. The effect of this manoeuvre was that the enemy, with scarcely the slightest resistance, quitted their strongest positions, particularly Caesar's camp,[5] and the woods of Bourlon. Our cavalry pursued them nearly to Arras. The Imperials are masking Cambray and Bouchain, while the Duke of York, with the English, Hanoverian, Hessian, and 10,000 Imperial troops, has marched on a new expedition, the object of which is Dunkirk.

---

5. As this *Caesar's Camp* lies in the angle formed by the influx of the Senseé into the Scheldt (according to the map of the French general staff) it would be in the land of the Nervi, who border on the Atrebates, both Belgian tribes. It was probably instituted in the winter of 51-50 B.C., by the legate M. Antonius, while Caesar himself made his winter quarters at Nenatocenna (Beauvais), some sixteen geographical miles farther south. (*Bell. Gall.*, by Hirtius, continuing Caesar's Commentaries.)

On this march the 1st Grenadier battalion sustained two brilliant little encounters.

Of the first, we learn from the battalion journal, that after the troops had marched from Poperinghen, on August 20th in the afternoon for two hours, and had then rested out of doors till midnight, a force, consisting of the battalion, two Austrian Green Free Companies of Laudon, a squadron of Hanoverian Light Dragoons, a squadron of the Karaczai, three sections of Blankenstein Hussars, 250 Hessian Rifles, advanced to Oost Capell, and attacked and took the camp at 4 a.m. on August 21st, on which occasion one gun was taken by the battalion, two by the other troops.

A letter from Bruges of October 16th describes the second encounter.

Wormhout, August 28th: On the 23rd inst. three of our companies, to wit, Löw's, Bremen's, and Osten's (only 200 men strong altogether), drove as many French battalions out of this spot. As I happened to be among the first of those who occupied the market-place, I at once had the Tree of Liberty felled, which had been made mighty fine with a pike, a large tin Jacobin cap, and a tricolour flag.

Wormhout, September 5th: This morning we made an attack, of which, however, I do not yet know the result. A wound in the leg, which I received at the beginning of the fight, compelled me to return hither."

The battalion journal describes this action in the following words:

September 5th.—Attack by the battalion on a French post at Coffre, half an hour from Cassel, at which latter is placed a corps of 16,000 men. Several casualties. General Fabry of the Imperial army, in command, was wounded at the beginning of the action. Two other columns which should have also attacked this position were two hours late, on account of which the battalion had to bear the heavy brunt of the day. Surrounded in flank and rear by the enemy, we were delivered from otherwise unavoidable defeat by the determination of Captain von Bremer to cut the way through to the right to Eskelbeck. The battalion got back in the evening to Wormhout, after defending itself without cannon against a very numerous enemy, and for a long time occupying the position it was ordered to take. Killed, Captain Schlüter and 4 Grenadiers; wounded, Lieutenants von Ompteda and Bodecker and 74 Grenadiers.

On September 14th Christian writes from Bruges to his brother in Dresden:

You will have already heard the news through our brave brother Ferdinand, and been reassured about the wound I got in my right leg at Mont Cassel on the 5th inst. However, I write you these lines to say that I am improving as much as could be wished, and that I am generally assured a good and complete recovery. I may add the good news that our Ferdinand has behaved with distinguished bravery in a difficult rear-guard duty. I wish I could add that the condition of things in general was prosperous, as well as that of individuals who were dear to me.

Diary continued:

Bruges in Flanders, September 14th: I have had to be brought here in order to obtain more quiet for my convalescence. I am in very skilful hands, am quartered in a comfortable and quiet house, have no fever, and hope to be fully recovered again.

The Field Marshal has informed me, in very flattering terms, that my promotion to captain and adjutant in place of Charles Alten has been forwarded to England.

Bruges, September 20th: According to the assurances of my surgeon, my wound is in a surprisingly favourable condition, which I put down to the lucky direction of the bullet, and my own excellent constitution, which assists me better than anything else.

The French have had to pay very dear for the retreat from Dunkirk to which they compelled us, and have since been beaten several times, by which our former position is retrieved on the whole.

Bruges, October 10th: Just received my commission as captain and chief adjutant.

In a further letter from Bruges of September 29th, and October 4th, he complains about the field postal service, which for four weeks had delivered no letters.

I will write you no details about the last events of the campaign. The public papers have much to say about them, and I am trying, as far as I can, to drive the recollection of this unhappy war out of my head,

The conviction of the true character of the conduct, events, and sacrifices of the campaign, reveals itself more and more to the young warrior. The Hanoverians and Hessians had lost 4,000 men. Christian laments the heroic but vainly shed blood, and wishes, for the sake of his fatherland, that this wasteful and senseless campaign may quickly come to an end. In the meantime, his recovery progressed but slowly. His injury consisted of a fortunately incomplete perforation of the tibia, so that the *ridge of the bone* (anterior ridge ?) was uninjured. He seeks to fill the enforced leisure of the healing process by freshening up a few light sketches of his own warlike experiences.

Christian to Louis, Bruges, October 16th, 1793: I must tell you something about a fortunate affair—it was still the good times then—which I took part in when we invaded French Flanders in August. After we had crossed the Scarpe (Christian is talking of an engagement preliminary to the great attack of August 6th—8th) and surprised and taken a French entrenched camp at Oost Capell, the advanced guard, mainly consisting of our battalion, followed the enemy along the road which leads to Bergen St.Vinox. We believed we had quite driven them back to that place; but when the head of our column approached that village a few cannon-balls which they sent us convinced us. that we should not be able to have our dinner that day until we had done some more work. Our battalion guns were immediately brought up along the road to reply to the enemy's fire. The latter were behind an entrenchment which defended the entrance of the village by the road. Moreover, the enemy supposed, and not unreasonably, that the village was unapproachable owing to the structure of the ground. And I think you would be inclined to agree with them, if you imagine the Hoya marsh where it is most cut up by small enclosures, deep ditches, and high-growing hedges placed before troops only accustomed to regular movements. In the meantime our battalion was formed in lines, in a place where the ground to some extent allowed it, on the left of our guns, and we then had the experience which I hold to be one of the greatest trials of patience—viz., to look on passively at a cannonade which was pretty lively, but of which the shot, although frequent, fortunately flew over our heads without causing us loss. I thought directly in my mind, 'This won't do,' and fortunately there finally happened what I should have liked to sec earlier. They ordered us to attack the enemy in flank. The battalion first moved some distance to the left, then marched to the front. How such a march is carried out when it has to be worked through the above described obstacles I leave to your imagination. All I know is that in this and several subsequent successful attacks we had to cut our way through the hedges with swords, sometimes getting over, sometimes breaking through, and helped each other hand in hand through the ditches. But the parade exactitude of the line was destroyed, and we were lucky to be able to hold together in any military sense. With a body of men so formed I was happily able to find the way into a byroad, which led to the village. The French were there very numerous, but our fire, our unexpected appearance, and our lively advance, with the Hanoverian hurrah, persuaded them that the game was up. They fired on us out of houses, and from behind houses, but as this did not stagger my Grenadiers, and as I drove them the more rapidly forward the more I perceived the enemy to waver, we pressed into the village, and the French then merely sought safety in the lightness of their heels. We came upon them so swiftly that they left three guns in the lurch which they had already withdrawn from the entrenchment without firing them at us, although they were loaded. But all three were ours, and the pursuing cavalry who advanced into the village as soon as we had made the coast clear took another. This was the first occasion on which I had the great pleasure of seeing and sharing the active service of our Grenadiers. I also had the pleasure of having at my side Charles Alten, who dismounted to accompany me as a volunteer.

Of my promotion to captain and chief adjutant with Field Marshal Freytag you are glad to hear, I know. I hope it will conduce to completing our household arrangements when we are next in Hanover, unless you are going to provide me with a sister-in-law, in which case I will return to *bachelor's solitude*.

> On the 15th and 16th of October Jourdan attacked Prince Coburg stationed at Wattignis, to the south of the fortress of Maubeuge, in order to relieve the latter. It was an undecided struggle. The French were only hindered from retreating inasmuch as the Austrians were prevented from compelling them, after a courageous encounter, because the Hereditary Prince of Orange refused his support. Confused rumours of victory reached Bruges. Christian speaks of it in his letter to Louis of October 25th, 1793.

What first upset my wavering belief in this good news, which was afterwards in no way confirmed, was a printed leaflet, apparently official, which mentioned vague details in a description devoid of coherence or common sense. I am convinced that this leaflet was a device on the part of the French, or their numerous hangers-on, to keep our *cordon* on the frontier. Or it may be due to one of those fatal *Emigre's* who crawl everywhere at some distance in the rear of our armies, like noxious vermin, and largely quench any feelings of sympathy one might have for their condition by their own despicable conduct. In the afternoon some wounded came in of Löw's company, of my own clear 1st Grenadier battalion. This was stuck about by companies here and there on outpost duty in a number of villages on the frontier, from Commes to Poperinghen, and therefore nowhere in sufficient strength. These companies, attacked singly by superior forces, were compelled to retire with loss, from their different airy positions, on Ypres. How many brave men this luckless campaign has already cost us!

In consequence of the advance of the enemy the sick quarters were removed to Flamisch Hoeft, opposite Antwerp.

On December 19th Christian was so far advanced in his recovery that he could inform his brother:

I am extremely comfortable here in one of the best inns. I spend the day now out of bed, and although my wounds are not yet healed I make continual experiments in order to accustom my leg gradually to use. Still my movements are one-legged, my faithful Hegener fulfils the function of a second leg.

During the next ensuing months letters fail. Still we can follow Christian's movements by means of a fragment of his Diary fairly well.

February 20th, 1794: My wound has not yet closed, although for the most part healed, and as I cannot yet ride, I must limit my duties (as chief adjutant) to such as can be done sitting.

February 23rd to March 28th 1794: Bruges and Courtray. Rest in winter quarters.

London, April 8th, 1794: General Wallmoden has sent me here with despatches for the King and the Field Marshal.

The latter had left the army on account of his discordant relations with the Duke of York. Wallmoden was his successor.

I left Courtray on Saturday at 3 a.m., and took ship at Ostend on Sunday, 4 a.m. The passage to Margate lasted twelve hours. Thence I took only one night to cover a distance of seventy-four English miles.

On April 15th Christian was very *graciously received* by King George III (who had recovered from his first illness) and Queen Charlotte, and on June 10th again *most graciously* was allowed to take leave. On June 13th he got back to the headquarters of General Wallmoden in Thielt, and at once took part in a fight with his old 1st Grenadier battalion at Rousselaere and Hooglede.

The fragment we have of his journal concludes with mention of the intended retreat of the English-Hanoverian and Austrian troops at Ghent, June 30th, 1794.

The latter were pressed by Jourdan towards the Rhine; the Duke of York had to give way before Pichegru, to Holland. His *combined English-Hanoverian Hessian army*, after a series of reverses without battles which must have deeply wounded every soldier's heart, took up its winter quarters north of the Waal, between Arnheim and Nymwegen. The Hanoverian Guards, under Brigadier-general Prince Adolphus, Duke of Cambridge, were encamped in huts at Elste. Instead of finding quiet winter quarters, which the troops, exhausted and demoralised by the continual retreat from Belgium to Holland, greatly required in order to restore themselves, and become to some extent again fit for war, they encountered new hardships. The prevailing extremely cold weather made the line of defence of the river wholly untenable against the now superior and triumphant enemy. Disease prevailed to a shocking extent, especially among the Hanoverians. On account of the incapacity of the English for covering and outpost service, the Germans could never be relieved from the defence of the advanced posts. Whole weeks long the infantry lay out of doors, in rough weather, without wood or straw. No wonder that the serviceable state of the troops diminished fearfully from day to day. From the original return of the Hanoverian infantry of 13,500 men and 477 officers, there remained, on December 31st, 1794, 4,650 men and 211 officers fit for service, therefore not quite a third part. In the regiments of Guards there were in the 1st battalion 177, in the 2nd battalion 141 efficient. The 9th Regiment of Infantry had in two battalions 79 men under arms.

1795

There began now a sad and disastrous retreat to the northeast, towards the German frontier. In Scharnhorst's Memoirs this complete collapse of the army is strikingly described. He was, as Quartermaster-General, the soul of Wallmoden's command. The latter followed Scharnhorst's advice, so far as his own moral anxiety as responsible commander of the combined armies permitted, in all except dangerous undertakings. The horrors of the winter's march through the sands and moors of the poor provinces of Gelderland and Over-Issel were not less than they would have been under a complete defeat. An eye-witness, who at a later period took part in the Russian campaign of 1812, compares the episodes of that time with those of the later horrible war.

Scharnhorst expresses the opinion that all the troops were in a state of dissolution, but that even that had its limits. The worst were the corps of *Emigrés* in English pay, the Hussars and Chasseurs of Choiseul, Rohan, Salm, Hompesch, and the rest, whatever their names may be. Without officers who were of any use, they consisted partly of the worst people in the world. By their plundering, which was worse than that of Cossacks, they brought all the troops with which they served into evil report, and invariably drove the inhabitants into the arms of the enemy. If they rode on patrol a single half-hour beyond the line of outposts, the peasantry fired at them. Naturally the information they brought was not to be depended on. They gave wilfully false intelligence in order to cloak their own marauding, and there were always among them a crowd of hostile spies.

The English troops had the character of very brave fellows, impetuous in attack, steady under fire, willing, and never grumbling under fatigue. But the officers treated the war as a superior species of sport; they did not feel the duty of morally elevating men collected from the dregs of the populace. The latter therefore sank quickly and deeply under the pressure of want. It sometimes happened that in order to gratify their immeasurable thirst, they sold their uniforms at ridiculous prices, and came back nearly naked to their quarters. Nothing was safe from them. Hessian officers sometimes had to drive out English plunderers sword in hand from the house of the General in command. Want of discipline deteriorates the condition of an army as much as bullets and diseases. In December 1794 the English and the *Emigrés* amounted only to 11,000 men, about a third of their original number.

If the behaviour of the German troops was rather better, they nevertheless consisted, for the most part, of fresh levies, and the want of discipline was very contagious.

Scharnhorst's description of the fate of the poor sick and wounded is particularly shocking. They remained with their regiments, and in the retreat had to be ferried over the Waal, and then dragged into the nearest houses. The boat never disembarked a load among which there were not some dead.

The defeats which were suffered to occur, Scharnhorst regards as a disgrace to the whole people. He says:

> Political and military incongruities united to weaken the martial honour of the Germans, and to discourage the princes; nowhere was rigour, nowhere animation, and nowhere a direct approach to a high purpose.

He fears lest the spirit of the German nation should be deeply wounded by this war, and that unless other measures be taken "a fearful ruin should await many a good institution."

> I cannot speak of the thing without losing my temper and forgetting myself.

On crossing the German frontier, General Wallmoden, who had the nominal Command-in-chief of the combined forces, issued an order, in which he says:

> I must mention with pain and shame for the army, the unspeakable plunder, even robbery, and occasionally also murder and fire of which many have been hitherto guilty. I can therefore, now that the army is on the point of treading German ground once more, with every possible emphasis, order that no one in the army shall be guilty of plunder, extortion, or robbery.

Until May 1795, the troops lay inactive in the bishoprics of Minister and Osnabrück. On April 5th the Peace of Basle was concluded between France and Prussia, and the army evacuated the Ems. The two battalions of Hanoverian Guards had quarters in the town of Oldenburg.

Among the victims of this sad, and finally disgraceful campaign, in which loyal and brave troops, who proved their honour under arms in the face of the enemy, were destroyed through blind, many-headed policy and incapable leadership, was Christian Ompteda. Immediately after the commencement of the retreat, the *sequelæ* of his severe wound, of his long sickness, of the discomforts of the ensuing winter, and the, to him, extremely distressing undeserved humiliation of his own dearly beloved troops, exhibited themselves in the saddest form of obscured and disturbed mental condition, ending in marked *melancholia*. He obtained an extended leave of six months. In the *Kur-list* at Carlsbad we notice under the date June 11th, 1795: "Herr von Ompteda, Captain in the Hanoverian Service, lodging at the house of Herr Anton Gerber on the market-place." But the expected recovery did not at once take place.

To the solution of this life-crisis, treated with such tender-hearted comradeship by all who had to do with him, and brought on by a cause so creditable to the sufferer, we are introduced by the following correspondence, most unusual from the strict service point of view.

Report of Captain Christian von Ompteda, commanding a company in the Foot Guards, to Major the Prince of Schwartzburg, in temporary command of the regiment.

Oldenburg, August 13th, 1795: To Your Serene Highness, as in present command of the regiment which has the misfortune to include me in its numbers, I am compelled to state the following facts.

I have been six months absent from the regiment as sick, or as some believed, as having a mental disorder, *without this having been the case in any way whatever.*

If I spoke (falsely) of this (illness) to some persons, who took a wholly undeserved interest in me with unshakable friendship, then I would accentuate my symptoms, and by a certain kind of silence, by deceit, and by the use of drugs, yes, even to the undergoing of a cure-process at a distant bath, deceive even the medical men who attended me, although they appeared to perceive very few of the customary signs of my alleged complaint.

The true confession of a deception such as this will be sufficient to furnish an idea of the proper punishment for it, without going further into the labyrinth of causes, of which the deepest *(although they lie in me only)* would not be elicited by any judicial inquiry.

I see before me most clearly all the fearful consequences of this present step. But equally clearly I recognise the as good as mathematical certainty, that what is built on deceit can only be kept up by further deceit, that disgrace engenders disgrace, and that a dishonoured and dishonourable man is as little use for any good purpose as a cripple for walking. On that account, and in order that the service of the regiment and the company may not suffer further (as suffer it unavoidably must through my connection with it), and that no one may be further deceived by me, I herewith tear off the tissue of infamy, and hasten that civic annihilation which must sooner or later overtake me, since resolution fails me to face the great crime of making an end of everything *here*, although I have hung on the miserable thought, as on a last resource, for long months, with ridiculous obstinacy, and have for that very reason become incapable of responding to the demands of honour and duty.

I await the orders of Your Serene Highness for my arrest, until the matter may be settled by a general court-martial.

C. *von Ompteda*

Prince Schwartzburg, a warm friend of the sufferer, placed this lamentable self-accusation before the officer commanding the forces in Oldenburg, Prince Adolphus, Duke of Cambridge, and he sent it to the then Commander-in-chief of the Hanoverian army, General Count Wallmoden, with the following comment:

Your Excellency will observe the unhappy phase of mental distress into which Captain Ompteda has relapsed. When Prince Schwartzburg showed me the enclosed letter, we agreed that the best thing would be for the Prince to go and see him, and talk the matter over in a friendly way, and convince him, as far as possible, treating the matter as if nothing had happened. This was tried, but without result. The Prince said to the patient that there were only two paths open to him. One was to go voluntarily to his relatives, and there await his recovery, and take care of himself, in which case his letter would be treated as non-existent, and his return to health expected in the course of time. The other was to inform Your Excellency of the whole thing, and await your decision. Although the Prince put before him that if he determined on the latter course, Your Excellency's orders would probably be in accordance with the tenor of his letter, he could be in no way dissuaded. As since his return there is little or no trace of improvement in his condition, and the letter shows every sign of continued insanity, the Prince did not very well know what to do. So he made him give his word of honour to make no attempt at suicide, he took over all the Company papers, which were correct and in good order, and told the captain to consider himself under arrest in his own house. His servant, who is a reliable fellow, is put over him under pretence of being a sentry, to keep the unfortunate man under his eye. I hope that these steps and measures, which have only been taken out of sympathy for a most deserving young man, will meet with Your Excellency's approval, and I have the honour, with your approbation, to suggest that Your Excellency should send me a written order to send Captain Ompteda to Regensburg, by Hanover, and to take such measures for that purpose as I may find requisite.

As the Deputy Ompteda (in Regensburg) has offered to use every possible means for the recovery of his cousin, I think this is the only way to meet the purpose. I could in virtue of such an order (which I could show him if needful) send Captain Ompteda to Hanover under escort of his brother Ferdinand, and could forward him thence, with the help of relatives or friends, to Regensburg.

Adolphus Frederick

Christian's seniors and friends had undoubtedly recognised the true nature of his mental disorder. What we learn is, that there was every symptom of this form of malady present: unwillingness to admit himself to be suffering from a real disease, mistrust of himself, a feeling of incapacity to manage otherwise familiar affairs passionate irritability against his surroundings without cause, imaginary self-accusations, which prey on the feelings, and obstinately defy every attempt at consolation. In such cases the best cure is removal from the customary surroundings. Before, however, this could be carried out, on account of the then slow rate at which things progressed, the first signs of recovery were already visible. Perhaps the after-effects of the Carlsbad cure were beginning to manifest themselves.

On October 8th, 1795, Brother Ferdinand writes to Brother Louis from Oldenburg (the latter having in the meantime been appointed to a *chargé d'affaires* in Berlin):

I have the greatest pleasure, dear L., in being able to inform you that our brother has extraordinarily improved, so much so, that we have an almost certain hope that it will not be necessary to carry out the Regensburg project.

For some time already I had observed a gradual change in him; he went through the whole of his Company accounts, occupied himself as much as was possible for him in his then situation about service matters, and when I asked him why he had without any reason put himself on such a disagreeable footing in the regiment, just at the time when we were expecting to get his best friends back, Drechsel and Charles Alten, he replied that if he remained with his company in the future, he would not only make in it changes tending to improvement, but would also try as much as possible to set himself again on the old footing with his comrades.

I made use of the opportunity when Prince Schwartzburg came to headquarters, about a week ago, to talk to him of these great changes, and to propose to him, and to Prince Adolphus, that General Wallmoden should be asked to send an order which should contain something of this sort: That since nothing in the slightest could be found in Christian's words or writings that showed him to be in any way guilty, he was therefore to be pronounced wholly at liberty, and might return to his duty with the regiment as before. But at the same time I suggested that in case he, contrary to expectation, should not accept this, a second, but quite separate order, should be added containing the command that if he persisted in his behaviour, he would be looked upon as an invalid for the future, and in order to restore his health, was to go to the Representative at Regensburg. General Wallmoden fully approved of this plan, and promised to send the order very shortly.

Drechsel, who had seen Christian a few days before, was quite astonished at the improvement which had taken place in him during the short absence of the former. He was ready at once to release him from arrest, but I did not advise this because I was afraid that Christian, knowing that Wallmoden, had the control of the matter, would take no decisive step on the mere authority of the regiment, and things would again go wrong. He now is pleased when any one goes to see him, and every one who has not seen him for a long time is astonished at his alteration. He reads and writes all day, and smokes his pipe, which Hegener assures me he had not done for a long time, and has also a good appetite.

The order setting Christian at liberty came immediately afterwards, and drove away the last traces of his disorder.

The restored one speaks in October of his illness to his brother Louis as of something lying wholly behind him, and rejoices, though perhaps with a certain shyness, in his restoration to the clear light of day.

Oldenburg, October 1795: Whatever my history has been, is, and may become, I feel that my sympathy with the happiness of those persons who are nearest and dearest to me has not been quite vanished. Therefore, brother, let me congratulate you on your promotion. That I have not written to you or to any of those with whom written intercourse formed previously so essential a part of my happiness, will not estrange you if you could imagine yourselves in my condition (which I do not wish you for a moment to do), where no thought arose which could give joy to others or awake it in myself. Whatever I have done destructive of my moral existence, one joy is left to me, and that I must share with you. All my old comrades, with Drechsel and the Prince of Schwarzburg at their head, have given me proofs of friendship, and even respect, which are infinitely precious to me, and will assure them in every possible condition of my life my warmest acknowledgment and thankfulness.

There are still excellent people in the world, and particularly in the regiment. I hope it may some time be my part to do something for them, worthy of their acceptance. Vrints, too, in whose house I dwell, who knows my condition, treats me with quite the old friendship.

I have recently had news in the most unexpected way of one of our other former good friends. I speak of Cepoy. The young Lieutenant Robertson of our regiment came back not long ago from Bourges, where he had been a French prisoner.

He formerly became acquainted with Cepoy at München, and met him quite unexpectedly in that far-off inner district of France, on the highroad. In spite of his dilapidated costume, which Cepoy, more from necessity than choice, had to accept like the rest of the French, Robertson knew him directly. Not so Cepoy, who, in such a place, and in the ragged teguments of a plundered prisoner of war, never imagined to see Robertson. After recognition, Cepoy, with the warmest sympathy and remembrance of his old relations with us, took up Robertson, and though he himself was in very pressing difficulties, shared his linen with Robertson. By this trait he may be easily recognised. His further history is this. He was for some time with Dumouriez, though not as aide-de-camp, made the campaign in the Netherlands with him, and became finally Lieutenant-Colonel des Chasseurs a Cheval in the garrison at Antwerp, and marched out with them from there in the retreat which took place under the capitulation of April 1793. Soon afterwards, Robespierre's measures depriving all former nobility of their rank in the army, deprived Cepoy of his. His family lived in Paris, but he dared not go there. So he had to take a position in the commissariat, most unsuitable for him, in which it became his business to ride about the country and buy up forage for the army in la Vendée. He is in poor circumstances, and made no concealment to Robertson of his bitter dissatisfaction with the whole state of things in France. His present address is: Au Citoyen Bouvier, Préposé aux Subsistances Militaires, à Saumur. I hope this capital fellow will see better days. Good-bye.

Besides several of no importance, there is a letter of this time, which in some sense closes the melancholy period, which he reviews with impartial self-analysis in a cleverly sustained parable.

Oldenburg, October 31st, 1795: Dear Brother—Very valuable to me was your letter of the 27th inst. received yesterday, and full of kind consolation what it told about the continued good opinion and friendship of those with whom I formerly associated.

Let us suppose a man to be possessor of a house, which attracted the notice of experts and non-experts more by its external appearance, by the brightness and elegance of certain parts of its furniture, than by the inner solidity of the foundation of all parts, or by the general utility of its arranged and constructed totality, and in many aspects perhaps even deceived the former. Not precisely from evil motives but from weakness, inattention, a certain mixture of vain carelessness and melancholy depression, it came about that the owner, wishing, on a special occasion, to make a general illumination of the house, accidentally let an important and dangerous part of the building catch fire, and was in extreme danger of seeing his whole property a prey to devastation. Further: What accident caused to break out, what failure of his own precautions against the danger made worse, drives his own senselessness to the highest pitch of approaching ruin. In distracted despair over his originally only partial loss he stares, sunk in passive mood, on the now flaring up, now obscured, devouring fire; half mad, he throws out into the chaos of general ruin the once valued household goods which happen to fall into his hands. Soon there stand round him only the main walls of the whole structure, and they threaten to fall in soon.

Among the bystanders, the severe and excited judges say: 'The miserable creature of an owner ought to be taken by the head and thrown into the fire, which he can take so little care to prevent.'

Others laugh at him, and all go their way, some with the suppressed chuckle of pleasure in another's misfortune, others with the half-sympathetic, half-ironical shrug of contempt.

But there remain a number of true friends, whom neither the view of the continually increasing ruin can frighten away, nor the incredible inactivity of him whose interest and duty it ought to be to stop it, without any personal risk or damage.

Some of the noblest and best among them are distinguished by the warmest and most loyal zeal. True nobility wrecks not its own natural tenderness, nor the demands of delicacy. It rises superior over every possible gossip of the higher and lower kind of mob. With rare correctness of view, with patient tolerance, with affectionate sympathy, as well as with fully deserved severity, it advises, cheers, consoles, and blames, and all that for a considerable time almost in vain.

However, there ultimately arises an appearance of hope of that which all these combined efforts for a long time could not accomplish. The householder gradually comes to his senses again; he begins gradually to clear away the almost consumed ruins; he seeks to extract from the refuse what is of any value; he begs back from his friends the goods lent them; a sad lesson has gradually taught him how to undertake the rebuilding of his house; he even thinks of improving the foundations; he at least grasps the good principle to erect everything more purposefully and solidly in future. Though he is inwardly troubled by the loss of many objects, and among them the not easily credited but only too possible destruction of goods entrusted to strange hands, he nevertheless hopes with his new structure to inaugurate a work which shall be to him a shelter, and now and then to his friends a refuge not wholly without its charm.

Brother, the application of the parable I leave to you.

A person who is in a condition to look on his own disease from so external a standpoint may well be treated as recovered.

The correspondence here ceases for a long time, nearly two years. The regiment went back to Hanover; and the country spent several peaceful years of growing prosperity behind the shelter of the line of demarcation laid down by the Peace of Basle, in a state of doubtful security.

Christian Ompteda was now thirty years old, a soldier, sobered, but educated, by three inglorious trying campaigns, a man matured by severe internal spiritual storms. For him now began an existence externally consisting merely of garrison and social life, interrupted by *cordon* service and travels while on leave, which undoubtedly had a favourable effect in smoothing and levelling the after-swell of the waves left by the storm in his soul. The above *cordon* service was under the following circumstances:—

The *line of demarcation* for North Germany was practically ignored by both sides. In the year 1796 news came to Berlin and London that the French Directory was planning an attack on the Electorate of Hanover from Holland. To meet this, the Prussian garrisons in Westphalia were strengthened to 27,000 men. To these were added 15,000 Hanoverians under

Wallmoden, who had chosen Major Scharnhorst, already distinguished in the Netherlands, again as Quartermaster-General. The *Combined Prussian-Hanoverian Army of Observation* in north-west Germany lasted from 1796 to 1801. The Hanoverian Guards were stationed during this period in Bücken, near Hoya, on the Weser, from October 1796 to January 1798, and then later in garrison at Hanover.

The essence of Christian's letters during these quiet years (1796-1802) before those of his great lifelong wanderings began (1803-1815) will be here briefly set forth, so far as they are worthy of the interest of those born in later times.

In January 1799 Christian visited his brother Louis in Berlin, where he frequented the society of that place with pleasure, but without gaining political sympathies. On his return home, he writes to Louis, February 14th, 1799:

Much as Hanover attracts me in a thousand various ways, and prized by me as are the style and manner in which my friends here have received me, the memory of the many delights associated with my stay with you is too lively for me not to experience sensations of regret at having them no longer. Forgive me the remark, dear L., but I cannot refrain from expressing the conviction that you yourself would value many of the advantages of Berlin more highly, had you, as I have, opportunity of making many comparisons. Not that I undervalue the advantages of my own country and home, or feel its influences less, which have become so dear to us by being interwoven with our earliest existence; but Hanover is, in many respects, particularly in those of social life, no longer what it was; an observation which will be confirmed even by those who have not quitted it.

He then refers to a great masquerade in Berlin, and continues:

I had on Tuesday an experience in shocking contrast with it. A fine young fellow of our 10th Regiment, who had murdered a company surgeon a few months ago, was condemned to the wheel that day, and I had unfortunately the command of the party present to keep order at the execution. I hope that will be my first and last experience of that sorry side of the service. If I wanted to continue the chapter of *horreur*, I might proceed to deal with politics. But all talking, writing, and I might say, reading, on that topic, make me perfectly sick, and all there is to do really is to wait and see whether it will come to blows again in the end or not.

Hanover, June 6th, 1799: I doubt, dear L., whether I shall be able to write so fully today as I could wish. I must, however, at least mention my return from the Prussian camp of exercise at Petershagen (on the Weser, north of Minden), in which neighbourhood I have been from the 28th ult. to the 3rd inst. The leading dispositions of the different days will be known to you. Both Royal Personages (Frederick William III. and Louisa) behaved themselves thoroughly in consistency with their known love of popularity, but as they directed their attention mainly to the military, a few of the Tondertentrunk families (probably a nickname for the local Westphalian nobility), and the spiritual and temporal bodies of Minden, must have been rather less satisfied with their share of attention. All the more had the very numerous body of Hanoverian officers, with no less than seven generals at their head, the highest reason to be charmed with the reception they met with.

Besides individual cases of distinguished notice, there was the one that applied to all of us—*i.e.,* being invited daily to dine with the King.

Perhaps that provoked some jealousy among the Prussians, who were there in smaller numbers than we. As far as regards me personally, I was remembered, especially by the Queen, in a most gracious manner, as a Berlin acquaintance. I found myself very much in the good graces of the chief lady-in-waiting (Countess Voss), which I was, however, modest enough to put down to a special *tendre* which she cherishes for you. *Elle ne jure que par votes,* and entrusted me with the sweetest greetings for you. The clear Moltke was very nice and agreeable, as she always is. Above all other acquaintances I chiefly took pleasure in seeing Hoischfeldt and Tagow again. In a general way life among the Prussians recalled to my mind nearly as many pleasant recollections of former days as did my stay with you.

Behme I spoke to one morning during the manoeuvres, but

Haugwitz I merely saw. Unless I am mistaken, his serenity was not so unshaken on this occasion; but that may be not unnaturally put down to the present political situation.

The hearty rejoicing with which we welcomed the two consecutive pieces of good news from Switzerland and Italy (fights of the Austrians and Russians against the French) was in extreme contrast with the marked effect in the opposite

direction which these events had on the greater part of the Prussians. But all these phenomena you can observe with greater completeness and ease than I can describe them.

Hanover, June 9th, 1799: According to my promise I will add a few more details in connection with the appearance of the Royal Prussian pair in our neighbourhood. I think I said that Hedemann" (chief of the household to Prince Adolphus, Duke of Cambridge, then residing at Hanover) "had been sent to Brunswick, partly to pay compliments, partly to inquire on behalf of the illustrious travellers how they would be treated during their short halt here, and particularly with regard to the persons whom they wished to meet at the Prince's. The result was that the fullest *incognito* was adhered to, in respect to the arrival, to the extent of omitting all ceremonies. With regard to the table, Prince Adolphus was left free choice to invite whom he pleased ; and yet we knew here that it was the Queen's wish to meet persons she knew, more especially the former companions of her childhood.

> The Queen was born in Hanover, where her father, the Duke Charles of Mecklenburg-Strelitz, had been a general, and spent her childhood there.

In consequence of this, an attempt was made to make the most appropriate possible combination for the claims of our notabilities of the first rank, and for the less etiquette-regulated notions of the Queen, which was facilitated by a praiseworthy abnegation on the part of several respectable individuals (as, for example, Mrs. Privy Councillor Beulwitz, and Mrs. Chief-chamberlain Grote, who declined the invitation). On the other hand, the Privy Councillor, and Chamberlain Grote, who was not invited, applied most seriously, by a written complaint that he had not been asked, and guarded himself in a solemn protestation against all resulting prejudice, to one of the Prince's Equerries!

The King was extremely genial, and the Queen recalled with the liveliest interest several details of the scene of her earlier youth. She consulted Dr. Wichman, and made to him the communication (which perhaps had better been suppressed) that it was not without the most heartfelt joy that she saw herself again in the house in which she had been born, although with this feeling was mingled the recollection of a very dear person, whom, under other circumstances, she would have been glad to find there.

The Princess Frederica, sister of the Queen, and widow of Prince Louis of Prussia, had been engaged to the Duke of Cambridge; but had at the beginning of the year 1799 very suddenly and surprisingly married a Major Prince of Solms-Brauenfels.

Prince Adolphus told me when I had my quarters in the same village with him during the Prussian encampment, that the first meeting with the Queen had moved him extremely, but that they had thenceforward entirely restrained themselves by silent agreement from all painful and useless explanations.

He had at first addressed the Queen as *Majesty*. But this she did not like, and desired that they might treat one another on the old footing as *Cousin* and *Cousine*. The Queen expressed the wish that he should think of a marriage after his own heart. He spoke on this subject very reasonably, but with something of the feeling of a burnt child who dreads the fire.

Advocem Minden, I must mention another person concerning whom your curiosity is entitled to expect news. I mean the Prince Louis Ferdinand. His whole behaviour there reminded me of Falstaff's *alacrity in sinking*. Although he behaved himself fairly carefully in the presence of the King, still one clearly saw what his state of mind was, and the sight was not pleasant. The King's demeanour towards him was as it should be, mostly serious and cool, although he drew him quite good-naturedly into his conversation with others. I find him, since I last saw him a year ago, much altered in appearance for the worse by his extraordinary compound of so many unusual and contradictory qualities. I expressed this to a Major Quitzow, a very sensible man, who replied with fitting candour, 'What can you expect? He looks like what such a loose fellow should look like.'

At night he played madly high with several of our officers at the canteen. He paid eager court to the Duke of Brunswick, but was paid out for that, when the Duke criticised harshly the badly beaten regiment of Bremer, by taking it into his head to assert that regiment to be the bravest in the army, and reminding the company of the occasions when they went under fire with such distinction with him. I think that is a characteristic trait.

In the year 1800 the Brother Louis was recalled to Hanover and nominated Postmaster-General. This office had then been just instituted. Up to then the Post had been administered only by a special minor department of Government, managed by a subordinate. In Ompteda's place the Privy Councillor of War, von Reden, was sent at his own pressing request to Berlin, who had been representative at the Congress of Rastadt, where he had had no opportunity of reaping any laurels.

The new Postmaster-General was most surprised at his appointment, and on personal grounds not exactly pleased. His brother Christian sympathises with the genesis of these feelings in his characteristic style:

I hope a future historian will derive from this useful reflections on the practical way of preventing and warding off misuses of authority. The late Post-director was enfeebled with age, and a few *plotting men* perceived the opportunity of setting up a new State-Almshouse. The leading personages in the Government were won over by the prospect of unusual profits. The thing came to maturity, and the Hanoverian postal department, stronger by two heads than the directory of the French Republic—*viz.*, two Ministers and five Privy Councillors—was presented for approval in London.

When all this was in process a fiery zeal burned among certain well-instructed and well-meaning persons, who felt strongly that the object of this institution was not so much the general welfare of a department which badly wanted purification and improvement, as a regular *job* dictated by private interests. Besides which it was felt to be monstrous to put seven people at the head of a public office which would be best managed on the principles of a military monarchy, in which unity, discipline, and prompt despatch are the chief *desiderata*. Nevertheless all the passionate complaints of these onlookers would not have hindered the consummation of the scheme, had it not come back most unexpectedly from England *revu et corrigé* and with the nominations of persons so arranged as is now officially known to you (one director and two councillors). This outcome proved a great disappointment for large numbers of those who either on the stage or behind the scenes, or merely in the pit, had taken part in the original plan. That has been, however, no reason against the selection of you giving almost universal satisfaction. You know now yourself that your appointment is the King's own work. This favourable attitude of the monarch, who has deserved true respect, as much by his correct estimate of mankind as by the quality generally conceded to him by the English, of a truly honest man, has increased and strengthened the warm individual attachment which I feel for him, since I have known him.

Beyond this the promotion was very moderate, in a financial sense; the salary of the Postmaster-General being 1,200 marks (about £60).

In December of the year 1800 Louis married the widowed Countess Christiane zu Solms-Sonnenwalde, born Countess of Schlippenbach. He spent this and the next year of his office in Hanover with his brother. The latter had scarcely anything to do in his own service, because in consequence of the general peace of Luneville (February 9th, 1801) the Corps of Observation had been demobilised. The regiment of Guards counted in both battalions only 240 heads. No correspondence took place between, the brothers. So we learn, unfortunately, nothing from Christian's pen of the provisional occupation of the Electorate of Hanover by Prussian troops under General Count von der Schulenburg-Kehnert.

The object of Prussia was to cover the line of demarcation and protect the country from an occupation by the Russians and French, directed against England.

The Alliance of these powers was called into existence in consequence of the driving of the French out of Malta, and Russia's demands concerning the *neutral flag.*

"It was," as Treitchke says, "a decided step which it was correctly supposed in England that Buonaparte would never forgive." But among the Hanoverians it provoked a mixture of depression and bitterness, with fear of coming events which had far-reaching after-effects. From this uneasiness of mind Louis Ompteda, and for him his brother Christian, had personally to suffer. The former speaks of it in his manuscript, *Recollections of My Life* :

> The first Prussian occupation of Hanoverian soil took place at this time under the command of the Prussian General of Cavalry and Minister, Count Schulenburg-Kehnert. He took up his headquarters in Hanover itself. Any resistance would have been useless, and would only have exposed the country to greater hardships.
>
> That the Prussian Commissioner should not be welcome in Hanover may be accounted for by the nature of his errand. To that may be added a certain personal mistrust, although Count Schulenburg was particular to observe outwardly the manners of a courtier, and took pains, as far as external forms lay, to alleviate the wounding nature of his charge as well as he could.
>
> Nevertheless he was avoided as much as possible. But as it seemed almost unavoidable, in order to keep up as good relations with him as possible, to at least show him a few civilities, which were, however, limited to a few stiff banquets at the houses of the chief persons of the town, which every one did his best to avoid, it happened that I, through my long stay in Berlin, and through the fact of my wife being a born Prussian, was regularly invited to these festivals. Beyond this, Count Schulenburg was ignored by everybody, and had no social intercourse except that prescribed by duty, in which, however, he was in the habit of exhibiting a tone of reserve. As a refined man of the world, he was fond of society, and it was his favourite recreation to spend the evening in a small social circle in intimate conversation, to which

he usually made the principal contribution, which could not fail in interest from a man of his keen intellect, his knowledge, and his experience.

So it happened, therefore, that Count Schulenburg often came to tea with us. As he was invited to other houses, I could not shut my house to him without distinct rudeness. I had received many distinguished attentions in his house in Berlin. He knew my wife from childhood, who had been brought up at the same school as his daughter, and in many important and complicated matters Count Schulenburg had been of valuable service to my wife's family.

At the same time my house was open to other acquaintances, and if nobody came, because they expected to find Count Schulenburg there, it was not my fault. People could easily have convinced themselves that no treasonable projects were being hatched under my roof. Count Schulenburg was particular in avoiding in conversation any allusion to his business in Hanover.

Nevertheless I had occasion to remark that this social connection gave offence to some zealous patriots. Friends told me of it; I received anonymous letters. I paid little attention to them, because my political character must be known. I have never been at all an *Ultra* in my public behaviour. Besides that, the political intention of this military occupation was not altogether unknown to me.

Finally, however, my patience was put to too hard a proof. My wife received a lengthy impassioned letter from a lady in Hanover, who stood on an intimate footing with distinguished personages (with the Duke of Cambridge, as was known to everybody, except perhaps her husband), in which my relations with Count Schulenburg were so described as to throw an ambiguous light on my calling, my patriotism, and my faith to my Sovereign, in which I was warned of the possible consequences for me which my attitude might produce. That was too much, especially from such a quarter. In my first irritation I sat down and wrote a letter to the Ministry, asking for unlimited leave to make a distant journey as the only means of avoiding undeserved slander, which seemed to be rising against me.

But before this request had reached its destination, Count Schulenburg received a despatch by express, announcing the murder of the Czar Paul, on the night of March 23rd, 1801.

Next morning the General had disappeared. In a short time all the Prussian military had followed, and we breathed more freely.

"The trouble over, this undeserved mortification," remarks his son here, "whitened in a few weeks the eyebrows of the thirty-three-year-old man. Serious people, however, took quite another view of his behaviour, because shortly afterwards Louis was offered the post of ambassador in St. Petersburg. As he declined out of consideration for his family, Count Münster was sent thither."

Later Hanoverian diplomatists have since met with similar insinuations and slanders from such passive kind of *patriots,* more zealous than reasonable, because they knew how to avoid being *Ultras* in social behaviour.

By November 1801 the whole Prussian force was withdrawn, and the old conditions in Hanover restored.

In the meanwhile, by the Peace of Luneville (February 8th, 1801), Prussia had acquired a certain expectation of the succession to the Bishopric of Hildesheim.

At the same time it was supposed in Hanover that this piece of ecclesiastical booty of the Prussians lying before the very gates, as it were, might be exchanged against the Bishopric of Osnabrück, more remotely situated from the point of view of the Electorate. For such a confidential and delicate negotiation the Government considered the Berlin Ambassador, von Reden, less qualified than the Postmaster-General, Louis Ompteda, who was therefore sent, in February 1802, to Berlin with this important and ticklish proposition, which he himself regarded from the outset as hopeless, with the ostensible mission of winding up the maintenance-accounts of the Prussian occupation of 1801.

His position there alongside the uninstructed, jealous, and officious Ambassador was extremely awkward. It appears more painful still when we call to mind the extremely intimate friend-ship of both brothers with von Reden's wife. Between the two former there develops at this period a lively correspondence.

During the year 1802 there are about fifty letters from Christian's pen.

The great delicacy with which this rocky situation was treated by those concerned, and their care to extend the great-est possible forbearance to the Ambassador von Reden, was re-markable. Moreover, a firm resistance was found necessary in the face of his struggles to withstand a so far from flattering Doppelgänger, while the fine sense of justice with which Mrs. von Reden observed the weak position of her husband, and acknowledged the forbearing behaviour of the Omptedas, as well as the written testimony of all these things, exhale so noble and pure an atmosphere, that short quotations from the letters of this period cannot be wholly spared in these pages.

On February 25th, 1802, a few clays after Louis' departure from Hanover, his brother writes to him:

I received yesterday a letter from Berlin, in which your ap-proaching, and at that time enigmatic, arrival, was touched on with friendly delicacy. I am now inclined to strengthen myself in the belief that many obstacles presenting resistance to the shock will be levelled—in that quarter, at any rate. What to expect of you I know; I therefore repeat with the greater insistence my pressing request for the fullest confidential explanation with her. She, on account of her frame of mind, and her influence on the whole future fortunes (of von Reden), unites with the need of the fullest confidence the most justifiable claim to it.

Hanover, March 4th, 1802: From what you tell me of your first meeting, I hope that all will fall into an easy track in respect to R.'s attitude towards you and position with you. The most con-soling feature will be that your mission there is only temporary. How joyful a thing it would have been for me, had you been able to tell me something about Her, you can easily imagine. A woman who feels keenly and correctly, and sees with unclouded gaze the situation and its consequences to the whole future ca-reer of herself and hers, who has no one with whom she can share these impressions—I only need indicate to you these features in order that we may try, as far as in us lies, to comprehend and soothe all her bitter feelings, great and small. I have your promise, brother! And I know you. Enough now of these too sensitive matters."

> While Louis was inducing the Ambassador, not without a struggle, and not at the last without official pressure from Hanover, to surrender the privilege of this mission to him, Mrs. von Reden writes to Christian:

>> Your sister-in-law has showed me a most consoling sympathy; I love her with my whole heart; she was so affectionate, so good to me, that I owe her thanks for ever. I have just come from your brother. I shall introduce your sister-in-law to my friends; beyond that she will require no help to make her way in society. I must now close. You can judge from the tone of this letter that I am at peace again, and breathe once more, but I have had to go through some stormy moments.

> Christian sends this to Louis, adding:

But the above is too much for a distance of seventy miles, and the Presence will make you feel much more convincingly what nothing in Absence will completely express." (An exchange of letters between Berlin and Hanover in those days took, as a rule, from ten to twelve days.)

In the following letters also Christian's feelings are repeatedly alluded to, always divided into sorrow for the reaction of the painful, personally intolerable position of the Ambassador and of his pre-eminently excellent lady, and recognition of the patience extended by his brother towards his colleague, with a justifiable wish that Louis could officially accept the position he was practically occupying.

The painful situation found its natural solution in this way, that Reden was appointed to the post far more suited to his personality in Regensburg vacated by the death of the long-time Reichstag Deputy Theodore Henry Louis Ompteda. Louis Ompteda now became formally as well as actually the representative of Hanover in Berlin, and that, with a few interruptions due to the involuntary fluctuations in Prussian politics, for twenty years.

Before I go on, to serious things belonging to general history I may put in two little pictures of life of the period in Hanover.

Prince Adolphus, Duke of Cambridge, had gone to England during the Prussian occupation of Hanover, and was now to return to the German residence of his house.

Hanover, May 27th, 1802: All here are living in expectation of the Duke, who should be here, but has been delayed by the east wind. On all sides one is met by preparations for the illuminations. The lights, transparencies, pyramids, and temples are standing waiting in all the deformity of daylight. A wondrous thing is the way of human feelings. Enthusiasm seems to have but a momentary duration with most people. The moment once gone, it often turns to the opposite extreme. To begin with, there was joyous goodwill all round. Now that there is a delay in the completion of the thing the deadly *but* is beginning to be heard. On an occasion of rejoicing (which might be otherwise regarded by the quiet reflection which follows the first inconsiderate impulse) it is certainly a pity that the rise in the price of bread-stuff should have reached almost famine proportions here. The poor people have often to hang about the baker's for hours before they can get anything to stay their hunger. Often numerous *Queues* have to stand at the shops as in similar situations in Paris. The Government does what it can, but the circumstances are adverse. To go back to the question of the arrival and its accompanying festivities ; there are those, in the lower classes especially, who say that the present is by no means the moment for public rejoicings. The Wolfshorns (then a notoriously low quarter of the town, now the *Grosse Packhofstrasse)* had to be prevented from putting up an illumination in which a doggerel distich ended with *Adolph! give us bread*' In order, when possible, to make matters worse, the aristocracy is making an ass of itself. Truly these unteachables can never learn the fact which they could grasp with their hands even—viz., the feeling which surrounds them. In this way the security of conciliation and oblivion of past grievances is being turned into a new fountain of gall-imbued bitterness, and these people are doing harm to the general welfare and wounding the honourable feelings of patriots.

The trouble lay partly in the feeling against Prussia, also in the fact that Hanover always had helplessly to suffer the consequences of England's continental policy, after the manner of a whipping-boy.

Hanover, July 15th, 1802: For the common amusement of yourself and wife, let me relate to you a little about the festival of yesterday, which, however, did not amuse me much. Mrs. von Decken (wife of the minister) had projected a *fête champêtre* for Monday, which was to be accompanied by something very *récherché* and novel in the way. of entertainment, in honour of the Duke. *Hay was to be made* in the field behind her garden. The bad weather on Monday came in the way. A rather better appearance yesterday morning brought about a renewal of the invitations, but from midday onward the weather was like November, with a ceaseless downpour of rain. But clever people are never in want of resources. After I had anxiously but vainly awaited a second postponement, I set forth in the most awful weather for the appointed *fête*. I was conducted into one of the rooms on the left, where I found the only ladies to be Mesdames Field Marshal Wallmoden, and von Arneswald, with Prince Charles of Mecklenburg, Count Lippe (Bückeburg), with an equerry, Kielmansegge, Ferdinand Ompteda (a cousin, Lieutenant in the Foot Guards), and papa and mama of the house. In the next drawing-room I heard the melody of *God Save the King* resound to moderately decent accompaniment, as a preliminary rehearsal. At length the hero of the day appeared, and the lady of the house conducted him in at the central door of the hall, where the three Hedemann girls and the two belonging to the house, dressed as peasants, made hay on the paved floor and sang couplets of *Das Hebe Heu* (The Lovely Hay). Then garlands and wreaths were offered on bended knee, and whatever other new and original surprises they could think of, all to the high edification of the onlookers, especially to mine. Another happy, and to me, alas! much too startling part of the programme, was that I had to take the direction of the dance. However, I came off with relative good fortune, for the worthy Lady Field Marshal Wallmoden said that she had at least saved me from the danger of figuring as a masked old man in the pastoral scene, and having to babble poetry.

Just think! Although the extremely vulgar proverb of the Ass playing the Lute could not possibly be more appropriately applied than to me, I made the best of a bad job, and made them dance Schottische, English, waltz, perigondine, minuet, hopser (a quick kind of waltz), and kehraus (literally *turn out!* a final dance), and even—yes! at times seized the fiddler's instrument, although my violin had been at rest for a year, and kept time with the miserable muddle they made. Eleven struck the hour for relief, long and wistfully waited for, and who was happier than I?

One more characteristic point: when the first scene was over, the lady of the house led up her eldest daughter to the Duke for a dance, with a naïve, affected curtsey. She was forced upon him, which reminded me of the Thousand and one Nights, where an enchanted prince is obliged to accept at the hands of a well-meaning fairy an ugly princess, whether he liked it or not.

We observe that if Christian was externally well inside the most distinguished circle of Hanoverian society of the period, he was nevertheless internally well outside it.

During the second half of the year 1802 the letters concern themselves almost exclusively with politics. On August 3rd, the birthday of King Frederick William III., Prussia took possession of the Bishopric of Hildesheim, and had allegiance sworn. It was the so-called compensation for losses on the left bank of the Rhine. This proceeding was looked on in Hanover with much tension, because it showed that the desired exchange for Osnabrück had obviously broken down. Christian, who was acquainted with his brother's secret commission in Berlin, considered himself bound to provide the latter with the most authentic information concerning the behaviour of the new neighbour. First, as to the taking possession:

Hanover, August 5th, 1802: On the 3rd inst, at 8 a.m., the Commanding General (Count) Schulenburg (-Kehnert) assembled his whole army corps before the gate.

The way was led by an advanced guard of Hussars in the same formation as they would take at the head of a column of attack. Then followed infantry, artillery, and lastly, the rest of the cavalry. The town magistrate met the friendly conqueror at the gate, and handed him the key of the city on a silver salver. One Horseman, Burgomaster, was orator, and let fly a rather silly flourish, comparing the Hildesheimers to the population of a conquered city; to which Schulenburg at once replied, 'That they were conquered in no sense whatever, but in consequence of a general agreement' ('of the whole country' my informant adds, but I do not believe His Excellency capable of so impudent a lie) 'were to be regarded as allotted to His Prussian Majesty as a compensation, to become henceforth an integral part of the Prussian Monarchy.'

Then the entry took place, during which a few voices of the inhabitants raised a 'Hurrah!' whereas the majority observed the novel spectacle in sullen silence. The column marched past the house of the Prince (Bishop Baron Francis Egon of Furstenberg), who beheld this cheering entry from his window.

Then the princely and civic military guard had to be informed, that they might leave their posts, which were immediately occupied by strong Prussian detachments, without giving the Prince a sentry, which he is said to have obtained at last in the afternoon. At 10 a.m. there was a full parade on the Cathedral Square, where further strange things went on. Schulenburg sent to the Imperial recruiting officer, Captain Begg, to demand his appearance at the parade. The same appeared, with a determined, perhaps rather excited deportment. Schulenburg indicated to him that 'he and his levy might depart forthwith.' Begg replied that 'he took orders from nobody except his own authorities,' whereupon Schulenburg said he would place him. under arrest. Begg replied shortly, that 'against force he could not contend, and would calmly await protection from Vienna.' Here-on he departed with an extremely confident demeanour.

It had been stated some time before that Begg had orders to resist to the uttermost, and to let himself be compelled to give way by superior force only.

The Emperor had, in point of fact, forbidden the *Provisional Occupations* until the *General Congress of the Realm* had been formed. This congress—for the purpose of estimating compensations—met on August 24th, 1802, and sat till May 10th, 1803.

Just to keep the onlookers in a breathless condition, there was another spectacle presented in the afternoon. The entire military force of Hildesheim, princely and civic, was marched up before the Town Hall, where it was disarmed, declared released from its duties, and provisionally taken note of by the Prussians, after which it was dismissed. At midnight, however, all these poor fellows had to get out of bed, and be forthwith distributed among the Prussians. They may have wanted the reinforcement, for during their victorious march the desertions had been considerable. The Prince looked on at everything with apathetic indifference, and is said to have walked about as a spectator during the disarmament. But the evening before, when the nobility bade him farewell, he shed tears. On the following day these gentlemen took steps with Schulenburg. His Excellency dilated much over native royal kindness, and allowance to retain all the privileges of their condition, *so far as the circumstances allowed*. The whole affair does not look *provisional!*

To these political cares were added military difficulties. These were connected with that pest of military life of the period—desertion. A long chain of communications was kept busy carrying out the measures taken on both sides in this connection, which came pretty near to a small frontier war. This irritating state of things was naturally destructive to the purpose of Louis' efforts, wherefore he sought to hush it up, and particularly warned his countrymen not to let these differences make themselves felt in personal intercourse. Christian does not find it so difficult for his brother in Berlin, but, "If a man has a feeling of honour for his fatherland left, it is hard if it does not recall in him, with the memories of the year 1801, *Remember!* as the ghost of Hamlet's father did to his son. I cannot quite take your distinction between individuals and government as valid, when will and intention of both are most likely working in the same direction." But on reflection his opinion turns towards the other more serious side of the question, and he throws on it a marvellous prophetic light:

Whether it would not be wise, in the evil condition to which stupidity and cowardice have reduced us, to have recourse to the weapon of weakness, viz., dissimulation, it would be a question easier to say yes to than (in the case of many, at least) to carry out. Dear L., whatever your present, and perhaps for the moment (God grant it!) correct view may be, here is my conviction, and you can think what you like of it. The Prussian Cabinet, and all Prussians, will always regard *the possession of our country* as their great aim, to which all their efforts are directed. They will not attain it now, because it does not suit the convenience of their aider and abettor. But let there be any European commotion again, and we shall probably repeat the second part at least of the history of Saxony during the Seven Years' War. They have learnt to know us too well. That it should have to be so!

We conclude here with this, for 1802, certainly rarely inspired foreboding, founded on a breadth and depth of historic and political insight, in which the young Captain in the Guards then (and much later) stood, it may be said, alone among his countrymen.

The other numerous letters of the winter 1802-3 treat mainly of current news of the day on life, and things in Hanover with which Louis was to be kept *au courant*. There is perceptible in their prevailing tone an uncanny calmness before the storm. Not the slightest hint of approaching disaster, no indication of a certainly impending outbreak of war between France and England, threatening the Electorate, or the intention of Buonaparte to reply to the refused evacuation of Malta by England by occupying Hanover, or of the fact that the English Government would undoubtedly deplore the invasion of Hanover, but pay no further attention to it in their policy.

Even as late as March 1803 people were only thinking of Hildesheim, and its desired exchange for Osnabrück in course of negotiation.

So closes the second phase of Christian Ompteda's life, From henceforward its course is one of unrest and pilgrimage, through twelve long years of danger, hardships, and struggle. But when at last this noble high-beating heart found rest, he had earned the imperishable reward which was the fulfilment of all his longings: the reward, high and everlasting, of the loyalty and self-sacrifice of a true unselfish man, and a brave obedient soldier, from the God of Battles, which can never be taken away.

CHAPTER 3

The French Conquest of Hanover
March 21st—July 13th, 1803

For the easier comprehension of the events in Christian Ompteda's life embraced in this section, it will again be well to recall the facts of general history bearing thereon. This may be the more necessary, inasmuch as the conquest of Hanover by the French in the year 1803, and the annihilation of its army, depended on complicated and bygone political conditions scarcely conceivable by people now living.

When George I ascended the throne (1714), the most intimate personal union with England was distinctly established. The constitution, government, and interests of Hanover as a member of the general German realm were unconditionally separated from the English by Act of Parliament. Nevertheless, Privy Councillor Von Hattorf, after bringing about the Act of Succession of the Brunswick-Lüneburg House to the English throne, had already made the prophetic announcement as to the future fate of Hanover: "I have done a thing which the world has not expected, at which my countrymen wonder. But I fear future generations will condemn it." And so it was.

The Electorate had, in consequence of its actual, though not constitutional, dependence on England, to suffer powerlessly through a century all the rebuffs of English policy.

Already in 1797, after he Peace of Basle, the French Directory stated in its official papers with respect to Hanover that the Republic *devait chercher son ennemi partout où on pouvait l'atteindre*.

For Buonaparte, Hanover was, moreover, the Achilles-heel of the enemy, whom he could not otherwise get a hold of. So he broke the German Electorate, under the illusion that he would bend the King of England.

Immediately after this complete ruin of Hanover and its brave army, a bitter paper-war arose, a regular deluge of mutual incriminations and justifications poured out to and from all sides. It was natural that the ill-used army attributed its disruption, which it looked on as a disgrace, to the two heads of the Government, Field Marshal Count Wallmoden, and the Cabinet Minister von Lenthe in London. But even allowing for the weakness and incapability of both these men, one as army leader, the other as statesman, and to their sins of omission, one has to look still deeper for the reasons of Hanover's helpless and disarmed state—viz., to the political demoralisation of Emperor and realm, in one word, of our whole nation. Hanover in itself was not essentially worse governed than Prussia was till 1807, or than Austria was till 1811, and so forth. It required first, as we who are of the present day know, twelve years in the hard school of adversity to wake our folk again, so that it should rise in youthful might once more, and shake off inward and outward fetters, so that the immortal German soul might clothe itself again with a young and growing body. The men, too, who had to represent with their personally honourable names decaying age, and a state of things abandoned by all the Great Powers, above all the three commissioners to the Convention of Sulingen, appear to us to deserve sympathy rather than blame.

The old Hanoverian army, regarded as a military organisation, had fallen no less into senile decline than the other German military bodies. It had decreased after the Revolutionary War, the third part of the establishment in the year 1803, about 15,000 men on paper, being on almost perpetual leave at their homes, and an infantry battalion having an average establishment of 215 men.

In England extensive preparations for war were being made, in spite of the Peace of Amiens (March 27th, 1802). In reference to this Talleyrand presented Lord Whitworth, the English Ambassador in Paris, on March 11th, 1803, with the verbal note, which did not become known till later:

> If we receive no satisfactory explanation of these armaments in England, it will be but natural consequence that

the First Consul must send 20,000 men to Holland. And if these troops once arrive in that country, it is obvious that they should form a camp on the frontier of Hanover.

Surely the hint was clear enough. Yet Minister von Leuthe, residing with the King in London, trusted to the Line of Demarcation, of the Peace of Basle, and the Peace of Lüneville between Germany and France. He *would* not see any real danger. On the 15th and 22nd of April both he wrote to Hanover that "Peace will be maintained." The Duke of Cambridge, serving as Lieutenant-General in Hanover, sent an adjutant, Major von der Decken, in March to London, in order to get a clear view of things, and at the same time to represent Hanover's condition. King George III gave him to understand that his wish was "to endeavour first to obtain the support of Prussia; failing that, the troops were to be assembled at Stade, and from there finally shipped to England." At the same time the French corps in Holland received the official designation of *Armée de Hanovre*. Decken then negotiated vainly in Berlin, supported by the War-Councillor, Louis Ompteda. To diplomatic intrigue in St. Petersburg may be ascribed a Russian note delivered in Berlin, to the effect that "the Czar would be very unwilling to see Hanover occupied by Prussian troops." This decision was in a curious way mainly called forth by the Hanoverian Ambassador, Count Minister, who was treating according to instructions from Minister Leuthe, who was again reckoning, quite groundlessly, on Russian support. Such apparent double-dealing in Hanoverian policy annoyed the straightforward mind of Frederick William III., who had already felt deeply the misinterpretation of his benevolent intentions in occupying Hanover in the year 1801. The King then said to Field-Marshal Wallmoden: "Here am I put in difficulties, through this cursed war we are again threatened with, on account of a country which does not deserve my interest in the least, having repaid me with so much ingratitude for what I did in the face of pressing obstacles, *Anno* 1801, and slandered me afterwards into the bargain."

In the meantime Field Marshal Wallmoden had, under increasing pressure from the Government since April, ordered the immediate mobilisation of the army, the burden of whose neglected condition fell mainly on his back. He was personally a brave, cultivated man, with a strong sense of duty. But he had the misfortune of not being a really professional soldier. Favoured by his natural relationship to the Royal House, he had very rapidly gone through the *Prince career*, which advances by leaps. Born in 1736, he was nominated in 1759 (then only twenty-three) from Chamberlain to Colonel of the Life Guards, whom he commanded in the Seven Years' War. After many years as Ambassador at Vienna, he was promoted in 1776 to Lieutenant-General, in 1784 to General of Cavalry. In the campaigns of 1793-5 he commanded the Hanoverian Corps (after the departure of Field Marshal Freytag), and lastly the so-called *combined army*. Then he became Master of the Horse, and finally, as senior General, Commander-in-Chief and Field Marshal.

During this dilatory and topsy-turvy mobilisation, Wallmoden developed an activity for which he must be given due credit. But the testimony applies to himself, which he bore in his later published justification, *Account of the Position in which the Hanoverian Army was found in the months of May, June, and July 1803,* with reference to the Corps of Officers. "That what human power could do in those critical days was accomplished by the officers; that hours could certainly not make good what years had ruined and destroyed."

"Wallmoden," says one of the Field Marshal's contemporaries, "was by nature rather careful, and dilatory in his resolutions." Scharnhorst's criticism of him we know already. One thing mainly responsible for this condition of things was the obstinate refusal of funds for several years, and the constitution of the different provincial governments. These latter had requested that the sons of the soil might be protected by binding guarantees from being further used as English auxiliary troops, and, as in 1793-5, made the victims of English policy.

But the helpless Government machine, dependent on London, only introduced incomplete, stupid, and dilatory measures. It was not till May 16th that the Ministry issued a proclamation, which was, however, drawn up with such incredible awkwardness that the impression the country derived from it was that a *general armament of the nation* was what it was intended to convey. It therefore provoked active opposition. It had only been intended to demand an immediate increase of those liable to service provisionally of about 30,000 men.

A fugitive pamphlet of the period, of which Chamberlain

Frederick Ompteda (died 1819 as Ambassador at Rome) was the author, satirises the measure in the following terms:

Levy for the Defence of the Land
A. All court-servants and other loafers.
B. All the poachers in the country for a Jäger corps.
C. All those who despise rank in order that they may get it.
Any one not able to stand fire to hold his tongue.
D. All customs officials, to act as spies.
E. All respectable convicts, gaol-birds, and mole-catchers. Any one who does not wish to join can have his leg broken. This will cost, according to the new medical tariff, four thalers six groschen to cure. Trephining comes cheaper: without brains, three to four thalers. If these be damaged, they can be supplied from ten to twelve thalers; extra-super, fifteen thalers.

But all resolutions to strengthen the army came much too late. At the end of the month of May the Hanoverian troops began to move towards the Weser; by June 1st there stood there about 6,300 men and 2,700 horses. But at the same time negotiations were quietly going on for the capitulation of the country and the troops. The Duke of Cambridge refused any co-operation, resigned his command, and went to England.

On June 3rd the notorious Convention of Sulingen was concluded between General Mortier on the one side, and the Hanoverian plenipotentiaries, Court and Provincial Judge von Bremer, Lieutenant-Colonel, commanding the Life Guards, von Boch, and, as their assistant, Councillor of Commerce Blandes.

The Electorate was left in a defenceless state. The troops were to withdraw to the right bank of the Elbe (into the then Hanoverian Duchy of Lauenburg). Then came the retreat over the barren Lüneburg heath under great difficulties and privations. Exciting rumours of being shipped to England—to the West Indies—were spread among the troops. A part of the cavalry in particular showed signs of mutiny. Desertion became rife, *as there wasn't going to be any fighting.*

Local deputations from the country came to Lauenburg to beg that an end might be made of useless resistance. After severe inward struggles Field Marshal Wallmoden gave way, and concluded with Mortier at Arthenburg, on July 4th, the second Convention.

Article 3. of this stated: "The Hanoverian Army is (hereby) dissolved."

Article 4.: "The Hanoverian officers can go on parole to such places of residence as they choose, on condition of not quitting the Continent."

On the day when the English transports were to start to take up the Hanoverian troops in the Elbe, the Convention of Arthenburg reached London. The King ignored it, as he did that of Sulingen.

Thus, for the time, these brave and renowned troops were scattered to the winds of Heaven.

Framed on the above brief *data,* the relation of Christian Ompteda's adventures in the following letters is comprehensible, so far as his personal experience and information go, and as far as he could criticise from the standpoint of his personal views and feelings.[1]

Christian's letters of this, the third period of his life, begin from March 21st, 1803. They continue almost without interruption to June 29th. Between that date and July 7th, and from then to July 13th, there are *lacunæ* accounted for by the fact that Christian was with his brother at the time. The latter came on July 1st to the headquarters of Field Marshal Wallmoden at Gülzow, went back on July 3rd to Berlin, and appeared again at headquarters at Mölln on July 9th.

An account of these proceedings by Louis, written many years later, may serve to complete Christian's experiences, and to close this section of the latter's biography.

The time was now going to be ripe which Christian had so long and impatiently desired, the time of renewed, lasting, fresh military activity, unfettered by the earlier generally lamentable political conditions. But when it dawned, when the young officer stood on its very threshold, he knew it not. No one around him was willing to acknowledge it. His first letter to Louis of March 25th seems still almost without a foreboding. It was not till four weeks later that the desperate condition of Hanover was clearly revealed to him.

Christian to Louis:

---

1. *The Conquest of Hanover by the French* obtained an exhaustive description, found among the secret archives at Hanover, by the late Royal Privy Councillor Frederick Baron Ompteda (Hanover : Helwing, Court Bookseller, 1862).

Hanover, March 21st, 1803: On Thursday (March 17th) I was dining with the Duke. After he had withdrawn, and most of the guests were gone, Decken (Adjutant to the Duke of Cambridge) took me confidentially on one side to ask me if I had any commissions for England, whether there was anything there I wanted done then, because he was about to go there. Afterwards he distinctly mentioned London *and Paris*. I thanked him most sincerely for his confidential communication. That opened the way, and we exchanged our opinions on the important matters of the moment; and out of it all the result came to about this, that in the first place Decken was going to England on a Government mission.

People are now convinced that our *postulanda* in Berlin, particularly with regard to Hildesheim, will never be granted. Wherefore it is proposed to bring the negotiations there entirely to an end, and apply to the great fountain head—Paris. France and Russia are supposed to have promised that Prussia should agree to a cheap exchange for the needful Hildesheim cession. The great thing is how to get these promises carried out. Decken seemed to feel oppressed with the weight of the difficulties, expressed great unwillingness to undertake the journey, and said he would willingly give a, thousand thalers not to have to do it, if it were possible.

We had got so far with our little plans, and Decken was just gone, when the English post came in of March 10th, with the news of the King's Messages to both Houses of Parliament, and their unanimous reply, the considerable fall in the funds—in a word, the manifold symptoms of a fresh war. My dear fellow, all that gave me, and I will not deny it, a feeling of joy and relief. When one has got so far as to be unable to take any satisfactory interest in the politics of one's own country, it becomes a great source of joy to see a foreign nation treat matters in such a way, and to hear its most distinguished men of all parties speak in such a way. I remembered what Sheridan said on a former occasion: 'In calculating the strength of a nation I do not ask for their numbers; but show me the mind and spirit of the people, and I will tell you whether they will be subdued or not.'

The same feeling echoes in all the English speeches, and in truth, in case of¯ necessity, fleets and armies will not fail to respond to it.

By-the-bye. Should Buonaparte become more tractable under pressure of the prevailing English tone, it is possible to hope, from the apparent sympathy of the English Ministry, that their method of negotiation will have an advantageous after-effect for us, in which case the miserable views of the howlers here will be put to shame, who never could find salvation in anything but jeremiad's. But among these great foreign events I must not forget my own small ones. Among them are some of extreme interest, and I will come to them at once after once more taking up the thread of Decken's discourse. Talking of the *negotiations* in Berlin, we naturally came to speak of the *two* negotiators there. In that connection the following extremely important disclosures came to light, which I repeat *to you,* and to *you only*: Decken said he was present when our King took into his head the idea, of his *own accord,* of sending you to Berlin. *Your* despatches are the only ones which he reads, and is glad to read. The Reden despatches are in evil odour with him since Rastadt, and could not be laid before him, and Decken seemed to believe that it was only through the holding of them back that the King got the idea that Reden was no longer in Berlin. Wherefore people here (the Duke of Cambridge) are convinced that our Embassy in Berlin cannot last longer on its present footing. They would be willing to give Reden credit for his other good qualities, and to build him a golden bridge with triumphal arches, if only it would facilitate his withdrawal. In any case the condition of things *must* be changed, and they have no one in their eyes but you, as the man for a post which is always so important. What will be the upshot of all this for Reden. Heaven alone knows! I suppress all that I might add of *my own* views on this subject. That my inmost sympathy would be therein expressed in a *two-fold* respect you can suppose. In regard to *yourself* only, I beg that you will so consult for your future condition, as to utilise all its unquestionable advantages, and not sacrifice yourself in the face of such decisive prospects.

Brother Louis was perpetually expressing unwillingness to continue the diplomatic service forced on him by fate, and preferred his employment in Hanover.

Decken said, among other things, that you and Minister were the only persons whose future advancement the King contemplated with real pleasure.

The post of Cabinet Minister in London is alluded to, which both men held in succession at a later period.

You owe it to yourself and yours not to renounce such prospects, even if they must be purchased by a temporary sacrifice of your inclinations. The possible demise of our King would undoubtedly bring about many changes, but even in that case— *olim meminisse juvabit.*

Pardon me if I add a repetition of my request to keep these disclosures, so important for us, *exclusively* to yourself. Not from any kind of mistrust of her with whom it would be most natural for you to share them (L.'s wife), but because I know—perhaps from unfavourable experience of my own—that in later distant times people are liable to make known confidential outpourings of one's heart, under the impression that it does not matter *then*, confidences harmless in themselves, but capable of being misunderstood by others, and that at a time when explanation from the original source is no longer possible. Here I conclude. To add something more, lying still nearer to my heart, is more than I can do.

Hanover, April 17th, 1803: I utilise an opportunity which has been presenting itself for some time to give my pen an unrestrained course. And if these pages do not shed any fresh light on the grave crisis of the moment, they may serve as a response to the disclosures you confided to me, which I value at their full worth.

That the state of our country may be termed desperate, in the event of a real outbreak between France and England, is an opinion which I share with everybody capable of a little reflection. But it may be remarked, in passing, that it is surprising what a quantity of people here display the characteristics of the ostrich, that peculiarity of that creature which consists in hiding its stupid head in a hollow tree in order to hide itself from the approaching peril of the hunt. The paternal *mothers* of the Fatherland do not seem, however, to share this illusion. There seem to have been Cabinet-Councils *sub rosa,* and attended by the Field Marshal, too.

The last English letters came in at the beginning of last week, and some people are inclined to augur well of their contents; because they chose to detect a special elation in the Duke after he had received them. About the same time the bankers here got private news from the house of Hope in Amsterdam, which contained assurances of peace, whereby the weak-minded and credulous were revived as by an Evangel. Many circumstances have, in the meantime, compelled me to suspend my conviction for a while. I was extremely pleased to find that you adhered to the point of view, according to which no fair-minded person can refuse to the English his warm approval of their measures, or his best wishes for an honourable consummation of them, be the event what it may. But should we, in the worst case, have nothing but such passive sympathy? Are we destined, if it comes to war, to become the victim of the shameful injustice of the West, or the more shameful perfidy of the East? Is there no other prospect save to bury the few still glimmering sparks of courage and patriotism in *this* country in cold ashes? Will they, *can* they think of no other course than the completest surrender to the might of circumstances? Well, then there would be at least one way out, one way to rescue the last living twig of strength and honour of the country, and that would be to plant it on a soil more favourable to growth than its native one. To speak less parabolically, if there is war, England will surely want an army and arms, be they only so few thousand; in that case, hail to the measure by which they would be called on to fight in foreign lands for the cause of justice and honour, instead of seeing their hitherto honourable names perish in deep disgrace in their own land; whereby they might maintain the claim either to bring back its old good fame to their Fatherland or *never to see it again.*

One more point *of a political nature* I must touch upon. Is it not possible to open the eyes of the King of Prussia to the true nature, if not of the situation, at any rate, of the way in which it was treated in 1801, *and its natural consequences!* Of his integrity (I use the word *Biederkeit* only because it is here appropriate) I had never any doubt. But perhaps he is the only man in his kingdom who takes the view he does of his relations with us, and really we should not deserve the interest he used to take in us, had we been able to behold the events of which we were eyewitnesses (1801), with other feelings than those which will not be easily blotted from our memories.

Hanover, April 25th, 1803: A thing has happened which surprised me, and that is, that we all—artillery, cavalry, and infantry—were warned by a general order of the Field Marshal eight clays ago, that perhaps at the end of the drill season the troops might have to be assembled in small camps of exercise, wherefore we were to direct our attention forthwith to the; replenishing of field requisites, and the provisional acquisition of the vehicles necessary for purposes of transport. The drill is in a fine mess, and the cavalry and artillery in particular have by no means mastered their new systems. Candidly, I only look on this ostensible purpose as a mask to cover preparations for something serious. But with what aim? That is the question, and particularly whether something is being contemplated of the sort which I prefigured to you in my last letter. That several among us are speculating, and reasoning, and unreasoning to that effect, is a matter of course, but, on the other hand, regrettable, if I mention that they are already announcing a battle at Bentheim here with 50,000 of Buonaparte's heroes knocked on the head. *Il n'y a de décidément victorieux chez nous que la bétise.*

Hanover, April 30th, 1803: Decken came back from England the day before yesterday evening. I sat next to him at a dinner at the Duke's yesterday. He said nothing of the original object of his journey—Hildesheim to wit—and of course I asked no questions. But in the event of anything new turning up, you will hear of it more authentically than through me. I gather that our King is as well as ever in mind and body, and deeply interested in the prospects of our country. Decken seems as much in favour as ever. If he uses it with intellect and honesty he will have my entire approval.

Hanover, May 16th, 1803: Louis Wallmoden will bring you this letter. I gain thereby a means of free communication, the subject-matter of which has acquired a very definite character since my last. Decken's appearance in that quarter will, I hope, have been not wholly surprising to you, in consequence of the preliminary hint which I was enabled to give you accidentally. I doubt if he will be the saviour and deliverer there, but fortunately my views and principles *here* are not more those of one crying in the wilderness than before. A better spirit has at length prevailed, I do not myself quite know how—over the passive surrender of pusillanimity. The lamentation and howling is now confined to the females of both sexes, and the resistance of the egoists to any kind of effort or sacrifice must not get abroad. That measures be taken, in the case of a hostile attack which, in the worst event, may justify us for the laconic saying, of Francis I. of France after the Battle of Pavia, seems to me to be mainly the work of the Field Marshal.

As to preparations and arrangements, which are being put on a proper footing with most praiseworthy secrecy, I have to say the following:—

The report of last month, which I saw yesterday, admits that, thanks to our exquisite organisation, and lack of any rational territorial system, we can put a little over 12,000 effective troops in the field, of which about a quarter are cavalry. At last the Government and the local authorities have opened their eyes, and the latter, of whom the great majority are in favour of a stout defence, agree to a levy of 18,000, of whom 10,000 to be raised at once. At the same time 2,200 invalids will be armed and made into four battalions, mainly destined to occupy Hameln. The total garrison will thus be raised to 3,400, and provisioned for four weeks. A principal magazine will probably be established in Stade. All the available horses are being counted up, the number, with the foals excepted, coming to 120,000 in the whole country, and, including the unavailable ones, to 160,000 (?). I only mention this with the view of pointing out the strength of this particular resource. Better than all this is the excellent spirit animating the soldiers especially, and, as far as I hear from several quarters, the population at large. Our men look on the *quæstio an?* of fighting the French, *Wenn hey nich ruhig syn kann*, as quite settled, and their natural feelings give them a far better grip of the whole matter than those whose less pure passions (notably that of fear, the strongest) obscure the correct point of view.

If he can't hold his peace—*hey* being obviously the Frenchman.

I hope you do me the justice to believe that I am fully aware of the inequality of the contest, as a whole, or in the long run. But if we are to do nothing with the materials which are at our disposal except make a disgraceful submission, the country had better at once be covered over with yellow or blue on the map, to denote the devouring matter, for it would be no longer worth while to carry on the old name. In this connection it has been a pleasant surprise to me to see how the actual sight and assurance of strong measures wakes everybody up, and directs all forces to a common purpose. What the general plan of operations will be, in case of an attack from the west, I have too few *data* to reckon from. I have made my own speculations on the subject, and shall develop them. If they are of no other use, they will do on the next safe opportunity to conduct you on a military promenade through part of our country, in which you will at least find more novelty than at the Berlin and Potsdam manoeuvres.

May 17th, Morning: I have just received your letter of the 14th. Thanks for the expected agreement to my opinions; I could be sure of that from the outset, from *you.*

Dear L., he who does not abandon himself will never fail to find backers in a cause so just as ours is. 'Make a first stand with a manly spirit,' and the bulk of the defence often grows in the quarter in which it is least expected.

Hanover, May 20th, 1803: The dice are cast, at least as far as England and France are concerned, and we are here for the present in a state of doubt, which is more unpleasant than dead certainty.

Perhaps you already possess the accompanying important proclamation. It will receive your complete approval, and such is the case also with most people. Still one often runs against egoistic critiques and reservations where they least ought to occur. Our national spirit is, despite all its hereditary failings, good. But whether the people can be got out of their customary easy-going state—that's where it sticks. Still, even the *vis inertiæ;* itself may be electrified with greater energy. But as for the two great levers which quicken nations out of themselves, reasons to inflame national enthusiasm, or *a leading man* whose spirit and fire penetrate the multitude with lightning speed, whose steadfast courage gives them resolution and endurance—there is nothing of that sort visible.

But to come to particulars. In consequence of the proclamation, the lists were made up on Wednesday of those available for service in the district of the Mayoralty (Hanover New-town, and Garten-gemeinde), and in this district alone were enumerated 2,000 men. The results in other districts I do not yet know. There can be no lack of numbers, but what I do not clearly see is how these masses are going to be organised and utilised. The realisation of this, and the general *lack of rapidity,* is what strikes everybody, and naturally not to advantage. A burgher was giving me his views on this point yesterday, with the flattering addition that if I were only to assume command of a battalion out of the mass for purposes of organisation, there would be no lack of candidates for it. Very flattering, I am sure; and if this favourable opinion were not very individual it would be a valuable prejudice in my favour. But I tell you that I have more confidence in the battalion I *do* command, and hope to do more good with it than with a legion of mere national guards. As to our regular force, we shall advance, in case of necessity, without being mobilised at all. The field baggage must be taken in vehicles. What will be done about the artillery horses I do not yet quite know. There is indisputably much that is unpleasant about this method, but necessity has no law, and under the circumstances in which we are placed each of us will willingly do his best to overcome difficulties. Otherwise long marches will be quite out of the question.

I have just heard, from a good source, that in three days there will be a *real levy of recruits for the regular regiments* in consequence of the proclamation, which is, however, not generally understood. The same informant assures me that the Field Marshal is opposed to all projects of *Landsturm* (= national guard, more or less), and I think he is right. *Cela s'en va en fumée et nuit au vrai feu.*

I close in haste. A thousand loves and good messages to all yours. You will act *there,* I know. A common success—there and here—would be a consummation greatly to be wished.

Sunday, May 22nd, Morning: When I came back from drill with the battalion yesterday morning, I saw Job's message on all faces. It consisted of the fact that war was formally declared in England on the 16th, and furthermore, that the French were on the march, and were already at Bentheim. This received double and multiple weight from the interesting detail that the Minister's servants went round very early with despatch boxes, and told one another that the news was very bad.

Yesterday afternoon we began to revive again—shall I say fortunately? Henze, the courier from Berlin, had come. Soon after that the *public knew* that Prussia had definitely declared the intention of taking our part in case of an attack, and for that purpose had already sent orders to the Westphalian regiments to take the necessary steps. Although the contents of your letter of the 19th, received by the above-mentioned channel, do not seem to give much occasion for triumph, and although I try to preserve a sober moderation, as I am bound to do, more particularly as I do not know whether this statement comes from you or Decken, still it is a good thing to start the current of popular feeling in a better direction.

With regard to the news from Bentheim, I have not been to ascertain how much or how little foundation it has. Vincke has been there for some time *on the look out.* Yesterday several couriers are said to have come from him, but the Field Marshal is supposed to have stated that they were to the effect that the French were keeping quiet as usual. In a general way, I repeat, he toils without ceasing, and meets in every direction with organic defects in our Constitution, and the indescribably slip-shod way of conducting business now acknowledged even by civilians. It cannot be concealed that our condition here does not look favourable for the country at large. Now that people expect salvation from us they wish we were on a better footing. When I go about among my men, and gather from every little expression what might be done with troops of that mind and temper if what cripples us were not a cause so deeply rooted and beyond our power to remedy—really, brother, it leads to reflections which I will not write down, for you will read them in my soul.

A non-commissioned officer who has been to Hameln under orders has just reported to me, and says that they are taking active measures for .the setting of Hameln in a state of defence, that he met with a good spirit everywhere, heard people cheering for the Duke of Cambridge, and saw in Münder a shield put up with the inscription to that effect—'Vivat! Long life to the Duke of Cambridge!' Indeed, the good comes from below upwards, while from above downwards they are doing their best to prostrate it—always excepting the Duke and the Field Marshal, who has been so long struggling with our domestic obstruction. A temporary assembly in the neighbourhood of Nienburg, on this side of the Weser, seems contemplated. We here will probably be the last to quit. We have orders to provide leathers for the accoutrements of double our present establishment. Our regiment has got them in store, but others will have the greatest difficulty in furnishing themselves with the same.

An important and needful step is a proclamation about to be issued, whereby all authorities will be put under severe responsibility to deliver all requisites for the troops without delay. If the Field Marshal could only become Dictator in the widest sense of the word!

Hanover, May 22nd, Sunday, after 1 p.m.: As you have been told nothing officially, I hasten to add a second appendix to the letter which is already on its way, to inform you that the crisis, in our sense of the word, seems to be approaching. Again, through the women—particularly Sophie M., who addressed me in the street about it, with tears in her eyes—I first learnt that evil tidings had come in since yesterday, and that the French were on the march. But where I cannot make out, but from all I otherwise learn and see, the news has a foundation. It was to be foreseen. But as everything depends upon time, and we have lost months and days, and are losing them still, you can understand how doubly we feel the paralysis which cripples us, not by our own fault, but certainly by the fault of others.

But all this, and a thousand more such things that I could say, will, I hope, not prevent me from remembering Ariosto's words: 'Ruggiero spake: "Let us give over care, and let us do as if all hung on *us;* the rest be left unto the Lord of Heaven."'

I will add, on those also whom we trust in the earnest moments of life; and since I reckon you among such, I will perhaps take another opportunity of telling you at greater length.

Hanover, May 26th, 1803, *2 p.m. In great haste:* The reality of the declaration of war between France and England is now confirmed by half a dozen expresses, who reported to me all at once, while I was writing to you this morning. There is no express direct from Holland. It is therefore supposed that the French do not let any pass through. Our news is from Bremen, where it was placarded on the Bourse. Moreover, the English mails are not come, though the wind is fair. They say there is a general embargo, so strict that it extends even to the packet boats.

Your last letter distinctly said that Prussia and Russia do not yet know what they are going to do. I hope *we* know what *we* are going to do. But would to God we had found it out a little sooner! and then we—*i.e.,* the Executive—would not be so weighed down by internal obstruction, which we have made a determined struggle against, but which, at the same time, must cripple us in our struggle with the external enemy.

Fifteen thousand men have been raised in the last few days, and will be apportioned among the infantry. Just think of the disproportion to the old stock of the regiments, in explanation of which I enclose our yesterday's regimental state,[2] and the catalogue of recruits which has been delivered to it.

---

2. This has been lost. According to authentic accounts the strength of the regiment of two battalions of eight companies at the dissolution was 43 officers, 823 non-commissioned officers and men—*i.e.,* about 50 men to a company. The recruits were then already dismissed.

We have really received only 18 men per company, but the others will of course follow in a few clays. But just think what it means, to make a soldier out of a ragged clodhopper, if only approaching at all to our old ones, if only able to stick in their places in the ranks! Wherefore we are lacking in many articles of extreme necessity, especially sufficient uniform cloth, and are overwhelmed with work. And yet we have to get them clothed in from eight to fourteen days! But shall we have the eight to fourteen days to do it in? *Eh bien! Nous marcherons en demi-sans-culottes,* and if the fellows have not been able to master the art of letting off a musket, they can go in with the bayonet and the butt.

I shall most likely write to you again from here by the next post. I have, indeed, been confidentially informed that a battalion of the 2nd Regiment, which lies here, is to leave in a few days, but we shall probably be the last of all—*last, but, I hope, not least.*

The printed notice (that of May 24th, to the effect that no *Landsturm* was intended to be raised, but only a levy of recruits for the regular forces) would have prevented a good deal of harm if it had come out sooner. You know how I told you it would be, at the outset. We had to send out three parties yesterday to bring the peasantry to order, who made a disturbance about the levy. The strongest has marched to Loccum, and consists of 100 infantry and 30 horses, under Captain Wurmb of ours. The whole thing is only intended to frighten, and, it is hoped, will have no other result; but compulsory levies are detestable measures, and give rise to legitimate complaints. And we might have been saved all that by a rational Cantonal constitution, in which only will was wanting.

But on the whole, the spirit among the recruits obtained under such circumstances is better than might be expected, and it will not be *our* fault if everything necessary is not done to keep it up.

PS—I have been so taken up, in my letter, with the internal difficulties of our own organisation, that I entirely forgot the external. So I write these further lines to tell you that the most probable thing I have heard about the French army (which they must needs now call *l'armée d'Hanovre),* is that they have extended their position this side of the Yssel, between Zütphen and Zwoll. They are said to be in great lack of stores, particularly forage, for which reason the cavalry have to get green forage, and so appear at times before Bentheim, which is only about four miles to their front.

The hatred of the Dutch for the French is said to be without bound, so that a Frenchman dare not go out alone at night time. They will have to leave a whole army behind in that country.

Oh, if they only would!

I hear today a rumour that the French will occupy Emden with the consent of the Prussian court. But no! Baseness cannot go so far.

Hanover, May 30th, 1803, 5 a.m.: Everybody is on the move, and the General Advance is beating. But I have a few moments left. We march today to Neustadt, to-morrow to Nienburg, where, it is said, we shall make a halt. It seems the main body is to be cantoned on the Weser, the advance guard the other side, and our Light Dragoons in Lemförde. If we had only eight to fourteen days for the numerous recruits they would be ready, if their training in all military senses were equal to their good spirit. However, the thing has got to be done; and that is the general belief among the troops, what with all the hindrances from within, which give us much more trouble than what may happen without.

I hear that since Werner Bussche had been sent as courier to Bentheim the day before yesterday, Lieutenant-Colonel Bock and my friend Brandes set out yesterday in the same direction. Their object would be only to make polite inquiries as to the particular purpose of these numerous visits (of the French).

The Duke remains here still to-day, on account of the Government; it is said he will probably follow us tomorrow. The Field Marshal is still here too, where, in the centre of authority, any serious internal precautions may be more readily taken. Again, farewell.

Nienburg, June 1st, 1803: We have been here since yesterday. Last night the French, whose advanced guard reached Wildeshausen the day before yesterday, entered Diepholz. General Hammerstein is in front of Sulingen with four battalions, six squadrons, and one battery of Horse Artillery. You see we must soon come in touch. The main direction of the enemy seems in the meantime to be, as I always supposed, towards Bremen. The General commanding the advanced guard must have notified this, to some extent. Werner Bussche, for example, who passed yesterday on his way back as courier to Hanover, informed us that Captain Vincke was sent by General Linsingen to Wildeshausen to ask (the French) what they really meant. Whereupon the French general replied briefly and somewhat doubtfully that he was surprised at the question, as the war with England was a notorious fact. Vincke retorted that Hanover was not an English province, but a German state, and under no definite bond to England. The other replied that they could make what they liked out of that, but that he was not concerned with these distinctions; that he had orders from General Mortier to march on Bremen, and that he was going to do it, and did not care about anything else. And, indeed, it was a good soldier-like answer.

You will have learnt already from Hanover that Bock, Judge Bremer, and Brandes have gone to the French headquarters. They have not come back yet, and I have heard nothing further of them. I hope they will not detain them there to gain time.

We are under the immediate order of General Drechsel, who commands, in addition to us, the 8th and 14th Regiments near Stolzenau, the *Garde du Corps,* and the 8th Dragoons and a heavy battery behind Nienburg. but is himself, with all the above, relegated to the command of General Hammerstein. We are glad to belong to the corps of this fine old warrior. For the rest, you can see from all this, and from the fact that some troops are still in the neighbourhood of Hameln *not* destined for its garrison, and that Schulte has got a corps of his own of some lowland regiments in Stade, that my idea of concentration has not yet reached its proportions. But I gather that now, indeed since yesterday, such an intention is entertained. It is clear that we, as an army, can make no resistance worth mentioning, if we are to be strewed all over the place in little bits.

But if we can only get united soon enough, we shall still be able to concoct plans which will make each advance of the French to the Elbe uncomfortable, if their superiority in numbers is not too disproportionate.

The bridge here (over the Weser) is fairly well defended, although this part of the work, like all the rest, is distinguished by slowness and *vis inertiæ*. The spirit of our recruits is good, but that is all.

Nienburg, June 1st, 1803, 12 at night: The French got to Diepholz today. At the Vechte Dam there was a slight skirmish, in which a Dragoon and a couple of horses were wounded on our side. Thereupon General Linsingen, commanding the most advanced cavalry, fell back on Hammerstein's corps at Sulingen, and this evening the withdrawal of all the baggage of this miniature corps, which passed through the town, made it seem likely enough that Hammerstein himself will retreat; and he really cannot alone undertake to oppose all that is pressing against him. This evening was marked by two other noticeable arrivals, that of the Duke and Decken,—upon whom the encounter with Hammerstein's retreating baggage on the road cannot have made a cheerful impression,—and that of Bock, Bremer, and Brandes, the three deputies to the French headquarters. They have been to see Mortier at Vechte, and were in conference with him the whole of last night. The result does not seem to have been very favourable, in so far as no change has taken place in the measures directed against our country.

They speak well of Mortier, who is said to have expressed his regret that it should fall to his lot to lead an expedition, the odium of which he was fully alive to. They are less impressed with Berthier, chief of the general staff, brother of the Minister of War. He is probably the man who replied to the representation that we did not belong to England, that our last proclamation settled that question, for it ran "George III., King of the United Kingdom of Great Britain, etc." It was quite frankly admitted that their plans were first to take possession of the country by three columns sent to Stolzenau, Nienburg, and Hoya, so that after that the estuary of the river would give them little trouble.

They did us *(i.e., the troops)* the honour to mention us with respect. They said our reputation was known, and that perhaps we might beat this army, but a second, and in case of necessity, a third army would immediately follow, until their purpose had been attained.

It would certainly be difficult to collect so many armies on our side. But as our attention is at present confined to the one before us, everything reduces itself to a very simple question. As to the real strength of the force marching against us, Decken, who ought to be very accurately informed, puts it at forty to fifty thousand men. On the other hand, I have told you what we can rely upon, here, and in the neighbourhood. Now calculate! If we were all together, *as we might have been,* then, indeed, the point we were placed at would not be so easily endangered; if it were well chosen, and the enemy advanced too rashly, which they would be sure to do, towards the Elbe, then we could at-tack—an idea which even *in our disjointed state* may soon be able to be carried out. But scattered as we are—there! I won't swear. But I approximate more to your doubts again, what you said the other day about not being able to understand why I said so much in praise of a certain man (Wallmoden). Here we are in four little bodies (exclusive of the fortress of Hameln)—namely, one here, a smaller one at Walsrode under Diepenbroick, one under Schulte at Stade, and a fourth somewhere in the neigh-bourhood of Hameln. Even to these magnificent rendezvous (for out of respect to our superiors we must suppose that is what they are) some troops did not arrive till the fifth instant! At last Decken has insisted on a general concentration. Probably it will take place behind the Aller, whither I see in my mind's eye our own proximate departure.

Why was not all ready two months ago? Then we should be at the points where one ought to be with our most important defensive appliances, I mean the numerous recruits. Although we have with us only 600 out of the appointed number, and they have plenty of courage and goodwill, yet, with the exception of about 50 who have served before, they are an indescribable bur-den to us. Without uniforms, without discipline, without drill, incapable of the commonest movements which require precision, what use can they be to us? They take up the time of our non-commissioned officers and senior men, who are indispensably required for other purposes. Just think of what they consume uselessly! And in their present condition we cannot think of using them against the enemy—in fact, Hammerstein sent his back yesterday as far as Lemke, though he did talk of using them as a reserve, an idea which occurred to me at the same time. But what is possible in an attack, where the use of the bayonet would not be a mere *fanfarronade,* would in a retreat be absolutely out of the question. They cannot fire, and their mere disorder constitutes a great danger, as it may carry everything away with it. This is so obvious, that the idea is already suggesting itself to dismiss them, to limit ourselves to the old dependable nucleus of our men, and then to try what a second retreat of the 10,000 will be like, and w*here* it will lead to.

The Prussian General Blücher was yesterday at Hammerstein's quarters. What *are* the Prussians going to do? Decken seems to despair of them. I still maintain some hope that, now the thing has come to a regular disturbance, unexpected results may come out of the bluster and turmoil of the elements, and as revivifying as our course hitherto has been beneath all criticism, which (course), if continued, would cast down the best of courage. But no, *dum spiro spero.*

Lüneburg, June 8th 1803, 1 p.m.: Just as I came in here with the regiment, and reported to the Field Marshal along with Langwerth and Alton, the first-named detained me to tell me very kindly that he was sending Vincke to Berlin, and that I could avail myself of that opportunity to write to you.

Should you not have been informed of the events since my last from Nienburg, Vincke's presence will relieve me from the sad task of writing you *a long tale of despair.* I can only speak briefly, and will reserve for a more convenient moment a short and *surprising* journal of the last eight days.

If you can manage, by your manner of description, that the impression which our fate must produce should not recoil on those whose only remaining feeling perhaps is that no justifiable blame can fall on *them,* you will have done good service to truth, to your countrymen, and to the soldiers, who have already proved, before Nienburg, that if required they can fight the enemy without returning their fire, can stand quietly to be shot at like targets, and even now at this moment, crippled hand and foot, have but one idea—to do their duty and have their revenge.

With suppressed rage I have got so far. Since I have seen the tears of the noble, excellent, and most unhappy Lady Wallmoden, the curse sticks in my throat which I, in common with all my comrades, was about to pronounce over the original cause of our downfall (the Field Marshal and an over-parsimonious War Office).

Farewell. Probably we shall soon cross the Elbe. I was going to send you this unique Convention (of Sulingen), but my hand refuses its services to write such a thing. Most likely you have got the precious document already.

Goodbye, and embrace all yours from me. You have now at least escaped the immediate storm. Tell the Berliners the question is now arising: Will you be as safe among them in twelve months' time?

Cantonment of Lütau, Two Hours from Lauenburg. (on the Right Bank of the Elbe), June 16th, 1803: You will have seen from my last Lüneburg letter that it had something of ostensibility about it. For several reasons it was bound to bear that character, on account of its connection with him who invited me to write it, and that perhaps only for his own purposes. In spite of him, it expresses my real opinion as far as what it says goes, but my *whole* opinion I thought it imprudent to reveal through that channel.

But in a general way, brother, there are situations in which silence is the strongest expression of feeling for those who understand one another. All your later letters prove to me that our bases of reasoning, our views, and our perceptions are in agreement.

'We speak little of you, but our thoughts meet,' you say at the conclusion of your letter of the 12th. Here also I expect we are agreed in opinion, so I can limit myself mainly to a recital of the bare facts, which will enlighten you as to the extraordinary occurrences which have, in the last fourteen days, compressed together the results of a whole century, as far as I can clearly see; for in the present dark-lantern illumination, which perhaps *might* clear up *everything,* I can only see a twilight glimmer.

As soon as the Duke arrived at Nienburg, on the 1st inst, the news began to circulate that the Field Marshal had resigned the command and handed it over to the Duke. It was said that he did this by the delivery of a Royal rescript which he had been already provided with for some time. The Duke took the command too; issued, during the few hours he held it, as many orders as time and circumstance permitted, and received on the 2nd, at 4 p.m., an express from Hanover conveying from the gentlemen there a pressing request for his immediate appearance at the Curule seat on account of requirements of the extremest urgency. I think I should have asked those gentlemen to be at the trouble of coming, all and every of them, or as a deputation, to my headquarters. However, different minds take different views. The Duke went away, just at the moment when the news came in of an engagement at the outposts, and gave over the command on the Weser to brave old Hammerstein, who as far as he could know what the state of things was, handled the troops as an intelligent and good general knows how, though he very possibly might have operated differently had he been in the secret of the larger conditions of the situation, and certainly would have played a different game had he had an independent command.

Of the further fortunes of the Duke you are probably informed. We know that he was taken almost by force in his travelling carriage to England, and that he felt *very* unhappy. A letter which he wrote to Charles Alten before his embarkation, in which he said that he had no choice left but to take his dismissal, certainly implies such a feeling. He is really to be pitied. The bases of characters cannot be altered. It would therefore be futile and unfair to expect another Charles XII, or even George II., or George III., to flare up. Well, *quiescat in pace !*

The Field Marshal has taken command of us again—that is, the general command; for until arriving at Lüneburg we were all under the special command of Hammerstein. What this meant you can easily estimate; in case of need, however, Hammerstein would only have the spirit and not the numbers of the troops to depend on. So we all shared the soothing and elevating feeling of being under the command of a man and a soldier, both in the highest sense of the words.

It was about 6 p.m., on the 2nd inst, when I was talking to Charles Alten on the Nienburg bridge about the defences of the town, when Hammerstein appeared alongside us, in haste to get to General Linsingen, who was with the advanced corps at Lemke. He had already given orders to Alten, who had been with him, and for whom lie had rightly entertained a special regard since Menin (celebrated attack led by Hammerstein and Scharnhorst in 1794), to dispose our regimental fragments, the only ones at hand, with two guns of the 6th Regiment, for the defence of Nienburg. Now the General told Alten to ride back with him, and as Langwerth, our commander, was busy with the internal arrangements of the place, the command of the 3-pounder regimental and the garrison artillery fell to me. I believe I have already told you something of the ineptitude of the defensive works. Thanks to the *inertia* which animated the engineer officer there, half an invalid, everything was about in the same state as on our arrival. The *flèche* [3] in front of the bridge was unfinished, no platforms or embrasures for guns, which in any case ought to be able to be placed there. I had the latter prepared at once by parties from the regiment as well as we could manage, although the above engineer, perhaps influenced by the interests of the town, which trembled at the idea of being defended, made wilful difficulties and delays, and did not even know how to procure some necessary planks. Now remember the situation of the Weser Gate. Right on the roadway, to the right, a house, from which hostile *tirailleurs,* who would undoubtedly have occupied it, could have poured in fire à *brûle pourpoint* on the men in the *flèche,* if the burning of the house had not been provided for beforehand. A little further along the road a big tavern, near the toll-house, blocking the direction of our cannon-fire. In the mind to do

---

3. A field-work consisting of two sides inclined to one another presenting the resulting angle to the front, the plan roughly resembling an arrow-head, sometimes called a *bonnette.*

what was practically possible, I had the guns so placed on the open rampart as to enfilade the dangerous house by the gate, to obtain the widest range possible in the direction of the road, and to clear tirailleurs out with grape, from the hedges on both sides, in advance of the bridge, to the best of my ability. One of our most excellent engineer officers, Lieutenant Schafer, whom I fished out while engaged in these precautionary measures, gave me the most willing assistance, and did me the satisfaction of fully agreeing with my opinions. Our (regimental) artillery officer, Lieutenant Witzleben, justified the excellent opinion I have always had of him by the most lively activity, the most zealous goodwill, and the fullest appreciation of details. In order to cover the gunners to some extent, on the open rampart, I ordered them to make a trench for themselves and guns. The men at first requested me, through Witzleben, to forego this precaution, as they were most willing to show themselves worthy of their craft. But as I nevertheless found it necessary to stick to my order, the work was all finished in half an hour, and everything in readiness as far as circumstances permitted.

I have entered so far into these (unfortunately so fruitless) details in order, by a few simple strokes, to give you a fair sketch of that good spirit of which those hopeless convention-smiths have not the slightest conception, in the place of which they have installed their own rotten egoism, in using which perhaps a second or a third French army, but not Mortier's, might have imposed conditions on the country, not worse than those we are suffering at present.[4]

Another piece of news which will interest you where you are. On the 1st inst. General Blücher came through Nienburg, came in to General Hammerstein's headquarters, and had a conversation with him, in which he is said to have expressed his undisguised sympathy, as I can easily believe from his character, and set out on his journey through ours and the enemy's posts,

---

4. Terms: Occupation of the Electorate. Interning of the Hanoverian troops in Lauenburg. Giving up of arms and ammunition, the treasury, and the private estates of the landlords. Appendix: The existing Government to be transformed, contributions to be imposed, horses and clothing to be provided *gratis* for the French troops.

in the course of which he also visited Mortier. At our foremost infantry outpost he naturally halted. His horses were tired. He asked the officer if he could not have some bread for himself. 'We have got nothing here' (this is the literal reply), 'but you will be with the French directly, where everything you require will be doubtless at your disposal' I do not quite approve of this reply myself to General Blücher, for I consider him to be an honest man, even in our sense of the word.

So I hope he will take it with excuses under the circumstances, and that he will not feel himself individually insulted from a natural general feeling.

From this episode I return to the course of events, whose complete development is more suited to the proportions of a whole book, than to be comprehended in the limits of a letter. I will follow chronological order, and only dwell circumstantially on such facts as have especially struck me as noteworthy.

According to such order, I ought to have mentioned before, that on the forenoon of the 2nd inst, as a serious crisis seemed imminent, we sent back our recruits, of whom we had about 560 in the regiment. All the regiments on the Weser did the like. After their departure, every one, from the C. O. to the private, felt really relieved, and we rightly considered ourselves just so much stronger through the restoration of our usual organisation, in proportion as our numbers were weaker. We had that confidence in ourselves, which was, perhaps, through the contrast, never greater among the troops than we found it at that juncture.

Now we will go back to the Weser bridge. We had just finished the preparations I have described, when General Hammerstein came back from Linsingen's advanced corps at Lemke. I went up to his horse to report to him that his orders had been carried out. His hasty answer was: 'That's no good *now*.'

Really, I believe that before he rode out to Lemke, he had grasped the necessity of retreating behind the Aller, and that all the dispositions he ordered were simply for show. And just for that reason I admire the correct view of that original man, who had before his eye the effect on the troops which he commanded, which it was most important to count on by hours and minutes. Compare, on the other hand, the effect the Duke's departure was bound to produce at such a moment, and did produce.

The march to the rear of the Aller started at midnight. In accordance with the general scheme, the troops went into confined cantonments and bivouacs between Hudemühlen and Hademstorf, where Hammerstein's headquarters were. We and the Life Guards formed the rear-guard of this column.

Of the details of our retreat, which was carried out in the greatest order, in spite of a dark and rainy night, the following from personal observation. Uncertain how it was going to be in the morning on our rear or left flank, we made the regiment load, as a matter of precaution, before the stroke of midnight, when we marched. As relatively few possessed the secret of the intended retreat, a belief was raised among the men by this measure that an attack was intended, but as on the next day our direction developed itself continually more and more to the rear, indignation and dissatisfaction were the main themes of discourse among the rank and file. Weather and roads partly through fenny country impeded the march, which, for our regiment, came to an end, after several necessary halts, at 6 p.m. on the 3rd inst., at Eikeloh, where we found very confined quarters.

Unaware of the results of the blessed negotiations, and still reckoning on a general concentration in rear of the Aller, we were undeceived on the night of the 3rd—4th by receiving the order to march next morning by Hudemühlen to Soltau.

We spent the evening of June 4th in Soltau. It was at the small chemist's shop of the place, where I and the officers of the 1st Grenadier company were quartered, that we clinked our glasses to the welfare of our (in the unhappy German Fatherland so badly represented) King. (June 4th was George III's birthday.)

Soltau was the place where I awaited with the greatest suspense the order for the next day's march. Decken had let fall somewhat of importance in Nienburg, regarding a project of sending our whole corps over to England. I tell you that according to all I could foresee—in part, for I had no idea of the full measure of our degradation—this way forth would carry out my fairest hopes. But I cannot conceal that already then, and more and more since, the general feeling of the men was not favourable to such a scheme, but decidedly against it. In married men (and this applies even to officers), and those who are yearning after their small landed property, this reluctance is intelligible. In the case of many others it simply proceeds from ignorant prejudice. But the subject is so delicate, that we must take great care not to give the finishing stroke to a vanishing valour in a decisive crisis, already being poisoned in slow daily doses, and various forms, by giving publicity to such ideas. In Soltau I had not yet acquired this conviction, so my whole attention was directed to the question: would the next march take us to Welle? Because that would have led us straight towards Stade, a point which I looked on, by conviction and preference, as that from which the honour of our corps could be assured, as it did not seem able to be maintained on the Continent any more than it was useful to our country. The orders came out, and the corps marched on the 5th at midday to Amelinghausen. From that moment I considered our fate as more or less settled, and yet not quite in the full sense of the Convention. The march from Soltau to Amelinghausen led by Stübechshorn. Imagine my feelings, when, under those noble oaks which surround that ancestral house known in our Royal House's history, I gave myself over to meditation on the mutability of all earthly conditions. (Stübechshorn is identified as the residence of Hormann Billung, the old Saxon Duke under the Emperor Otho I.)

We spent two days, the 6th and 7th of June, at Amelinghausen. Here it was where we were plunged in the most tearing passion by receiving the first intelligence of the Sulingen Convention, in the shape of a mangled copy which came from Lüneburg. And yet that copy did not contain by any means all the points. Many of us afterwards suspected that it was thought desirable to beat our fate into us à *petits coups*.

On the 8th we at last marched to Lüneburg, where, according to general report, the Field Marshal was to take over the command of all the troops there assembled, and enlighten us on the general state of affairs. Our adventures in this last important town which was in our possession west of the Elbe, will make the essence of our whole condition apparent to you. I have got further, in an accidental way, into the game, actually, than one of the treating persons themselves, through an event which occurred, in its way perhaps unexampled, so for one of these reasons and another I will make a further demand on your patience.

As we approached Lüneburg, we sent our adjutant, Lieutenant Ciero, in advance, to report our arrival at headquarters, and to obtain permission to enter, as well as orders concerning the duty the regiment might have to provide for. He came back with a cast-down countenance, and brought the reply from the Field Marshal that 'it would be perhaps best for the regiment not to march in *en parade,* but, for the sake of relieving the men, to dismiss them outside the gate; still, it was to be according to the pleasure of the Lieutenant-Colonel in command.' Further, there was no duty for the regiment to do, only to provide the ordinary staff-guard in its turn (about twenty-four men). You may imagine what an effect such an extraordinary answer had on us, especially as we were left in the dark regarding our future. But as in the meantime a certain amount of free choice remained to us, and the idea was so new and intolerable to us to sneak in this undeserved way with a regiment like ours into an important town like cowards, the two Lieutenant-Colonels and I soon agreed that we would utilise the appended concession, and march the regiment past the castle, as usual. As we went along I got more detailed information out of Ciero, and I learnt that he had found the Field Marshal incredibly changed, that he seemed to have suffered infinitely both morally and physically, and to suffer still, and that at headquarters everything presented an appearance of consternation and confusion. Moreover, that the Field Marshal was residing in the Schloss.

All this touched me indescribably, and the thought occurred to me: Ought not some sort of deference to be paid to the pretty obvious hint about the desired manner of marching in? I mentioned this, as well as my information, to the C. O., who took exactly my view, and decided to march the regiment along to a position between the Sülz and Red Gates of Lüneburg, with the town on the reverse flank, and there to send off the companies separately to their *chefs* quarters, but to bring the colours under guard, with the band playing, to his own quarters in Schütting. The alarm-post for the regiment was appointed at the market place.

As soon as we had entered the town, the two Lieutenant-Colonels and I went to report ourselves to the Field Marshal. He admitted us. We were soon convinced of the correctness of Ciero's impressions. But he received us in a friendly way, talked in his manner about our general situation, of the manifold deep-lying motives of it, and recommended us to keep our courage up—in a word, he talked platitudes, from which the many con-clusions were not as obvious to us as to him. We could at least be convinced of the gravity of the threat which Buonaparte is said to have uttered, that he would take all the prisoners he could get of ours, and send them to St. Domingo if we took the fancy to sacrifice ourselves for the English. We called to mind Robespierre's decree against the English and us of 1794, which, although a good deal severer in its terms, has still left a large number of us alive.

We listened, and were silent, and we thought, 'Be it so!'

On my departure I was detained, and received the invitation to write to you, which I carried out by means of Vincke.

I was officer of the day in the regiment. Besides ours, the 10th had got quarters in the town (Diepenbroick, the usual gar-rison of Lüneburg). How great was my astonishment to find, on visiting the guard in the afternoon, that the 10th had literally not a single man on duty! The citizens had occupied the Town Hall and all the gates, and the 10th had no orders, any more than we had, to relieve them. After all the bizarre proceedings I had gone through recently, I merely thought, '*Transeat cum cæteris!*' And having had very little sleep the night before, and being ex-tremely tired from numerous excursions over the bad pavement of the extensive town of Lüneburg, I gave myself up to needed rest towards eleven in my quarters, which were on the *sands* close by the Red Gate (one of the main issues, towards Ebstorf). I had scarcely got to sleep when I was awakened by a violent knock-ing at the front door, which was locked. I had already determined to take no notice of it, when I clearly recognised Charles Alten's voice. After many fruitless researches, he and Lieutenant Berger had found me out, and both came to my bedside. Berger's mission, the fulfilment of which was my duty, consisted of the order to occupy with strong guards from our regiment the three most important town gates on the Uelzen and Ebstorf side, the Old Bridge, Red, and Sülz Gates. The 10th was not thought of, although their local knowledge (which we naturally lacked) would have fitted them for such a duty much rather than us. As this occurred to us all three, and as we wanted instructions on several other points, we all went together—about midnight now—to Colonel Löw, whose room we at last found in the labyrinth of a dark castle, and him in it, in bed. We ascertained that when it was at last remembered that between Uelzen and Ebstorf and headquarters there was not a single sentry placed, an order was sent to General Hammerstein in Lüne to post detachments of cavalry in the nearest village to the upper routes, at the same time as one was sent to us to occupy the town gates. To the possibility of getting these dispositions made in the middle of the night, with the cavalry in a camp half an hour away from Hammerstein, no one had given a thought. This became very obvious to me even in the town shortly afterwards. In the meantime we suggested to the disturbed Löw, would it not be more fitting to set guards from the 10th, and at the same time put strong pickets of ours about the town, which would involve less difficulty? This proposition was accepted, and afterwards carried out. We mentioned the report that Ebstorf was really occupied by the enemy. 'I know nothing about that; only that they are in Uelzen,' was the reply. Still uncertain as to our attitude with regard to the French, as the news of the Convention was only a matter of unofficial conversation, and as *no publication of the same to the troops had been made up to this moment,* I asked: 'How are we to behave in case we meet them?' And Löw replied to that, that we must not begin hostilities, but only maintain an attitude of defence, if attacked. After these elucidations we took our leave. Alten and Berger went home, and to me was left the agreeable job, in the middle of the night, in a strange town, of finding and waking the adjutant, the sergeant, and the necessary men, in shut-up houses in different parts of the town, and all plunged in the safe repose of their first sleep—not the pleasantest of duties. The officer sent from the cavalry had lost himself in the night, and never got to his destination. Hammerstein put him under arrest, and was, as a matter of system, right; but it might be asked, *who*, with much more justice, ought to have been put under arrest, not to say *dismissed!*

Despite all difficulties, the whole of the guards and pickets were set by earliest dawn. I made a round of the three gates with Lieutenant Ciero, before they (the guards) could get there, and. found at each a civic corporal and four men with rusty muskets and halberts a century old, and the Sülz Gate so open, on account of some building going on, that it could not be closed against any approach. Fortunately there were three very able officers from the 10th told off, who combined professional with local knowledge. Although not under my orders, they seemed pleased to attach themselves to me, and I made use of their goodwill to help in setting out the posts, and arranging the patrols so as to be on the look-out as far to the front as is possible for infantry.

Until about half-past six, according to the report of the patrols, and information I obtained from an inhabitant of Lüneburg whom I met returning from Melbeck to his home during an extensive ride I took along the Ebstorf road, all was quiet, and there was not a sign of a French advance. On my return I visited all the guards and sentries several times, and as I found all in the best order, I was just going into my quarters for a little, when I met the mounted mail coming from Ebstorf. I halted the postilion, and obtained from him the very notable information: that the clay before three hundred French had reached Ebstorf who had orders to march to Lüneburg that morning. He had heard this from four officers who were quartered at the post-office, and the start was to be at three o'clock. I requisitioned this man at once from the then manager of the post-office, and took him off with me to Colonel Löw, whom I found still sound asleep. He was now convinced, and not to his *doux réveil*, of the accuracy of my earlier warnings. What was to be done? There was no definite decision possible. We might try to detain them at the gate while we reported their arrival (as if they were a troupe of travelling mountebanks). Morally and physically tired out by all my previous proceedings, I calculated that without wings these unbidden guests would not arrive before eight. Having therefore instructed my posts to report to me at once anything that might occur, I hoped to get at least an hour of most-needed rest. It had not passed when a non-commissioned officer from the Red Gate appeared with the report that four French officers had arrived at that spot. I hurried thither, and got there just at the time when these gentlemen were getting out of a *Viennese* carriage with four post-horses outside the gate. I fell in the men under arms on each side inside the gate, went up to the Frenchmen, and after mutual salutes of extreme politeness, I asked: '*Messieurs, qu'y a-t-il à voire service ? Qui êtes-vous ?*' The senior replied: '*Je suis le Lieutenant-Coalonel de Longe, commandé par le général de division Montrichard avec* 300 *hommes de la* 27me *demi-brigade légère pour prendre les quartiers à Lüneburg!*

For further authenticity he dictated this reply for me to write in my note-book. Thus it appeared that they, quite à *leur aise,* had gone in advance of their detachment, which was following at some distance. My reply was something as follows: '*J'ai entendu parler d'une convention entre notre gouvernement et votre armée, et quoique non authentiquement informé de ce qu'elle contient, j'ai lieu d'y croire. Votre arrivée ici ne petit done qu'être fondée stir tin mésentendu, d'autant plus que la ville est occupée par une nombreuse garnison, et que, pour votre convenance autant que pour la notre, il ne sauroit être desirable que nous soyons pêle-mêle ensemble!*

They replied, especially the second, a Major Berbier, a super-subtle fellow, who commanded his commander (who seemed an ordinary old blade): '*Mais, Monsieur, nous venons en amis; nous sommes amis maintenant; il n'y a rien qui empêche que nous nous trouvions ensemble, et les ordres de notre général sont précis!*'

And they again read out the written order, and showed me the particulars. I answered: '*En tout cas, Messieurs, la chose n'est pas de ma compétence, et votes sentirez qu'avant d'avoir fait mon rapport au général qui commandé ici, il est impossible que l'entrée de la ville vous soit accordée' 'Ah!* *rien de plus juste,'* was the reply, and then I bowed them into a very pretty summerhouse in the vicinity, at which the owner, widow of a Captain Ritter, prepared most readily at my desire a breakfast for these gentlemen, who were equally ready to accept it. Then there was a short animated conversation, *forced compliments* of the most flattering kind to our troops, and their regret at this disagreeable expedition, which was not to last more than three weeks—'*nous autres soldats, nous ne sommes que des machines qui doivent se porter là où on les dirige, et lorsque nous ne nous battons pas, nous savons estimer ceux avec lesquels nous sommes en guerre—nous sommes tous camarades,'* etcetera.

After seeing them fairly settled at breakfast for some time, and (unfortunately) having nobody to leave behind to entertain them but our Schwicheldt, in command of the picket, I hurried off to the Field Marshal on my not over-cheering errand. It produced its inevitable impression, but he tried to keep his countenance, and told me to reply to the gentlemen that he had General Mortier's positive assurance that our retreat behind the Elbe should be in no way impeded till the 13th inst. {*et que même quelques jours de plus ne signifieroient rien*); wherefore the order of General Montrichard must be founded on a misunderstanding; that the Field Marshal had sent Major Ende to Celle and Hanover yesterday for the fuller agreement of both Generals, by which this particular point would be made quite clear; that a countermanding of the orders for the detachment in question would be the inevitable result; and that he further particularly besought them to quarter themselves in some village in the neighbourhood, but not in Lüneburg, where it would be perfectly impossible to find room for them, owing to the number of men already there.

Before I left him, I asked the Field Marshal whether, in case it were demanded, I should bring the foreign guests to him, and that without the usual ceremony of blindfolding, and whether 1 might mention that he had his headquarters in Lüneburg at all? He assented to both queries, and at once agreed that I should take Lieutenant Bülow of the 9th Light Dragoons with me, as

I foresaw more *pourparlers,* and did not want to let these gentry out of my sight. I found them where I had left them, and gave them to understand what the Field Marshal's reply was. And they said: '*Monsieur, nous ne doutons nullement de ce que vous nous dites, mais il faudroit avoir cela par écrit.*'

As this request could not legitimately be opposed, I sent Bülow at once to the Field Marshal to ask him to carry it out, and that the more because I found that they were not deaf to my recommendations to take up quarters outside Lüneburg, but were apparently rather willing to do so. While Bülow was gone, I exerted my best powers of persuasion, tried to look at the matter from a jovial standpoint, and represented that they had assured me their quarters in Ebstorf were very pleasant, that they were quite comfortable in the post-office, and that they would find the most charming entertainment among the *jolies nonains* of the convent there, whereas in Lüneburg a thousand discomforts were to be expected. The attractions of Ebstorf really seemed to tempt them—*mais il seroit désagreable de rétrograder!* Ultimately I proposed, before Bülow came back, that the Major should draw up a conditional order for the detachment to halt where it was and wait for further orders. I at once put an orderly at his disposal to deliver it, and awaited with impatience the minute when the detachment would approach. At last Bülow returned, and brought a written answer from the Field Marshal. They read it several times with the greatest attention, and although they did not seem altogether to like it (I could only hear a few words and sentences), they decided to send off the already prepared order, while they also discussed sending an orderly to General Montrichard to tell him what had happened. As this orderly did not quickly appear, I suggested, for the greater acceleration of the order, that one of the four officers should ride back to their detachment, for which purpose I offered them one of my own horses, which was handy at the gate. The confidence placed in them implied by this proposal seemed to particularly strike them, and they declined the offer with expressions of obligation possibly implying a kind of remorseful surprise, after their customary treatment of other people's property. Finally we agreed that Schwicheldt was to ride with the order. This took place, and he hurried off, and fortunately got to the detachment in the neighbourhood of Melbeck, producing an immediate halt thereby.

Well content on my side to have brought matters thus far, I could bring forward no further objections when they, with repeated *mais,* represented the necessity of their having an interview with the General in command at Lüneburg. I gave Bülow a hint to hurry in advance to prepare for this, and had to confine myself to an irksome promenade with the Lieutenant-Colonel and the Major (the other two stopped in the summer-house) necessary in order to conduct them over the rather long road to the castle, which I could not avoid doing. Previously to this, they had seen our 2nd Infantry pass, marching into the town from Amelinghausen. This made them very attentive. *'Comment? est-ce qu'il y a encore des troupes de ce côté-là?' 'Mais certainement, et un corps très considerable.'* They became very reflective, as they generally do, when they saw a quantity of spectators pressing around, and soldiers in every direction, and seemed to be concealing some anxiety at this escort. I tried, by orders and persuasion (respectively), to drive away soldiers and mob, and we arrived ultimately without accident or insult at the castle. Everybody stared and wondered on the steps and in the ante-rooms, and the Field Marshal received them with that control over himself of which he is in so high a degree master, which has, however, perhaps seldom cost him more (effort) than in that moment. The result of the interview was the decision: That until further tidings from General Montrichard, the detachment should be quartered in Melbeck and its neighbourhood. There was still another *mais* left; the troops, that is to say, required provisions, which could not be obtained in the villages. The Field Marshal referred them to the town magistrate, who could manage that without difficulty, and handed over to me the task of arranging that matter. Then they took their leave, having behaved themselves with decency, although not with the expenditure of much ceremony.

We went to the town hall. Before one of the entries a chaise was standing, and I learned, to my great dissatisfaction, that an adjutant of General Montrichard was already upstairs at work with *amplissimo senatu*. He came from Uelzen, and had got in, God knows how, by the Lüner Gate, which still had a civic guard, so that he was present unreported, right at our headquarters, to which he had not given the slightest notification of his presence. With my two *camarades* I was introduced to the large and splendid hall of assembly of the magistrates, really of antique immensity, where the civic authorities were in numerous *corpore*, forming, with their different demeanours and expressions, a scene worthy of a painter. The adjutant, by name Noël Girard, a really handsome young man, of about twenty, muscular, well-built, resembling in face our former good friend Cepoy, with a profile in which I thought I detected a likeness to the usual portraits of Buonaparte, elegantly dressed, too, in overcoat, *cheveux noirs a la Titus,* a plume an ell long in his hat (which he had, however, taken off), stood there, like a new Caesar, impressing on the bewildered committee of the Senate the orders of his general, more particularly regarding future requisitions for subsistence and quarters. As soon as he saw his two countrymen, he advanced with a kind of superior cordiality (although he was only a captain), and said: '*Ah! Bon jour. Nous nous trouvons ici ? Votre bataillon y est-il? Quand pourra-t-il arriver?*' Following his example, I affected an indifferent recognition of his presence, and a slight mutual salute without a word was all that passed between us at first. The other two exhibited great zeal in displaying all deference to him, whence I concluded that he must be a person of influence with his general. They informed him of what had just been stipulated with the Field Marshal about their battalion. '*Ah non, Le bataillon doit être ici le 9,*' and thereupon he produced an instruction of the General in which it was solemnly set forth that this was so, together with the additional statement. *La presence des troupes Hanovriennes n'empêchera en rien l'exécution de cet ordre.* In all that he said or read out he adopted a heroic tone such as might have been used by le Kain in reciting one of Corneille's parts. At the same time, what with his above-described face and his sonorous, masculine voice, though there might be something extravagant about his general *allure,* there was nothing ridiculous. With these decided peculiarities he united all the keen mental cleverness of his nation. Think of my feelings in the presence of all these persons! But considering the actual situation of things there was nothing to be done except to exhibit the utmost coolness, or at any rate the appearance of it, and in such guise I awaited the issue.

The other two now began to go back on their agreement: *'Ah oui, celà est clair; l'ordre est précis; il n-y a pas moyen de faire autrement'* And then they went off into a corner of the hall to come to some conclusion among themselves. I remained quietly standing where I was, and observed, during the consultation, the very various feelings expressed by the countenances of the thirty or forty magisterial personages round about. Some exhibited the torpidity of passive surrender; some—probably swindlers in the revolutionary sense—a suppressed smile; while others seemed deeply moved. One at least there was—one High Bailiff Dassel, whom I scarcely remembered having met, who rushed at me and grasped my hand with excited fiery patriotism, saying: 'That we should have to endure this! My blood boils! If I could only go with you and smite them!' I replied, 'I am pleased to find you in that state of mind, but at present self-control is the only thing.'

In the midst of the turmoil waiters were rushing about, offering fine liqueurs and lunch, and were particularly attentive to the Frenchmen. Both the gentry and the servants seemed for some time to have no eyes but for *them*. To the honour of the company present, however, I must add that they suddenly seemed struck with a sense of propriety towards *my* uniform. Several invited me very pressingly, especially the Burgomaster Oldekop (who seemed otherwise encased in his natural phlegm), who wished to do me the honours at the select *déjeûner*. I declined, with corresponding demonstrations of politeness. The adjutant now approached me from the distant opposite corner of the hall, exhibiting in his whole bearing and manner greater deference to me, requested me to join the French trio, and invited me with fine soldierly grace, *'de prendre un ver de liqueur avec eux.'* Little inclined as I was to accept, I did not refuse, for I hoped to utilise this altered tone for an important purpose. After we had exchanged a few insignificant civilities, I said to him: *'M. de*

Longe vous aura detaillé les reasons qui motivèrent l'arrangement convenu par rapport a son détachement. Vous paraissez le considérer comme contraire aux ordres positifs de voire général. Peut-être cependant que pour la convenance il ne seroit pas de trop que vous parliez au Comte de Wallmoden sur ce sujet, et vous me feriez plaisir, Monsieur, si vous vouliez consentir, a ce que nous nous rendions tous les quatre ches lui.' *'Très volontiers, Monsieur'*, was his reply, and we went at once. On the road he gave me the fairest assurances, explained that a main point of his General's instructions was to maintain the best possible harmony with our troops, in case theirs were in the same quarters, which, in point of fact, had really happened at Celle and Uelzen.

'Je vous donne ma sparole a'honneur,—je vous réponds sur ma tête' (this with great emphasis), *'que de notre cote* (sic—*côté?) il n'y aura par le plus petit désagrément, et si vous voulez faire une discipline semblable, vous pouvez être persuadé que tout se passera dans la plus parfaite harmonie.'*

To give a more persuasive force to his argument, he mentioned, among other things, how their troops in Italy had been encamped with the Imperial troops often, and all had gone very well. Without discussing the question further, we again reached the castle, and were at once led through the crowd of adjutants, amid which Löw's star of the first magnitude, though eclipsed, was prominent, to the Field Marshal's room, and to him I had now, of course, to leave the definite settlement of the matter.

It was settled that the orders of Montrichard should be carried out.

As soon as I knew this I troubled myself no further about the foreign gentlemen, but devoted my mind entirely to two measures—first, to settle with the magistrate that the French should have a special location all to themselves, for which purpose the Sülz quarter was willingly assigned, .as the furthest off, and the poorest. As some of the streets there were full of our Grenadiers, I had them all removed and provided with billets elsewhere. The second measure, which Langwerth at once adopted on my recommendation, was the immediate telling off of a strong picket from the regiment, under command of a captain, to be in readiness in the market-place for anything that might happen. What with all these different arrangements to see to, the forenoon was nearly over, when about 11 o'clock, the French battalion, which had received from its commander the order to continue the (interrupted) march, marched in *tambour battant,* and wheeled the sections to the left at the corner of the market on the castle side, in order to march up with the left flank in front of the town hall, where the billets were to be issued. Our picket had been marched up to the market-place, and stood in a suitable position. They (the French) looked, at some distance, in very good close order, with a certain expression of reflective seriousness, which seemed to me to imply, *qu'ils ne trouvaient pas de quoi rire dans cette singulière expedition.*

By a fortunate coincidence, our superb *Garde du Corps* just then marched through the town with. music and drawn side-arms, so that they, passing between the town hall and castle, were close to the right flank of the French sections.

I could not help gazing upon this unique spectacle with close observation, and I did notice that both the *Garde du Corps* and our own men looked at the French with indignation and resentment. Near eye-witnesses said that the physiognomies of many of the latter betrayed visible astonishment and fear. Old troopers, who perhaps remembered Famars, wept with rage, and our Charles Alten, who came to me during the scene, had bright tears on his cheeks. I must admit that after all the detail of preparation, and the deep insight into the innermost nature of our situation, which I had had since last night the opportunity to obtain, my own feeling bordered on apathy. I again found myself in that condition" (probably referring to the death of his mother) "in which the busy occupations of funeral preparation annul, for the moment at least, the pain of an irreparable loss.

The Field Marshal, who had not meant to go with the general staff to Lauenburg until the afternoon, had gone off moved by these events, directly after his interview with Noël Girard, and left nobody behind except Estorff, who performed the duties of Quartermaster-General, and for the moment was entrusted with the carrying out of all necessary measures on this side the Elbe.

So we were mixed *pêle mêle* with the French, which need not have happened if the arrival of two expresses from Celle had taken place only a quarter of an hour earlier. In consequence of Ende's negotiations, General Montrichard had sent an order that de Longe's battalion should not enter Lüneburg till we had marched out, but halt, and in case it had marched in already, was to be marched out again. Two expresses brought the information (of this order) simultaneously to the Field Marshal and to the French. The latter had just been dismissed, and were gone to their quarters for their much-longed-for dinner. Noel Girard and de Longe now asked Estorff if, considering the difficulties of reassembling the men, and after the march already performed, they might not be permitted to leave the next day and Estorff, perhaps with too much consideration for them, assented. In a general way they (the French) behaved with apparent quietness and decency. They set a guard in the old watch-house in the street behind the Town Hall on the right, while we set the so-called castle-guard in the front of the Town Hall. De Longe had quarters at the house of Burgomaster Oldekop, and a sentry at his door. The latter omitted to salute one of our officers, a thing that was done as a rule, and with military punctiliousness by the others, and drew upon himself a heavy reprimand for this neglect. In the afternoon some of their officers came to Schütting, which was swarming with ours. The beggars drank rum like water, but behaved, except for a certain rather vulgar tone (consisting, as they did, in the demi-brigade from captains upwards of old non-commissioned officers), with proper deference. They complained of the irksomeness of their situation ; and while all honour and *enrichment* was accorded to the generals, they were punished for doing on a small scale what those were permitted to do on a large scale. I translated for their benefit the German proverb, '*While the little thieves are hanged,*' etc., and they quite agreed as to the application of the proverb. Of Buonaparte they spoke more with compulsory respect than with personal attachment. They were distinctly on the side of Moreau, whom, they asserted, Buonaparte feared more than any number of armies. A characteristic feature was their attention to petty details, and

140

their admiration of our uniform, and the costume of our men. Their men were healthy, at any rate—they came from Holland—and, in point of fitness for duty, much alike.

An important fact, which I extracted from one of the captains, was this: Their detachment was a *whole battalion,* and hardly amounted to 300 men, as was the earlier and honest statement of the Lieutenant-Colonel. So a demi-brigade would only amount to 600 men, and a division, consequently, to 2,400 instead of 12,000 men. According to these elements the entire strength of the enemy ought to have been calculated, in which case the calculation would have agreed with the results, now a matter of common knowledge. From which it follows that Mortier's whole command, including the force left in occupation of Osnabrück, was only composed of about 17,000 rank and file.

I have still to mention something of the relations of our men to the French. The impression made by the latter was, in certain respects, exactly what I should have chosen for a visible impression, particularly for those who had not learnt by warlike experience to know them already. The whole of Longe's battalion consisted of incredibly small men, considerably smaller than the Prussian Fusilier battalions which I have seen. A good part were young conscripts. Wherefore the general impression was the reverse of imposing. On the other hand, I state without disguise that the majority were robust and hardy sort of men. It is really incredible with what rapidity, with how few stragglers the French get in marching order. This same battalion, which had previously made the campaign of Italy and then been stationed in Strasbourg, had got from there to Flushing, and from Flushing here in a very short space of time. And part of them carried by no means light kits either. To give way to such opponents without a struggle was indignantly felt by our soldiers. Although we had given the strictest orders that there was to be no sort or kind of meddling with the French, we ascertained that a couple of private *rencontres* had occurred in which the French had been whacked by some of ours. Of one case I heard a few days after from a corporal of Grenadiers (whom I knew from experience of serious events in the former war to be one of the bravest and most trustworthy men under the sun), who said he had been present, and disclosed the matter to me in the following words, more or less:

'I came along just as Bosse (a sturdy fellow of our 6th company) was belabouring two Frenchmen. I knew right enough, sir, that as corporal it was my business to stop him, but as those chaps had passed remarks about the red coat, I just walked on and didn't see anything. Bosse gave them a fair hiding, and they took no notice afterwards.'

You can imagine whether the corporal or Bosse got reprimanded.

The other case was that of two Frenchmen who took into their heads to play the gallant to some Lüneburg beauties. The girls were frightened and ran away, and the Frenchmen were going to pursue them. But some of our soldiers came up, and these cavaliers had their appetite taken away in a very practical manner. But it is time to close this lengthy episode. I leave it to you to think with what feelings I, as an accidental accessory, beheld the whole of such proceedings as I have described. We retreated over the Elbe on June 10th, and crossed it in boats near Lauenburg On our march out from Lüneburg I found I had won great popularity from our countrymen in that place. In the densest crowds the spectators manifested feelings of sorrow, sympathy, and respect. This impression was the more welcome in that, as you know, the Lüneburgers have not hitherto had the best reputation for their attitude towards the troops.

On the same clay our regiment got quarters in Lütau, a village only a good half-hour from Gülzow. The houses must have had from thirty to forty men in each. In that condition the regiment remained, as did the others, for several days, and you may imagine that the results on our subsistence and order were manifold, especially accompanied as all this was by the exceptionally detestable weather which had followed us for weeks, as if man and nature had conspired against us. We first learnt from the *Hamburger Zeitung* the full measure of the mischief inflicted on the country and the army by that everlastingly accursed Sulingen Convention—as everybody with a spark of feeling or the slightest glimmering of sound sense left must regard it. From now to the 20th mainly, desertion set in in the regiments, after all the preliminary symptoms of licence and disorganisation. We hoped for a long time to preserve ours (regiment) intact, but a thousand reasons to the contrary poured ceaselessly in. Most prominent among these was the natural belief that everything was given up for lost; letters from relatives and friends in the country in that sense; communication to the same effect by letter carriers, who spread the belief in an intended embarkation (of the troops) to England, or to the West Indies; purposely favourable news about good treatment and safe homes held out by the French, who made the most seductive insinuations even to the officers in the smaller garrisons; ideas of self-ransom as prisoners of war, and above all the insufficiency of the daily ration of bread. This was fixed at only one and a half pound instead of the two pounds appropriate to the field footing. Of course the half pound is made good in money. But we know from experience that, even in garrison, the soldier is never complete without his supplementary ration. For that purpose potatoes, the only substitute, are lacking in quantity, and although there is a laudable superfluity provided of other kinds of food, it is nearly all too dear for the moderate pay of the soldier. The men get 26 groschen every ten days (=M. 2.08), and in spite of the careful attention we devote to the details of the *ménage* it is impossible for the soldier's dinner to cost him less than an average of 12 pfennig a day. Now reckon what is left out of 20.8 pfennig a day (=$22^2/_5$d.) for spirits, tobacco, breakfast, supper, and cleanliness. You know our nation must unfortunately eat, eat a *good deal,* in order to keep up good cheer. Discontent, true and false depressing rumours of all sorts, lack of something to do this bad weather, ceaseless thinking and talking about our situation,—all that must have some effect; so the disease of desertion broke out at last, and of a sudden, about the 20th, made its appearance in our regiment. We at once took a decided step, assembled the whole regiment under arms, and our commanding officer harangued them by companies in the most practical tone of sound reason and true honourable feeling, combined with impressive allusions to the strictness and serious meaning of the Articles of War. Alten and I supported his arguments to the best of our ability in our own battalions, and we have had fortunately since then no further losses, which amount in all to five hundred in the whole army, but in our regiment only twenty. But the brave hearts of the greater and better part of the men are now firmly fixed in the honourable intention of draining their cup to the dregs, or awaiting the moment of revenge.

Gülzow, June 29th, Morning: A decisive moment again seems to be approaching. We have known already for some days that our king, whose opinion has certainly always been correct, will not ratify the Convention. We have not the information directly from England, as, to our great disadvantage, there is no direct communication with England.

But I will pass to a more decided indication, our front, where *ifs* and *buts* do not hold out long. Mortier is concentrating all his forces at Lüneburg, and yesterday, probably, sent a strong advanced corps to the other bank of the Elbe, so that some of their columns have been clearly seen from our posts. The French have declared without concealment (in several partial conversations they had with our men on the Elbe, when the transfer was still taking place, some of the French having even swum over for the amusement of visiting our posts) that they would make the passage in the next few days at any price. I do not the least doubt this intention. Twice again was Bock sent over yesterday afternoon by the Field Marshal. We are trying for a different sort of Convention, but judging from the symptoms of the measures taken last night, it looks to me as if we were going to fight because there is nothing else left to do. This is also the general opinion; and considering the natural military advantages of our position, the passage ought, I hope, to cost them pretty heavily. In the meantime I am more apprehensive of internal than external obstacles, not in any way on account of the troops, whose spirit still survives in spite of the attempts made to paralyse it, the means of every kind which alone can aid and perhaps deliver us, if resolutely and rapidly applied. You know the character we maintain, and the means of assistance we have lost, or rather deliberately thrown away! Let our fate be what it may, I hope *that* will never be forgotten. By a varying and extensive system of dislocation some of our regiments have got as far away as Mölln and Hamfelde, and some still further, towards Ratzeburg. To bring these speedily up again is impossible. It is true that our whole cavalry is to hand, encamped since our arrival here in different detachments, of which the strongest, consisting of the first five regiments, including the *Garde du Corps,* is near Lauenburg. But to have infantry at hand would be still more important, and for that reason it would be a good thing if they were in the camp too. But *mobility*! For transport we could only count on the relatively small number of vehicles here. But we carry our own arms, and let us by all means cast aside all other *impedimenta* if that will set us with our arms in our hands at least under a free heaven!

I had the intention of saying much more, in a general way, on our internal situation, especially with reference to the Government of our country. But no more; of the nothing, nothing further, except a striking remark of General Mortier to Major Ende:'*En France, où, nous avons une république,* one individual governor, and *tout va bien. Ici où vous avez une monarchie, je vois que tout le monde se mêle de gouverner sans que les affaires en aillent mieux!* What a rich text!

Here is the place to add Louis Ompteda's account, alluded to in the opening, intercalating a few letters which place the state of affairs in a clearer light. His connection with these matters requires explanation. Although engaged at first only with the already mentioned negotiations in Berlin, he gained the confidence of the ministers both in Hanover and in London, as well as that of the King, to the extent that the other political affairs got largely into his hands. That the country also expected to gain mainly through his efforts the hoped-for aid from Prussia is evident from the above quoted letters, in various places. Sometimes alone, sometimes in support of Major von der Decken, appointed to act with him, he employed every means in various ways, but always in vain. He also received expert advice from his friend Scharnhorst, formerly Hanoverian Quartermaster-General, now Director of the Military Academy in Berlin. We have an autograph list by the latter of the available fighting strength of the Hanoverian Landsturm. Under it are the words: "In addition, I enclose for you the *History of the sortie from Menin*, which proves that *people can do what they make up their minds to do. Scharnhorst.*"

Now that the French had set themselves in movement in the direction of the Prussian frontier, one last messenger was sent to him (L. O.) to prevail on Prussia to interfere.

This situation of Louis Ompteda in Berlin was known to Field Marshal Wallmoden. The latter had already applied to the former in this connection from Lüneburg, at the same time when he permitted Christian to send the accompanying letter which has been quoted.

> *Lüneburg, June 8th, 1803*: The unexpected, incredible, and fearful condition we are placed in must be my excuse for approaching your Excellency with these few words. If our suppression and annihilation is to be accomplished, there is nothing left for me to say. But I have depended to a large extent on two things:
>
> 1. That you thoroughly apprehend our situation, and our motives, which are so extremely distorted and misconstrued.
> 2. That you also rightly divine the danger for others if no precaution whatever be taken for our due safety, at least at the stage things have now reached. No one can know of both matters to their full extent better than the bearer.
>
> I beg to recommend myself and our cause to your best considerations. *W*.

The bearer was his (W.'s) adjutant, Captain von Vincke, who reported himself on arrival in Berlin with the following note:

> *June 11th, 1803*: *My dear Friend*—I arrived here from Lüneburg last night as Mr. Müller of Cassel. The accompanying letters will inform you of the purpose of my journey. Things have got to such a stage with us that no officer of the army can leave without the consent of the Frankish chieftain. Hence the reason of my enforced concealment of my honourable name and position. Always yours, *E. Vincke*

Captain von Vincke had, however, to return empty away to headquarters reporting that Ompteda'.s renewed efforts had been fruitless. From there he wrote officially to L. O. by order of the Field Marshal on June 17th, concerning the state of things in Lauenburg, to which was added the following utterance:

> Under all these circumstances it is the express wish of the Field Marshal that you should strongly represent the danger continually and increasingly threatening Russia and Prussia, and the inconceivable results which cannot fail to ensue, if the French establish themselves on this (right) bank of the Elbe and making Ratzeburg (then fortified) into a place of arms, thus becoming masters of the Baltic and North Sea.

Enclosed with this was the following unofficial note:

> The Field Marshal has commissioned me to write to you officially. So please take care and do an answer I can show, and write what is only fit for us two separately. I say, think of this: On the 7th inst. there was an English frigate on the Elbe, provided for the Field Marshal to work our embarkation with. Great Heavens, if we only had not signed that damned Convention! We should, perhaps, be in England now, and saved for ever. There is tremendous annoyance among the troops about the Convention, which has very nearly led to disagreeable events.

The ratification of the Sulingen Convention was, in addition, spitefully refused by Buonaparte, *after* the Hanoverian Government had *carried it out* without delay. And then the last overwhelming storm burst on the little band, putatively secure behind the Elbe, half disarmed, but not discouraged. Every one now turned his eyes on Berlin, from whence alone deliverance could come. The Field Marshal again wrote on this point personally to Louis Ompteda, from Lauenburg, June 28th:

> All our information agrees that the whole French army is marching on Lüneburg, and since yesterday we know positively that they will all be assembled there by this evening. I leave it to you to imagine the effect of such a (malicious) failure to carry out a Convention at the present moment. The *pretext is said to be* that the *King*

has not ratified the Convention. We hear little public news here, but it seems that the French Government has made the ratification of the King (as King of England, not only as Elector of Hanover) a condition. I leave this point to your consideration.

Whether there is anything, and if so what, to be done {*i.e.*, in Berlin), and whether the loss of the Elbe is a matter of such absolute indifference to others, time will give us greater enlightenment. As far as I am personally concerned, I cannot go into further detail, but leave the rest to the care of your Excellency.

In consequence of these resolutions and challenges Louis Ompteda came to a determination. The following is his own account:

In order to inform myself more fully on the state of affairs, and to discover if it were possible in the first place to gain a little time, I at once went to Schwerin, where, at the time, a part of the Hanoverian Ministry was to be found. From thence I was sent to the Field Marshal Count Wallmoden, who had his headquarters at Gülzow, at the house of his son-in-law Count Kielmansegge. I learnt, on my arrival, that Count Wallmoden had assembled all the generals in a Council of War.

The question to be decided was, whether resistance was to be made to the attack on the part of the French with which we were threatened, or fresh efforts to be made to obtain a capitulation. Although individual members of the staff pointed out the danger to which the troops would be uselessly exposed, in their present almost unarmed state, before an enemy like the French, it was unanimously decided by the Council of War that any attack must be stoutly resisted.

Immediately after the Council of War I joined Count Wallmoden. He disclosed to me the determination arrived at with great apparent satisfaction. I, for my part, could only give my heartiest approval, as being in my mind the plan most conformable, not only to the honour of the troops, but also to that of the country.

The French forces, mostly assembled on the left bank

of the Elbe, were estimated at about 13,000 men. The Hanoverian army corps was of about the same strength. It had the further advantage of having its front covered by the broad stream of the Elbe, and of occupying the high right bank of that river, from which every movement of the enemy was visible, and in case the French succeeded in forcing a passage of the river, there were on the heights the excellent Hanoverian cavalry in superior numbers, who could not fail to make them suffer considerably.

In the afternoon the English Vice-consul of Heligoland, Nicolas, arrived unexpectedly from Hamburg. In case of extremity, the shipping of the Hanoverian troops to England was vaguely recommended.

Towards evening I took a walk with the Field Marshal Count Wallmoden, in the course of which he informed me in the strictest confidence that he expected to be attacked by the French that very night, and had determined to defend himself to the utmost.

In the evening I lay down to rest, though my sleep was disturbed by the constant expectation of the booming of heavy guns announcing an attempt to pass the Elbe.

On this suspense the morning broke, and all as yet was still, as several other persons, who saw into the condition of things with greater penetration, had said it would be.

The following morning I went to study more closely the position of our troops, and to see my two brothers who were with the army. War-councillor Kielmansegge lent me a horse for the purpose, and both he and his brother (then Chamberlain K.), who knew the *terrain* very well, accompanied me.

In the neighbourhood of Artlenburg, a village lying on the other side of the Elbe, we found the troops in a state of active movement. The Prince of Wales' Light Dragoon regiment stood saddled and bridled in bivouac. Part of the battalion of the Guards commanded by my brother Christian was thrown forward to the bank of the Elbe, and stood as furthest outpost by the ferry-house on this side. A few guns had been brought up to the bank.

The reason of these arrangements was this: The French had collected some ten or eleven large Elbe boats, and let them move slowly with the stream close to the left bank, confirming thereby the supposition that they intended to attempt a passage of the river on their left.

A *parlementaire* was sent over to inquire into the motive of these extraordinary proceedings. As the reply was of an evasive character, it was announced on our side that further movement down the river of these boats would not be permitted, and that as soon as they proceeded beyond a certain defined point below Artlenburg they would infallibly be sunk by our guns. This was the state we found things in on our arrival. As the road to the bank passed through a defile, we dismounted and left our horses at the entrance of this hollow, and walked on to the bank, where I found my eldest brother in command. Behind the hedges and fences of the peasant dwellings Artlenburg was just crawling with Frenchmen. The Elbe boats were lying up to the point indicated, in a row along the opposite side. They seemed to be empty, but one occasionally observed heads of Frenchmen of inquiring mind peeping over the gunwales, which were, however, always quickly withdrawn.

The French, seeing that in the face of our decided attitude the contemplated movement could not well be carried out, now appeared really to intend to remain quiet. When, after a while, we were more fully convinced of this, and my brother had taken some further military precautions, we rode back with him to the village of Juliusburg, where his battalion was cantoned. After cheerfully emptying a few bottles of wine there to the happy outcome of affairs, we returned to Gülzow, which we did not reach till evening.

Shortly after that there made their appearance in Count Wallmoden's headquarters certain members of the Hanoverian nobility, who had crossed the Elbe by permission of the French, and certainly not without the latter being aware of the object of their journey. This object was to adjure the Field Marshal to give up all idea of fruitless resistance, and to try for a fresh capitulation, in which very reasonable and honourable terms would certainly be obtained from the French for the army. And a good deal was said about profitless bloodshed, fire and flames heavy contributions, and suchlike.

The Count Wallmoden made me a party to this conference, as he declined to decide this important question on his own sole responsibility. With all my best powers of persuasion, I sought every possible argument with which our duty to the Sovereign, the honour of our army, and the general situation could furnish me, to thwart the purpose of these *Deputies of the Country*, as they called themselves. (The Ministers in Schwerin held themselves aloof, yet wrote recommending acquiescence to the wishes of the Deputation.)

But when I saw that all my eloquence was in vain, I informed the deputation, in the strictest confidence, that Prussia would probably be extremely loath to see an occupation of Lauenburg, besides which an immediate intervention on the part of Russia was to be expected.

These disclosures startled the deputation, and when I noticed the impression they had produced, I declared that I would forthwith despatch an express to the Secretary of Legation, von Hugo, who had been left in Berlin in order to get information of the latest phase assumed by the negotiations. "The deputation thereupon strongly pressed me to go to Berlin myself, because they were convinced that the purpose would be more fully achieved in that way. Count Wallmoden also took this view.

I yielded. In the light of subsequent events I have often reproached myself for giving way, though I cannot assert with certainty that I alone would have succeeded in frustrating the purpose of the deputation, and my main object was, moreover, to gain time. Besides, I had Count Wallmoden's *assurance* that he would do nothing till my return. I at once took post-horses, and hurried day and night to Berlin, which I reached in good time on the morning of the second day.

I at once sought the then Russian Ambassador, Herr von Alopäus the elder, a man of excellent mental endowments, whose special confidence I had earned. I described our whole state of affairs to him, and besought him to acquaint me with the attitude and intentions both of his own Court and the Prussian. Herr von Alopäus regretted that he had as yet got no instructions from his Court, but believed the Prussian Court would be found ready to take steps, at any rate to prevent further undertakings on the part of the French in the path of negotiation, if I were to make suitable proposals to that effect He advised me to hurry, and that the more because he happened to know that the Minister, Count Haugwitz, had an audience with H. M. the King of Prussia that very morning at Charlottenburg.

I immediately went to the Brandenburg Gate, took the first vehicle I could get hold of, and hastened to Charlottenburg. I was introduced without delay to Count Haugwitz, in whose room I found also the then Privy Cabinet Councillor Beyme and General von Köckeritz, First Adjutant-General, and confidant of the King.

My unexpected appearance created a considerable sensation, as it was known whence I came. I utilised this evident frame of mind to give a full and true description of our situation to these three gentlemen, and put the matter, with most pressing earnestness, before them. I exposed the nullity of the excuse which General Mortier was trying to utilise, in order to drive the Hanoverian army from its last refuge, and probably dissolve it, in spite of the Convention of Sulingen. I described what a surpassingly advantageous position our army was in should the French attempt to force the passage of the Elbe. I pointed out the dangers which would ensue if, nevertheless, the French were ultimately to succeed in occupying Lauenburg, in which case they would possess both banks of the Elbe.

The Privy-Councillor Beyme, a Hanoverian by birth, who happened to be well acquainted with both banks of the Elbe, bore out all I had demonstrated concerning the advantages of our position, and even General von Köckeritz, usually a very reserved man, was of the opinion that something or other must be done under these unpleasant circumstances.

After further discussion, Count Haugwitz finally told me that he would go forthwith and lay the whole matter before the King, and inform me of the results immediately afterwards.

Full of expectation and impatience I returned to Berlin. By four in the afternoon I received a note from Count Haugwitz, to the effect that H.M. the King had decided to write himself to General Mortier to restrain him from further proceedings, with the assurance that he would be undisturbed by the Hanoverian forces in the portion of Electoral country now occupied by him, and need apprehend no attack. The bearer of this letter was to start the same evening, and to be Lieutenant-Colonel von Krusemark, a man whose talents guaranteed a favourable result.

When I. had informed the Russian Ambassador of all that had passed, I immediately took post-horses, and started that day, July 6th, at 9 p.m., for the right bank of the Elbe, while Lieutenant-Colonel von Krusemark went through the Old Mark to the left bank of the Elbe to visit the headquarters of General Mortier.

But by this time the blow had fallen. On the day before, July 5th, the Elbe Convention had been signed. The following account, written on the 7th, proceeding undoubtedly from an entirely different point of view, but no longer able to reach its destination, was intended to give the information. Christian to Louis:

Cantonment of Juliusburg, July 7th, 1803, 8 a.m.: It is all up! Yet even now, at this moment, everything perhaps *could* be re-established. I am in too great a state of excitement to give a coherent account. The main points are these:

You know how things were at the time of your departure, in the direction of Artlenburg. The collection of boats from above and below, to the number of fifty-two, seemed to suggest that the French intended their main attack to be at this point. During the night of the 3rd to 4th they had, by a (rather *overdone*) disturbance with pontoons, guns, trenching tools, and timber, given rise to the opinion among us (and even in hitherto incredulous me) that there would be an attack from Artlenburg in the morning. Our regiment, and all the other available troops, were placed by daybreak in cover of the heights and ravines on this side in *determined* readiness to receive it. Yet the enemy remained quiet, and the negotiation business went on again. So passed away the 4th, and the next night we again waited vainly for an attempt on the part of the enemy to cross. On the 5th an interview was arranged to take place between the Field Marshal and Mortier, at first to be on this side, but finally in the middle of the Elbe. I stood that day with my battalion as extreme outpost above and below the ravine leading towards Artlenburg. Towards midday Wallmoden appeared with Löw. The Field Marshal was about to embark, when on a sudden two cannon-shots from one of our distant batteries, which could not be prevented, first informed us that Mortier, and all his generals, were already in the middle of the Elbe, in a big barge, waiting for the Field Marshal. They had forgotten to signal a truce, and so drawn fire upon themselves, but the balls fortunately—or unfortunately—only grazed the boat without hitting. By shouting and signalling we stopped any further firing. The other batteries were on the point of discharging, and would have simply sunk the barge. The Field Marshal rowed out with a guard, and the French, understanding the mistake, did not make any reply with their artillery. We now became spectators of a scene of a kind which does not happen twice. It had been (hitherto) most beautiful weather. Just as if the wrath of heaven were being pronounced, there burst forth, as the Field Marshal reached Mortier, a most violent storm, so that the boat could not remain on the Elbe, and we ultimately saw the Field Marshal and the French generals, who received him with marked courtesy, go over to Artlenburg. And there a second *Convention* was brought into existence, with which the Field Marshal came back to us, just as our Retreat was being sounded in proud rivalry with that of the enemy!

What we know up to now is approximately as follows:

There is to be a cessation of hostilities. We are not to lay down our arms, but to march to a place where we are to deposit them, and then give the men a year's furlough, while the officers will receive half-pay by way of pension. The cavalry are to give over their horses to the local civil authorities, who will deliver them to the French. The same will probably be the case with the artillery. Yesterday morning I had to give over my post below, by the water, to General Drouet in person. The items of the Convention are to be carried out in four days. I do not believe that to be possible, on account of the details.

As far as we hear, there is still nothing from England or Russia. *Can* it be that the whole world is deserting us? Here I close—and say nothing of those individual conclusions which circumstances only can decide. Embrace all yours from me; make the best of things if you still can; but what you do, do *quickly*, and very quickly! Thine, *C. v. O.*

Louis' narrative now continues:

While I was about to change horses, having just arrived, the following evening at Lentzen, the mail came in from Hamburg. The conductor stated that a Convention had again been concluded between the Hanoverians and the French, in consequence of which the French were already in Lauenburg, and on the right bank of the Elbe. I was unwilling to give credit to this story, until the conductor produced the last number of the *Hamburg Correspondent,* in which the so-called Elbe-Convention was already printed. And now information came in continually, though always of an inexact character, regarding these sad events which had taken place since my departure from the army at Gülzow, as well as the undoubted passage of the Elbe by the French.

My amazement was unbounded. Where the Field Marshal and his headquarters had got to I could not find out. I could not safely go further on the road I was going to travel under these circumstances. So I came to the conclusion to go to Schwerin, where there were still some members of the dissolved Hanoverian Ministry, in order to make inquiries as to the true state of things. But there also no one knew anything about Count Wallmoden. No one knew what had happened, or where the army was. At the same time the Ministers wanted me to go and find the Hanoverian headquarters as quickly as possible, so there was really nothing left for me to do but go and look for the Field Marshal by myself, and, for the sake of caution, I adopted the direction of Büchen. On the way, I was still unable to gather anything certain, and in this way I arrived in the night at the first (posting) station in Lauenburg, where, even amid the bustle of our advancing and retiring troops, I could obtain no definite information. In the evening, at Büchen, I found the whole post-house full of officers of the dissolved Hanoverian regiments, some sleeping in every corner, some endeavouring to find means of getting away in various directions. Here I first learnt that the Field Marshal had retired to Mölln!

I at once continued my journey to Mölln, where I arrived towards morning. Everybody was sound asleep, and when I tried to get shelter I found it impossible, owing to the houses being all overflowing with the Hanoverian military. So I got back into my carriage to obtain some rest there. But, heavy though the toils of the last few clays had been, no sleep visited my eyelids.

It was four in the morning when I came to the Field Marshal's house. Count Wallmoden was already at the open window. He stared when he became aware of my presence, and at once invited me to come up to him.

I found the old man in a state of excitement, which increased when I communicated to him all that which was now too late.

In the so-called headquarters of the Field Marshal there prevailed, except among one or two individuals, a tone of depression and discontent, which alone would have moved me to quit Mölln as soon as possible had not another special circumstance hastened my departure.

Soon after my arrival at Mölln, I received a courier from the Secretary of Legation, von Hugo, in Berlin, bringing me my nomination as Ambassador Extraordinary and Minister Plenipotentiary to the Royal Prussian Court. This was the more fortunate for me, inasmuch as it obviated the necessity of going back to my Fatherland in its then distressing circumstances, and created the possibility of being perhaps useful to it elsewhere.

As the disbandment of the troops was going on gradually, in order not to send back too strong columns at a
time into the country, and the Guards were among the
last regiments which had to submit to this sad fate, I
found my eldest brother still in Juliusburg with his battalion, where also the regimental staff were. Here I consumed a frugal dinner for the last time with the officers
of this distinguished regiment, out of doors, under the
fruit trees of a peasant's garden—as good as you could
expect to get in a village. A glass of wine, and the 'joy
of still breathing the free air of our own land, raised the
spirits of those present for the moment, and after dinner
my brother told me he wished in the first place to accompany me back to Berlin.

After he had finished his sad duties, I went with him
to take up my new appointment in Berlin, where we arrived July 19th.

CHAPTER 4

Campaigning with the
King's German Legion
Autumn 1803—July 1807

It was not long that Christian Ompteda was permitted to
enjoy the domestic quietude of his brother Louis' house. His
own desires, actuated by a sense of duty to his calling, the feeling of wounded military *prestige,* and the thirst for vengeance,
his intimacy with his old comrade and friend, Scharnhorst, who
mourned loyally for the old country, forgetful of its ingratitude,
together with his connections with his friend Charles Alten,
now gone straight to Husum from Lauenburg to superintend
the embarkation of the first fugitives, and thence to London, all
impelled him to be one of the earliest to take part in the attempt
to reconstruct in England the best fragments of the disintegrated
Hanoverian army, and from that starting-point to take the field
against the unspeakably hated hereditary foe. This Hannibal-like
hatred became henceforward the guiding principle of his life, and
he put into practice the axiom: "Make a first bold stand with a
manly spirit, and you will find help from unexpected quarters."

On September 21st he left Berlin, went through Mecklenburg,
and bade farewell to the lady to whom he was attached in Dam-
erow on the Reden estate, she now having to follow her husband
to Regensburg. From Bützow he commissioned his brother as a
parting message, "To give a thousand good wishes from me to
Scharnhorst; you know how I value this brave friend." To Louis:

Hamburg, September 25th, 1803: You can picture to yourself
how I felt as I entered Lauenburg, saw the dirty French sentries

placed with two of *our* guns in position before what used to be our main-guard, and afterwards traversed the whole extent of that district which had been rendered so notorious to us. My postilion happened to pull up at the *Haideknig,* one of the most miserable, lonely pot-houses possible to conceive, but only too memorable as being the place where Wallmoden held the last Council of War with the generals, on July 4th, in order to pronounce our unhappy fate.

The landlady told me some particulars. The place and the [female] historiographer were worthy of the hero and the theme. *Charles Alten* is gone to England, *in consequence of a letter from the Duke* [of Cambridge], with the two lieutenants During of our regiment Otherwise, they had, up to then, busied themselves with making arrangements for our bodies of soldiers in Husum who are going over to England; here (where perhaps, nevertheless, the work is going on quietly) it is very dangerous, on account of the strictness of the police, to have anything to do with recruiting.

> After a short digression to the family seat in Würden (on the right bank of the Weser, above Bremerhafen), Christian proceeded by Flensburg to Husum, and took ship on October 9th to England. There he made his appearance as the fourth Hanoverian staff officer. But progress was not made just then quite so successfully, as was reported in Hamburg, with the reconstruction of the force destined to bear the name of the *King's German Legion.*

> There was no scruple standing in the way on account of Article 4. of the Convention of Artlenburg, for to that the troops were not bound, owing to the hurry; moreover, it was not confirmed by the King, and subsequently expressly declared not binding. And the then French authorities in Hanover placed at first no serious hindrances in the way of emigration, being rather glad than otherwise to get rid of officers whose feelings were of the most hostile description. But the way chosen for the reconstruction of the force did not commend itself to the latter. A Letter of Service for 4,000 men was awarded to Major Decken, Adjutant to the Duke of Cambridge. This gentleman at once received the rank of an English colonel. His quick pro-

motion, solely owing to his connection with the Court and position on the staff of the Duke, combined with a certain abruptness of behaviour, inspired no extensive confidence in his comrades from the front. In addition to this a Scotchman, Major Colin Halkett, hitherto in the Dutch service, had succeeded, by private interest, in obtaining a Letter of Service as well. For every recruit the Government allowed these two favoured persons 300 marks. The advance money amounted to 150 marks. But when the formation of the Legion had been formally taken over by the Duke of Cambridge, and when his invitation to join, and at the same time the wanton oppression of the country of Hanover by the French, had operated for a while, the recruits streamed in so largely that it soon became possible to form two battalions of light infantry, and one (1st) of the line, as well as cavalry and artillery. In the 1st Line Battalion the former Foot Guards were collected, and Christian Ompteda became, November 5th, 1803, its second in command, the commander being Colonel von Langwerth. From this time to the close of the year we learn from Christian's letters and journals (the latter extending to March 31st, 1808) the following experiences and opinions worth relating. To Louis:

London, October 26th, 1803: Decken's unheard-of promotion to an English colonelcy has provoked such opposition among the English of the same category that the English staff, in particular, place every possible obstacle in his way, which is not promising for the construction of such a corps as the Legion. Generally speaking, dear L.,—*Et l'intérêt, ce vil roi de la terre*, stretches its sceptre in all directions, and often prevails even in those regions where the dominion of honour only should be recognised. *Get rank, get money*, is the first principle here, in pursuit of which Buonaparte, invasion, and who knows what else get forgotten. As my first principle was merely *to serve the good cause*, I do not know that I may not be thereby led to quite special forms of disagreement (with the other principle)."

London, October 27th, 1803: As Sunday is the most convenient day to be presented to the King at Windsor, I went there late on Saturday evening, and was ready punctually by nine o'clock, at which time he goes to church. As soon as the king saw me he began a gracious and lively conversation. I will only mention *here* what he said about you. When he named you he paused, and looked first at the Duke of Cambridge, then at those in attendance, and then at me, as if to call us all to witness, then said quickly, twice over, 'Ah, that is a very superior young man!' Then he asked if we had no other brothers beside Ferdinand (There were two cousins, Augustus and Ferdinand Ompteda, sons of the deputy at Regensburg, serving in the Foot Guards, subsequently in the Legion). When I replied in the negative he said, 'Now I know the two eldest, I will answer for *them*.' Then he asked if I suffered at all now from my wound. He then approached more recent events, and expressed the greatest sympathy with our bitter experiences, but with the fixed resolution of expression characteristic of one who is used to dealing with great catastrophes. He stood some time during this interview, and among other things, speaking to his gentlemen, paid a very flattering tribute to my command of the English language. Then the Queen and her ladies stepped out at the door. The King presented me to her, and she recollected our former acquaintance, and how she had then always seen me with a bandage round my wounded leg. When the Duke reminded the King that I had just come from Berlin, a variety of things was said about that, in the course of which I was pleased to bear witness to the personal integrity of the King of Prussia's motives.

From the Journal: A major's pay was nearly fifteen marks a day, that of a lieutenant five marks, that is to say, about 450 and 150 marks a month respectively.

All very fine in Germany; and advantageous also here, at least for the upper ranks, as far as the arrangements for the accommodation of the regiments go; and one may be able to live more cheaply and pleasantly in the provinces of England than in this great money-abyss of a London, where the expense is beyond all conception.

Journal, October 28th: Review in Hyde Park of the second half of the volunteers of the capital. The Dukes of Orleans, Bourbon, and Enghien, present as *émigrés*! If one could but obliterate one's memory! But to wander about alone among hundreds of thousands who are happy in the possession of a legitimate national pride, while I have every recollection to cast me down,—it is a hard, hard thing to bear.

On November 29th, Christian went to Hilsea Barracks, close to Portsmouth, to take over the battalion then in course of formation, which, according to the battalion journal, was formed on November 25th, in six companies of eighteen men each. Defective condition of the same. "No officers arrived except me, only five corporals turned up, no arms, and no uniforms." On December 5th, however, we find—"Drill this morning." The strength was about three hundred and fifty men. On the 16th, "Under arms for the first time." On the 24th, "Completion of the battalion as far as privates are concerned."

So closed the momentous year, 1803.

1804

This year was devoted to the completion and training of the Legion. The 1st Line Battalion was stationed close to Portsmouth until the summer, and later on, from August, at Bexhill, near Hastings, opposite Boulogne. This was because the time had arrived when England seriously expected an attempt at invasion by Buonaparte, and was preparing every force on land and water to resist it. Wherefore a quantity of troops of the most varied description were collected on that part of the coast of the Channel, and military movements of unusual activity were taking place. At the same time a satisfactory spirit of comradeship was developing, as the higher English officers quickly and readily recognised the efficiency and capability of the immigrated (Hanoverians), and looked on their officers as *gentlemen*. Even the residents in the large country seats in the neighbourhood displayed various symptoms of sociability to them.

It is a remarkable proof of the isolation of England at that time, as well as of Christian's absorption in his revived profession, that he only wrote three (certainly very comprehensive) letters to his brother in Berlin in all the year. The safest means was always employed for the transmission of these. As the French frequently intercepted couriers, it was a matter of anxiety lest those addressed in the Fatherland should be compromised. To Louis:

Hilsea Barracks, near Portsmouth, January 11th, 1804: The Duke of Cumberland commands this district, and General Whitelocke is second in command. The latter is a man wholly devoted to the service, and likes to see duty strictly carried out. He is a friend to us, being prejudiced in favour of the German system of discipline. In a general way, all the English with whom we come in contact treat us capitally. General Whitelocke first of all; he does for us what he possibly can, both as regards the service, and socially. The troops about here are some of them militia regiments, which, as you know, are in this country distinguished in many ways. We have been quartered for some time here along with the Merioneth militia (a Welsh regiment); and although, on account of the increase in our numbers, they have been put to some inconvenience in making room for us, the friendly relations which had arisen between us have in no way suffered. What I have seen of the natives of that part of England, in this and other neighbouring regiments from the same land (Wales), has confirmed and increased my good opinion of this genuine old remnant of the original Britons. They seem to possess the English magnanimity, candour, sense of honour, and hospitality to a marked degree.

He describes the fortifications of Portsmouth as very strong.

Under existing circumstances, this can scarcely be the point for friend Boney to select for his landing, however; notwithstanding that there are the men-of-war, the army, the militia, the volunteers, and your countrymen always in readiness to receive any such contemplated visit in a suitable way. Our dwelling here is not unlike a built camp, and the barracks form a military world of their own. Although not particularly attractive quarters, they are a source of considerable saving to us, and everybody has tried to install himself as comfortably as possible. We dine in English style at a general mess, where we get an excellent dinner with table-beer from a caterer for the very low price of two marks. Wine may be ordered according to individual preference. In other respects our life is rather monotonous. Drill twice daily, work indoors, and a walk between whiles get through the hours till 5 p.m. pretty quickly. The session at mess is protracted till eight or nine, after which one usually goes to one's quarters, or spends the evening with a comrade.

An old Admiral, Sir Roger Curtis, who has seen much service, has a country seat close to our barracks. During the last few days of last year Sir Roger called on us, and invited us in the most polite manner to more intimate acquaintance. Perhaps you may be aware that the customs with regard to the beginning of social intercourse are exactly the reverse here to those which are prevalent on the Continent. That is to say, the newcomer here does not take the first step, which would be regarded as an intrusion. But if he has recommendations of any kind he may expect to be called upon first by those with whom he is likely to be brought in contact, either by neighbourhood, similarity of rank or calling, or any other of those links which draw human beings together. Little as there might be supposed to be in common between the Admiral and us, he nevertheless soon convinced us, by the general tone of his behaviour during his first visit, that his invitation was seriously meant. The next day, in fact, he introduced some of our senior officers to his wife and daughter, and invited us a few days later to a jovial dinner. The daughter has studied music with success. As Baring (subsequently the hero of La Haye Sainte) plays the flute, and I, after three years' neglect, had to take up the violin-bow again, the little musical-evening's entertainment was able to proceed.

From all this you can judge that we have no reason to be dissatisfied with our condition. Nor indeed are we, up to a certain point. For it would be wronging the most careless of us to suppose it possible that these circumstances could make us forget for one single moment *the past,* or the present condition of things over the water. I only touch upon this chord because it is always stretched, and with or without special motive mingles in solo or unison mournful discords with the easy harmony of our present life.

The Diary at this time contains, in addition to an exact record of daily work and the general defensive precautions, the following remarks descriptive. of the position of the foreigners in England:

In the neighbouring country seats of the nobility, expectation, wishes, and apprehensions regarding the invasion. It is evident that a large number of the English are rather uneasy about the matter. If the defence depended merely on the national courage, or even on the number of defenders now actually under arms, the French need really not be feared.

July 26th: Muster by the Duke of Cumberland. Manoeuvres carried out well, and consequently successful. Spectators numerous. The English have not got much idea of manoeuvring strictly as such. Their evolutions are too exact to be applicable over broken country.

August 6th: Midday, first visit in the village of Bexhill (near Hastings, whither the 1st L.B. had been transferred). The people at this place, and about the neighbourhood, generally seem to look on us much as we do on Cossacks. The gentry round called at the camp. They seem to be beginning to discover that we are not quite outlandish bears.

August 13th: General Don has taken the command of us. He issued a flattering inauguratory order: 'Excellent officers, and gallant men, the composition of the Legion.' I look on this in the light of a bill drawn on us. Dishonour it, and you will be bankrupt! Later on he said, verbally, 'Now I have seen the state of the King's German Legion, I wish Buonaparte would come over to-morrow.'

To Louis:

Bexhill, September 20th, 1804: Our heavy cavalry at Weymouth is one of the main objects of the King's attention. That has, of course, its disadvantageous side for us, as opposing us to the English. Even the German tune *Landesvater* is said at times to have taken precedence of *God save the King*. Really moving are such incidents as these: The King walked in among the

165

ranks, went into home details, many of which were unknown to him—particularly much of the decisive part of our latest history. He then consoled the men over the present unhappy condition of their country, and exhorted them to be of good cheer and trust in Providence. In the latter regard, he instanced his own case, 'how he had a little while ago been visited by a severe illness (insanity), but had always placed his trust in God, who had delivered him out of that danger again.' Of the late Field Marshal Freytag the King always spoke as 'my late honest friend,' and his successor he called 'His Excellency the Count Wallmoden.' No more fruitless lamentation over our situation. *To give back as good as we got*, how and where it may be done, that is our only hope. One question: do you now read the English papers regularly?

Not that I would shut my eyes to their shortcomings and faults, but yet there is a rich field of useful instruction, liberal generosity, and of impartial truth, for which the press of this country seems the only refuge. Now and then numbers of the *Hamburg Correspondent,* that I once thought so excellent a paper, fall into my hands. Good Heavens! what a deterioration! And then to think that this is the most widely circulated and best of the papers which lead public opinion in Germany! A paper of a different kind, the *Anzeigen* of our own unhappy country, I also get to see sometimes, and each page affords me material for the bitterest indignation. You understand, but I cannot say anything further here.

> After the summer, during which the weather had been in many ways unfavourable in the land that is so rich in rain, really bad times set in in October, the description of which in the Diary will show what even the superior officers of the Legion had to put up with, and that in what was for the time a condition of peace.

October 11th: Violent storm and pouring rain last night and all day today. The ground where our camp is, bad any way, is now a morass, and the present quarters are bad for the men. Beginning to build huts.

October 27th: Storm last evening. Camp literally flooded. Hut-building delayed by the weather.

October 29th: The camp a swamp. Confined to my tent.

November 5th: Continued cold and bad weather. Being unwell, find my field-bed only a partial shelter. Ceaseless din of all kinds of bad music; meaningless shoutings and clamour. All this is trying to the patience, and leads to sullen stupefaction. This is the anniversary of the Gunpowder Plot, and Guy Fawkes consequently burnt with huzzas and jubilation in several bonfires in my proximity.

November 11th: Storms and rain do not advance my recovery. Obliged to exchange my tent for quarters (in a house) hard by.

November 13th: Left camp today; of all the uncomfortable ones I have known, the worst. Uninterrupted bad weather has turned the clay soil of our encampment into a sticky, miry morass, so slippery that one can scarcely escape the danger of falling down. The wet and stuffiness of my tent delayed my recovery, and I was obliged, unwilling though I was not to share our common hardships, to obey the warnings of reason and necessity. A neighbouring farm became my refuge. Contrast between the dwellings of the English and German peasantry. Comfort, even luxury, but of the most rational description. Agreeable impression of the innocent mirth of the family after the wild disturbances of the camp. Fresh experience. How easily a man can accustom himself to the sacrifices demanded by a military mode of life, as long as he is in good health, almost as easily as he gets spoiled by luxury. After that life (of hardship) the commonest comforts of life have an enhanced value.

November 15th: Morning call on the people of the house. Met Miss Mary Lansdale, the daughter of my host. Neatness of costume of this girl, who is, after all, neither more nor less than a fairly well-to-do peasant. Her politeness, in showing me over the house. Elegant appointments; mahogany chairs with horse-hair seats, carpet, mirror, a fine fireplace, and exotics in the room I occupy. Precautions that the labourers and maids when coming home from dirty work should not soil the house. Cleanliness of these lower orders. No shouting and noise. Four men and two boys do their work as quietly and cleverly as if they were skilled artisans plying a handicraft. The same quietude and goodness seem to prevail over the domestic animals and beasts of burden. No ill-tempered horse to be seen, nor goring horned cattle, and no barking dog to be heard. The female dwellers in the house are industrious, quiet, and cheerful; the tone of their hearty laugh, provoked sometimes by the antics of a favourite dog, does one good, being the expression of *nature's* own joy.

November 16th: Pure dry air and the return of natural warmth have in these few days brought about great progress in my convalescence. One of the most beneficent advantages of this place is its quiet, which I have been deprived of for a whole year in the incessant din of barrack and camp life.

November 20th: The weather being pleasant, I went to visit the camp. The ground has got worse. Had a look at the huts intended for the use of the battalion ; they are still a long way from being ready. Those already inhabited damp, natural consequence of using green wood.

The general state of health had suffered so much that all the officers who wished to find other lodging than the huts were given a special allowance to find quarters with.

November 26th: Reported myself again for duty. I expected to occupy my hut, but owing to the wet, one of the turf-sod walls had subsided, and had to be rebuilt.

December 1st: Left Woodgate Farm, and have got into my hut. The lime on the walls still very clamp, and the air uncommonly unwholesome.

December 20th: Increasing severe cold with rough weather. Our draughty huts afford a very insufficient shelter against such a climate.

These conditions had a deteriorating effect on the smart appearance of the men. We learn from the battalion journal later on that Lieutenant-Colonel Ompteda issued an order that "no beards were to be worn any more, and that the pioneers and drummers were to shave theirs off." At that time the troops still wore the pigtail, which was only dropped in 1808.

On the last day of the year Christian Ompteda became Lieutenant-Colonel and Commander of the battalion. As his seniority was not yet quite sufficient, the Duke of Cambridge became nominal colonel of the battalion, in order to insure Ompteda against the intrusion of any senior staff officer from among those newly come over in the meantime. That was a mark of distinction applying to the old Foot Guards as well as to their present leader.

1805

The year 1805 was also in greater part spent in training the troops, and in heightened suspense as to when and how the storm cloud threatening from Boulogne would discharge itself. The ever-regular clock of duty varied so little that whole weeks are skipped in the Diary for want of anything to write down; and what did happen was mostly not pleasant.

On March 4th the mess-house, only just finished, was handed over for the use of the 1st Line Battalion. I utilised this as a becoming opportunity to invite General Don, the English officers of the Prince of Wales' regiment, as well as the officers of the staffs of our battalions which are here, to dine at our mess. The festivities proceeded tolerably well till late in the evening, when, through a careless accident, a boiling tea-kettle got spilt over both my hands and legs. A bad scalding, much pain, and confinement for more than four weeks to my quarters, were the consequences. To cheer me, anxiously expected letters arrived, eleven being in arrear, all coming from Husum by the same mail.

On March 20th we hear of "continued pain from my wounds, and incapacity to make any movement worth speaking of." This went on nearly the same till April 4th. The person to blame for this *careless accident* is most generously left unnamed. Another accident, this time harmless, took place on April 11 th.

Out for a walk today I was almost grazed by a musket-ball, which was discharged by an Englishman who was letting off a firearm for the first time in his life. On my remonstrating, he assured me that it should not occur again.

Later on Christian had a fall with his horse, and received a contusion of the head, which again confined him to his quarters.

On April 28th there arrived in London forty officers from their country (Hanover). Says Christian, "Mostly elderly men of superior rank, and married. This does not look promising for the promotion of those who have been at work here some time already." This brief observation is connected with an extremely painful decision in which Christian was concerned.

His brother Ferdinand, recently Captain in the old Hanoverian 5th Infantry, had married at an early age Frederica von Behr Häuslingen, and was the father of four little boys. He had come back to Verden, his last station, from Artlenburg, and was living there with his family on half-pay, in distressing circumstances, and these not wholly of a pecuniary kind. What tortured this brave soldier much more was what he saw and experienced going on round him, together with the longing to share the efforts of his more actively engaged' comrades, and the dread of the stigma that might attach to him on account of his not having joined them in their expedition. He had written in the year 1804 asking Christian's advice on this matter. The latter had then decided that "considering that he had been relieved of his obligations to his country's service against his will, he must now first consider his sacred duty as a husband and father, and ought to sacrifice himself to the extent of abiding by that duty." But in the lapse of a short time the foreign oppression increased to such an intolerable degree, as to make the life of every honourable man a torture daily renewed. Not only were severe contributions extorted (in the twenty-six months of the first foreign dominion, till autumn 1805, about 26,000,000 thalers), but individuals were so maltreated, by secret police espionage, by impudent violations of the domestic hearth, and of time-honoured customs and manners, that even the calmest and most patient were unable to live any more in the old way. Ferdinand Ompteda, as the brother of two active and notable patriots, suffered confinement to the town and police surveillance, on the pretext that he had taken part in the recruiting. Moreover, the promised pension often delayed its payment whole months, while at the same time clumsy and insulting attempts to decoy him were made use of, which contained at the same time a latent threat. Here is a specimen:

De la part de MM. Les Officiers de l'état Major, les Officiers du 8ᵐᵐ Regiment, et les Employés aux Administrations M. le Capitaine Hompteda et Mde son Epouse sont invites à leur faire l'honneur d'assister à un thé qu'ils donneront demain Jeudi 20 Décembre à la maison de la Veuve Schmidt!'

The answer:

Verden, December 20th, 1804: To the Adjutant Major. Sir—I am fully penetrated with the sense of the honour to which Messrs.—— have repeatedly invited me.

But candidly and without circumlocution, I feel the sad fate of my unhappy country too keenly to deceive myself as to the depth of our misfortunes, which are felt by all classes, and especially by our ruined and impoverished troops. And though I am not so unjust as to lay the blame of that on the French soldiers, who are only doing their duty, it still seems to me hardly suitable for the blameless means of our ruin to be also the means of our entertainment. These are my real feelings, which slander has misrepresented, and given a suspicious colouring to General Rivaud, whom I have never failed to treat with the respect due to his military position.

In personal respect to you, Sir, I have placed before you the reasons which compel me to decline the honour of appearing in the society of the French officers. I beg those gentlemen therefore to excuse me, and remain, etc., *F. von Ompteda*, Captain.

Ferdinand sent this correspondence to his brother Louis to Berlin, explaining at the same time that he had given up, for the present, the idea of going to England:

.... hoping that in some way or other a change might occur in the course of this year (1805) in our hard fate. About our continual sad position I say nothing to you.

You know all the misery of our wretched country better than I do. Curse the originator of it! My sentiments towards our oppressors are unalterably the same, and will remain so as long as I live. My behaviour and dealings are, of course with proper caution, proportionate to those sentiments. I have carefully avoided from the outset any intercourse with these devils, and as I can be turned from that attitude neither by threats nor in any other way, they have at last taken to leaving us alone. The officers of the 8th Regiment were the only ones this winter who persistently bombarded us with invitations to their *thés dansants* in spite of our invariably declining. The preceding note to these gentlemen met with no reply, and the invitations continued just the same, as did also my refusals. Now, at last, all these precious festivities are over for this winter, I trust, never to recommence. *F.*

Nevertheless, Christian continued to dissuade his brother, and to disapprove of the coming over of married men, whether they brought their wives with them or left them behind. He writes on this point to Louis:

Were it not for the sufferings of our excellent Ferdinand under this infamous state of oppression, I should be proud of the noble stand he makes against this vile or stupid gang, who add indignation and contempt to the feelings already excited by our general calamities. This condemnation is not universal, but I am sorry to say the exceptions do not appear to be found most numerous in those circles where a higher conception of patriotism, and, I may add, of personal pride, ought to have been a guarantee against such unexampled, and often wanton humiliations. I assure you that this aspect of the ruin of the land so clear to us is the one of which I am most sensitive. Physical disorders can be cured by different remedies, but if the proper feelings suffer deterioration in those classes from whom one day help is to be expected, and if these perhaps go so far as to take pleasure in such deterioration, restoration in better days is beyond hope.

This sad prediction was unfortunately fulfilled later on in the *Kingdom of Westphalia*, and a lasting and severe agitation was required before the spirit of tame surrender and inert narrowness of mind which the wretched system of petty states had engendered in German life could be at last overcome.

In August says the Diary, "Expectation of the invasion livelier than ever; it is awaited every day."

So thoroughly had Buonaparte succeeded in deceiving the world, that at that very time his troops were on the march to South Germany against Austria. It was weeks before the English found that out. At last, on September 7th, the Diary reports the order to the troops "to make ready for embarkation." On October 18th, the fleet which was to convey the Legion to their old home left Ramsgate and assembled in the Downs.

The same day Mack had already capitulated at Ulm!

On November 5th the expedition put to sea, eighty vessels convoyed by five men-of-war. Then a perpetual east wind came in the way, after which westerly storms delayed the entrance into the mouth of the Elbe, so that it was not till November 17th that they were able to cast anchor in the roadstead of Cuxhaven. From there Christian writes with renewed confidence to Louis:

It is just a month ago today that we went on board at Ramsgate, and were detained by contrary winds in the Downs till the fifth. Then we made sail, and had a rough, and indeed, to some extent, dangerous passage, but, thank God! I hope we are all on this side of the water now. Our army is numerous and of good composition. We have some of the flower of the English troops with us, which are an honourable escort for that force which now stands re-arisen from its ashes, arms in hand, of a good courage, and well organised. I hope to God that much is about to be avenged, though I am not at all acquainted with the Continental situation.

Decken, who was made Brigadier-General just before our departure, is with us here, I am glad of that, for I entertain the hope that he will justify his unusual favours of fortune by some further display of merit than he has made hitherto.[1]

---

1. Gneisenau treats this person with unsparing condemnation, both as soldier and man, in his *Life* by Pertz, 1., 570. Later on, up to 1815, General Decken was always busy in the organisation department, but never appeared before the enemy.

The battalion was disembarked at Twielenfleth, and marched thence to Stade.

Diary: "November 20th:—On the shore, quantities of our country-folk of all classes, partly attracted by curiosity, and partly hoping to greet relatives. But what a sight! Not merely in contrast to fortunate England, but also in comparison to the better external aspect of the higher, middle, and lower Hanoverian classes three years ago! Oppression, poverty, dull lassitude, neglect of outward dignity or grace, dirtiness, force themselves from every side on the gaze.

The battalion remained at Stade till December 6th. During this period the battalion journal mentions a singular old military practice:

> Private Vieregg of the 6th Company was turned out of the battalion as a vagabond, for using highly objectionable and criminal language, and discharged from the gates of Stade with the Rogue's March.

Probably this had some reference to the losses by desertion.

Diary: The position of the Allies, or supposed Allies, was this. The Prussian army under the Duke of Brunswick was moving from Celle, Hanover, and Hildesheim, on Göttingen, and thence by Thuringia to the French frontier. The Russians were approaching the Weser from the Lower Elbe. A small corps under General Werdereffsky invested the fortress of Hameln, but only on the right bank of the Weser. The English and the Legion were on the right bank of the Lower Weser. The battle of Austerlitz, on December 2nd, with its consequences, upset all our calculations, and though that great struggle be not further mentioned in these notes, it, nevertheless, will be found sufficiently conspicuous to the memory and attention through its effect on subsequent events.

It fell to the lot of the brigade, especially to the 1st Line Battalion, to be the only troops of the Legion who actually came in contact with the long-wished-for enemy, for Hanover had been entirely evacuated by the French, and the Weser fortress of Hameln only was still held, by General Barbou, with a few thousand men. Christian subsequently wrote an account of his share in the matter to his sister-in-law, the wife of Louis the Ambassador, from Springe on the Deister, December 28th.

Dear Sister—Knowing your sympathy with me in my adventurous life, I am sending you a brief account of my experiences since we landed. On December 14th I marched through Hanover. There I had the happiness to meet our excellent brother Ferdinand, whose greatest longing has now been gratified, for he has got a company in the new 6th Line Battalion to be raised in that place. I entered by the (northern) Stone Gate, paraded before the Russian General in command there, and left again by the (southern) Calenberg Gate. And that was enough for me. The very looks of the people, high and low, whom we saw, was sufficient to confirm my saddest apprehensions, which must unfortunately be associated with two years of humiliation, be the latter compulsory or voluntary. We, who were so glad not to have to be immediate witnesses of the ruin of so much that we held so dear, can now for the time but swallow our bitterness.

Two marches more brought us to our destination. On the second, I had the unexpected and most welcome pleasure of meeting the enemy, almost under the guns of Hameln. It was quite an interesting affair, so I enclose the report I made to General Werdereffsky. You must not think me vain, for I attribute our success only to the excellent behaviour of the troops under my command. Nevertheless, the recollection of having marched over the battlefield of Hastenbeck with drums beating and band playing, under the eyes of General Barbou and the detachment which advanced to attack us and then dared not, will always be a pleasurable one to me. We must have given satisfaction to our ancestors who fell on that ground nearly fifty years ago.

At the Battle of Hastenbeck, July 26th, 1757, the commanders on both sides (the Duke of Cumberland, and Marshal d'Etrées) considered themselves defeated, and began to retreat. The French were the first to find out their mistake, and return to the field. The Duke of Cumberland, in consequence, had to give up his command. His successor was Charles William Ferdinand, Hereditary Prince of Brunswick.

175

After a few days, we were transferred hither, and last Sunday had another pleasing opportunity of improving our acquaintance with the enemy. Thinking us in full retreat, he made a reconnaissance in force to his front. I was on duty that day, so I speedily went for them with a detachment of Russian Cossacks, and cuirassiers. It was a brilliant skirmish, which only night put an end to.

He then proceeds to speak favourably of the Russians, and hopes that the Prussians will soon take an active share in the operations. "We shall, in any case, not relinquish our task, or omit aught that can be done right and left."

But even these petty hostilities were soon checked by the news from the great theatre of war. On December 4th peace was brought about between Austria and France, and the discouraged Czar Alexander set the face of his forces homewards, and so came to an end the brotherhood in arms of the Russians and English in northern Germany.

1806

On January 3rd the 1st Line Battalion left Springe.

Diary: Our departure from Springe was a source of genuine mutual regret, on the part of the Russians and ourselves. Werdereffsky and his officers had several times taken part in social gatherings at our battalion mess, which I had instituted in the post-house. On the morning of our departure our hospitality was returned by the Russians in the form of an extremely splendid breakfast, at which the floods of champagne, punch, and rum had the same perilous effect on the heads of some officers as the brandy and association with the Russian men so very often had on our soldiers at Springe. Late in the evening I entered Hanover in frosty moonlight.

In Hanover Christian learnt the worst news of all, that Prussia was treating with Napoleon, and that the Electorate was to be occupied.

On January 27th the Royal Proclamation appeared, according to which an arrangement was entered into with France that "the states of H. B. Majesty in Germany should not again be occupied by French troops, but on the other hand entirely evacuated by them and taken under the *protection* and *administration* of Prussia only, until the conclusion of a general peace." The Minister Minister left Hanover with a protest. The Hanoverian-English corps there, however, made no resistance, but withdrew slowly to the coast. It is probable that there was not so very much reluctance to this course in London, but on the other hand it was natural that the troops should be affected by the extreme feebleness of the issue of the expedition of liberation. Christian exhibits his soldierly indignation to his brother Louis in Berlin in passionate words:

Hanover, January 4th, 1806: I have left Hameln and been here since yesterday. Krusemark is here, too." (Lieutenant Colonel in the Prussian service, sent to the Hanoverian Ministry and to General Barbou with diplomatic proposals.) "I need not tell you that our retrogressive movements are Prussia's handiwork. I have just had an interesting explanation with Krusemark, who is a fine fellow, whom I personally esteem highly, and deserves a more honourable mission and to serve under more favourable circumstances, while it is not his fault that he has to deliver proposals of which he fully recognises both the pitifulness and the extremely dangerous possible effects on his own government.

My dear fellow, if this sort of thing is to go on, the Continent will soon be irrecoverably lost. The Russian and English armies will not long creep for refuge under the contemptible Prussian cloak, as Cathcart and Tolstoi are now inclined. We are here 40,000 men of the best and bravest troops. A swift movement on *Holland only* would have opened the road to certain success. Had there been a couple more battalions added to the force with which I was before Hameln recently, that place, from all the certain information I can obtain, would have fallen into our hands in perhaps eight to fourteen clays without a blow struck. As things are, we are rendered powerless; Barbou laughs in our faces, and will make the most absurd demands. Lastly, our friends far and wide are losing the very rare sparks of courage and hope yet perhaps left, and the neighbourhood of Hameln will be plundered with impunity, while our whole country will be plunged again deeper than ever in the cesspool of apathy.

And this is Lombard's and Haugwitz's work. I mention these personages in the order in which I think they should be classified.

The side of infamy is winning, and the adherents of the side of honour have at least one issue left, which is to play their part as honourably as possible to the last. Farewell, my dear brother. Indignation is not a joyful feeling, but nearly the only one left, in the face of public events ; yet one more, the determination, come what may, never to be defeated. Your Faithful Brother, C. O.

With this only too correct forecast for things in general, and this vow, carried out to the last, for himself in particular, the brave soldier turned his back on his own country, which he was destined never to see again.

A slow journey took place to the coast, and the battalion was embarked again on February 7th. On February 18th Christian again saw near Deal "the well-known lovely Kentish coast. Yet the memory of plans wrecked and hopes shattered almost beyond recall, mingled bitterness with impressions otherwise so agreeable. Happy is he who has a Fatherland like England!"

At Portsmouth Christian found orders to go with his battalion to Ireland. On March 6th the convoy weighed anchor. On March 8th they were off the extreme west of Cornwall, the promontory known as Land's End. The course toward the landing-place, Cork, was then north-westerly, but a keen north-easter drove the vessels in a southerly direction. Wherefore the passage assumed the character of an Odyssey-like ramble, in which we will accompany the adventurer by aid of his Diary:

March 10th and 11th: The nuisance of contrary winds was increased by a pretty violent gale. It blew hard two nights and a day from the north, and north to east. The ship rolled considerably, and we were all more or less affected by seasickness. It was a joyless day. We were even compelled to forego the comfort of a stove-fire in the cabin. The nights, too, were dark, and the danger of the ships running one another down was a source of serious anxiety.

March 13th: The wind abated in the night, and in the morning there was almost a dead calm, except for a light breath of wind now and then, from the most variable points of the compass, which filled the dangling sails for a brief passing moment. The Commodore made the signal to lay to, in order to reassemble the somewhat scattered ships. Ours was towards the middle of the fleet. While the laying-to was taking place, and the calm prevailing, the heavy rolling of the sea caused a number of the vessels to get a good deal too close to one another as they concentrated. They would not answer the helm, being unmanageable for want of wind, whence arose the extraordinary but very perilous circumstance, that several ships were on the point of running into one another, in which case the extreme roughness of the water must have occasioned their sinking, or grievous damage, by mutual collision. Fortunately, a breeze sprang up exactly at the critical moment, which enabled the imperilled ships to seek safety in separation in every possible direction. Soon after that we discerned land. It was an Irish cape of considerable dimensions. Our imagination followed our wishes, and every one pictured to himself Cork Harbour, which was our destination, as constituting the land that lay before us. Gradually the coast became more distinct. The general outline was of a rougher, sharper, higher character than that of the English coast, presenting therefore a new kind of interest. We were very glad to see several pilot-boats advancing to meet us. We very soon got a pilot on board, who disposed of all our illusions by telling us that the headland before us was Cape Clear, and with the north-east wind Bantry Bay would be the nearest place we could get to (on the south-west of Ireland). Towards midday we arrived there. The land enclosing the bay consists of rather rocky steep cliffs. Berehaven, in the north-west of Bantry Bay, was the destination of our fleet.

March 14th: After several hours of dreary tacking we at last came happily to anchor. The weather was fair, and my inclination never to neglect favourable opportunities of becoming acquainted with fresh objects impelled me to go on shore soon after our arrival. We landed between the cliffs near the only building of any consideration on this side (of the bay). It was the harbour-master's house, who lived here in the desert with a large family, and apparently not in prosperous circumstances.

We stepped ashore, and the father of the house at once came forward with that patriarchal hospitality, which is a beautiful and celebrated point in the Irish national character, to ask us into his house to partake of refreshment. We declined the latter, but went in, finding the house confined, and very plain, but clean: The daughters, four or five in number, were of a robust appearance, and justified the characteristic features of beauty attributed to the Irish, owing to an exuberance of contour.

After a time we got a guide, in order to traverse the neighbouring country, a lad as ragged as the other inhabitants about here, who came out in boats to sell their frugal articles of sustenance on board the ships. The first thing we beheld with real admiration was a romantic waterfall, which poured a stream of the clearest water down into the sea over the hills at the back of the bay. As they use *no wheeled vehicles* at all in this part of county Cork, but all traffic takes place on foot or horseback, we continued to walk up a path, partly very steep, which connects the military road from Bantry to the little town of Castletown. A large number of our officers hastened thither, but were disappointed in their expectations, owing to the extreme poverty of the place. We entered one of the country cabins which lay on our road; such miserable habitations are scarcely to be found among the most uncivilised nations of the earth. The whole building consists of a heaped-up, rough stone rectangle, sixteen to twenty feet long and about twelve feet broad. An opening, four or five feet high, serving as door, is the only aperture in the walls. Window there is none. Overhead, the cabin is provided with a badly arched roof of turf sods, a hole in which serves as chimney; but even that luxury is often absent, in which case the peat-smoke and the inhabitants have to use the same means of egress. On one of the narrower sides, usually the west side, a wretched peat-fire is kindled on the floor. Water and potatoes are the usual ingredients of the *cuisine*. Tables are seldom seen, at most a few chairs, and a shelf bearing the earthenware utensils required for housekeeping purposes. A sleeping-place, containing some coarse rags instead of a bed, apparently accommodates the whole of a numerous family. The costume of great and small, indoors or out, is simply that of beggars, with the customary addition of dirt, vermin, and bodily infirmity. In one word, it is a most pitiable sight. I ascribed it to the natural poverty of this region, of which the soil seems only capable of producing the barest necessaries. But Lieutenant Teighe of ours, himself of Irish descent, assured me that the condition of the common people was the same throughout Ireland. We returned on board our ship to our comrades, not much cheered by what we had seen, but refreshed by our excursion, and at any rate provided with some new impressions which would serve as subject-matter for conversation.

March 15th: The wind, still from the north-east, rose towards evening to proportions approaching those of a hurricane. Several ships, including ours, dragged their anchors even in this safe harbour, a state of things which, considering the rocky nature of the shore, was far from reassuring. A second anchor brought us to a standstill, and the night passed in anxious longing for the morning, amid great commotion and frequent apprehensions of collision with some of the other ships.

March 16th: This day, being Sunday, served to convince us that the good Catholic inhabitants of Ireland do not resemble their Protestant English half-brothers in their way of keeping that sacred day. Business went on as usual by the medium of boats from the shore. The articles dealt in were limited principally to potatoes, eggs, and butter, a little bread, which was dear and bad, rather better milk, thin pigs, ducks, and fowls, dried fish, but seldom any fresh. The most surprising thing that struck us was the general disinclination to accept English coins. Neither shillings nor pence could be disposed of, while it was easier to pass the German florins and three-groschen pieces. It would seem that the Irish value each coin by weight, regardless of the purity of the silver. This is said to proceed from the fact that Jewish speculators have flooded the country with base and light

English coins. Nearly every Irishman has a little set of scales of ingenious construction, by which both shillings and guineas are weighed. On the other hand, a passionate desire for *barter* on the part of the inhabitants gave an odd character to their intercourse with us. This peculiarity is attributable to their grinding poverty. Many of them, particularly the children, were almost entirely destitute of clothing, wherefore our old cast-off articles of raiment became a welcome form of payment to them. An old pair of trousers would generally purchase a sucking-pig. This gave our bargains the aspect of barter with some savage nation, an illusion which the ancient native language, the external appearance of the traffickers, and the rough surrounding country, served to heighten.

March 18th: Excursion into the neighbouring hills. All the inhabitants, whom we have hitherto heard speak of the great local landlord, Lord Bantry, talk of him in terms of respect and attachment. This happy attitude is occasioned by Lord Bantry's unselfish preference of his desert home to the attractions of England; the unfortunate condition of the native Irish being mainly due to the *absenteeism* of the great landowners, who live away in England, and let their Irish estates, which are subsequently sublet, often five or six times over. Each of the sub-lessees, of course, wants to make a profit, and the ultimate burden falls, in consequence, on the unfortunate peasants, who suffer under the extortions of the whole series of middle-men.

On March 20th a north-west wind enabled the strayed fleet to get under sail, and make its way by the next day to its original destination, viz., Cork,—a great relief "after we had been six weeks confined to the inconveniences of life on board a very crowded transport."

The 1st Line Battalion, now a thousand strong, obtained quarters on March 25th in the Kinsale barracks (on the coast south of Cork). The life there seems to have been destitute of incident, so much so that the Diary and the battalion journal have nothing to say up to June 14th. On May 10th the battalion received orders to leave for Gibraltar. From May 21st to June 14th it again lay embarked in Cork Roads. At the moment of actual departure Christian writes to inform his brother Louis, who had in the meantime been nominated Ambassador to Dresden, after the occupation of Hanover by the Prussians.

On board the transport *Windermere*, in the act of departure, I am on the point of going to Gibraltar. I have already told you that every destination is much the same to me, unless it leads to the probability of recovering our lost Fatherland. But the circumstance is not indifferent to me that I am now in command of a body of men which has survived many a hard trial, upon which I believe I can depend, and that I am supported by a body of officers of a thoroughly distinguished character. Wherefore we trust ourselves to Providence, and our cause to honour and justice. The coast is already growing distant, and the pilot wants my letter. Farewell heartily. C.

After a fair passage, the 1st Battalion, and with it the 2nd, landed at the Rock of Gibraltar on June 27th. Unfortunately, we can learn nothing of the impression this new station made on Christian Ompteda's adventurous character. The Diary is silent to October 6th, and even from that date we gather from it the general impression that his stay on the Rock, which lasted a whole year, was a life of quiet, occupied only by the perpetual course of duty, elevated by the magnificent surroundings, the view of the sea, and of the mountains of Spain and Africa; and enlivened by the mighty movements of the English fleet, which mastered and swept clear the Mediterranean and the sea-way to England, and perpetually ran in from east and west to the harbour of Gibraltar. A very peculiar state of things had arisen with regard to the hostile Spanish. As the map shows, Gibraltar lies on the eastward promontory of a deep inlet piercing towards the north, while on the west and opposite side is the fortified Spanish harbour of Algesiras. From that base the Spanish (then on the French side) carried on a troublesome, persistent, and courageous petty war with gunboats, which although they could not venture on to the open sea, kept up an unceasing and frequently successful chase of passing mercantile ships. North of Gibraltar, at the head of the inlet, was the so-called neutral ground, where peaceful *rencontres* with the enemy often took place, there not being in Gibraltar the same passionate hostility in the hearts of the English, and above all, of the Legion, against those of French nationality as in most other places.

It was a hard and painful deprivation for all these loyal men, especially for Christian, that during this whole year he vainly awaited letters from his brothers and sisters. The difficult and (as far as England was concerned) sluggishly conducted postal service he had to accept as the reason of this needless, and therefore the more painful, default of letters from the Continent, and his brother Louis only received three of his letters from Gibraltar.

Those of our contemporaries who enjoyed the advantages of the daily field-post in 1870-71 will appreciate the depression caused by the entire deficiency of this comforting institution.

By these brief explanatory remarks the general situation into which our adventurer's destiny had cast him will be, it is hoped, sufficiently comprehensible.

A few extracts from the Diary may serve to enliven, if not actually to fill, the blank outline of this year.

October 6th: To-day the rainy season came on with a sharp storm. Heavy volumes of water poured violently down the rocks. The effect was an immense relief after the uninterrupted heat and drought we have had hitherto, which had such a relaxing effect as to interrupt these daily notes.

The battalion journal, however, contains nothing worthy of remark from June 28th to October 18th, except that a few soldiers were condemned on July 18th to 1000 lashes for desertion.

October 8th: On my visit to the regimental hospital today, my sad conviction was renewed of the relatively grave character of our complaints under treatment. Even the convalescents recover with difficulty. A deep dejection, irrespective of their extraordinary bodily weakness, weighs down the patients, whose aspect demands the deepest sympathy. The 1st Battalion has been more fortunate than the 2nd, as the hospital of the latter shows, which contains even now, when the worst fever period is over, 120 patients, several of whom are not likely to recover. The immediate causes of serious illness are, the encouragement given, in a certain sense, to immoderate indulgence in unwholesome heavy wines, the setting the soldiers to public works in the summer months without proper regard to the hours of excessive heat, and, lastly, the defective arrangements for internal comfort in the barracks. These three main sources of illness *might* have been prevented.

It appears from remarks elsewhere that the then Governor was not fit for his office.

October 12th: Parade of the 1st Battalion. In spite of drill having been so long discontinued, the battalion really carried out all its movements excellently. Every one displayed quiet steadiness and goodwill, and it all made a truly satisfactory impression on me.

1807

January 1st: Here, on the extremest southern point of Europe, and in a certain sense in the last un-subdued stronghold of the Continent, I begin the new year. I have been without news for *eight* months from those who are most dear to me in my unhappy country, and recently (by the continental blockade) entirely separated from them. I am sufficiently aware (through the English papers) of the general misery of Germany to know that it is more or less crushed throughout, impoverished, exhausted, degraded, disarmed, dishonoured, and abandoned with scorn and contempt, to the amazement of the world and of generations to come. Yet here I am, in the place to whose renown my countrymen have contributed, associated with a little band of Germans who still hold weapons in their hands, making common cause with that unique nation which, still unconquered and unshaken, opposes the victorious fortune of the great malefactor. I have many storms to struggle with within ——, and so we go forward into the lowering darkness of the future.

January 15th: The following two facts cheered me very much, being proofs of an excellent military spirit, under which only is there any certainty of support on a path so full of sacrifice and hardship as that of a soldier's life. I had issued the precautionary order, in connection with yesterday's inspection, that the recruits of last year whose efficiency might not be quite satisfactory were to have no cartridges, in order to prevent irregularities during the firing. One of the young Hanoverian peasant-lads of last year's levy, included with apparent justice in that class, was further specially admonished by the sergeant of his company to observe the required conditions of equipment. It may have been that the double expression of the low esteem with which his military efficiency was regarded deepened his feeling of insulted honour, but at all events the lad replied with great bitterness: 'Very well. If they don't think me good enough to let off a musket like my comrades, although I have done firing exercise twice in Ireland and twice here, I will prove that I can make one sharp shot, at any rate.' It was then observed that he charged his musket with a ball-cartridge. The officer of the company, my cousin Ferdinand Ompteda, put him under arrest, and so the matter came to be reported. I had the prisoner brought in, whom I knew to be a good, simple, in no way hypocritical, peasant lad, and I talked to him seriously but not severely while hot tears ran down his cheeks. It was the expression of a noble spirit hardly to be expected under such an exterior. I gave the prisoner a suitable reprimand, and released him from arrest. I hope the character and prospects of a fine, brave fellow have not suffered from this matter.

The other incident was this. I offered a former drummer, now in the ranks, the chance of becoming a drummer again, which implied higher pay. He replied: 'I would rather carry a musket.' Such characteristics as these are among the experiences which increase one's value for one's profession.

January 18th: The Brigade attended Divine service on the parade this morning. Previously I read to the assembled battalion some judgements on certain officers by the general Court-Martial, which had recently been sent over from England. It cannot be ignored what a healthy influence announcements of this kind have on the soldiers' minds. The obvious conviction that the same justice befalls all ranks, and that the transgressions of the officer meet with the same severity as those of the private, softens for the latter the hardships he is required to undergo, and gives him that noble pride which arises from the feeling that he belongs to a calling which is a strict one, but regulated by impartial justice. And when the general effect is so evident which the French commanders can produce on their armies by proclamations and addresses full of bombast, one asks, 'Why are we so totally inoperative on that best of all levers of an army, its spirit?' Without the latter, your men are mere machines which will most likely leave you in the lurch, however ingeniously you may have calculated out the construction and wheel-works of the automaton.

It is not specially surprising that an officer who held such views at such a period should become a sympathetic and intimate friend of Scharnhorst, and later with Gneisenau.

February 1st: the evening the disagreeable occurrence of a drunken riot between the men of the 57th Regiment and ours. Bayonets and side-arms were used on both sides, and half a dozen were wounded of both corps, but not dangerously. As soon as I knew what was going on, I went to the scene of the disturbance, a narrow street in front of a tavern. I found in the meantime that, the rioters had already reached the parade ground, where I, for the time, made an end of the feud by driving the men of the battalion, one and all, back into barracks. One young man who seemed slack in obeying me I brought to order with some vehemence by main force, a thing which is, under such circumstances, indispensable, though it should only be done under them.

February 13th: The fine weather was so inviting to-day that I was tempted to an excursion outside the gates of the fortress. I rode along the coast of the Mediterranean Sea right up to the Spanish Fort Barbara, then to the very crest of the Glacis of the Spanish lines as far as Fort Philip, and finally by the shore of the bay, back to the fortress. The sentries in the Spanish lines presented arms most politely. What an extraordinary state of things between two nations who are at war!

In the meantime, Gibraltar had got a new, extremely strict, but prudent Governor, Sir Hew Dalrymple, who endeavoured to remedy the shortcomings of his predecessor.

February 20th: Sir Hew Dalrymple had a company drawn to-day from each of the four English regiments, and formed a battalion therefrom, which was drilled partly by himself, and partly by the other English staff-officers under his instructions. The intention was to impress on them the first principles of dressing and wheeling. They seemed to be imperfect in many essential particulars. Good as Sir Hew's idea was, the success did not seem to be answering. It is certain that for some time the English regiments, whether under special orders, or by the spontaneous requirement of their commanders, have been perpetually drilled. The patience of the men is something astonishing, and it is pitiful to see the purposeless exercises which are required of them, which remind me of Guibert's remark with regard to cavalry, *s'abimer dans la poussière du manège.*

When I see the quick, active, and smart Englishmen being perpetually tortured with the clumsiest system of Prussian regulation step, I reflect on the serious possible results such training might have, when opposed to the nimble and dexterous enemy. Indeed it is a sight which suggests very serious considerations. Great dissatisfaction is taking root among the officers, and in one of the Sicilian regiments seven or eight resigned in a body. Is it possible that they keep the men so continually under arms as a precautionary measure against the excessive drunkenness? But if so, the purpose will not be attained, for the unfortunate soldier will always find half an hour in which to sink his grievances in bestial oblivion. Really I incline more and more to the conviction that excessive drinking among the English soldiers and sailors is a result of despair proceeding from the situation in which they are subjected to a discipline indisputably the most severe to be found in any European army.

February 21st: I marched the first company of the battalion today up to Windmill Hill, to give them some instruction in the elementary principles of skirmishing, which are at the same time pretty exhaustive for a form of tactics so surrounded by obstacles. It afforded me real pleasure to see with what zest the men took up this exercise, and how quickly they grasped the leading ideas. I might look on this as the victory of free rational movement over the system of soulless mechanism. But it will not do to throw away the good with the bad. A system of strict ground principles of formation and movement of large masses of men is indispensable. There must be a compact mechanism, or the larger or smaller portions of an army must inevitably fall into confusion. But given that the individual is sufficiently accustomed to close formations to fall back into them as by second nature, then it becomes possible to instruct him how to utilise, in addition to his weapons and his personal dexterity, his own courage and brains. It is, moreover, inevitable that the direction taken by the more modern system of war, since 1792, taken with the character of the *terrain* in cultivated European countries, must give marked success to the application of light infantry tactics. The previous training of infantry of the line gives them much the same advantages' as the method of certain French dancing-masters, who made their pupils wear *sabots* for the most difficult steps and springs, so that after their removal, a proportionately higher degree of agility might be displayed. In accordance with that, the rule might be made that no one should be allowed to take part in light infantry tactics, until he has been for a given time exclusively restricted to drill in close order.

February 26th: Being invited to dine with Sir Hew Dalrymple at five o'clock, I handed over to Major Bodecker the duty of inspecting the men's kits, which were found in excellent order. This is one of the thing in which our soldier shows to advantage in comparison with the English. The latter has to be looked after almost every day, and, in spite of that perpetual attention, in spite of the certainty of earning a sanguinary bodily chastisement, will sell his last shirt for an absurd price to spend it in drink. Our men, on the other hand, are nearly all of such domesticated habits, and are so extremely attached to small articles of private property, that they can be safely trusted to keep their clothing and accoutrements in good preservation, and in many cases even have to be restrained from providing themselves with superfluous articles and things likely to prove burdensome on the march.

From March 6th to May 20th Christian was again seriously ill. The Diary was nevertheless kept up.

April 5th: The storm during the night attained a pitch of extreme violence. I never saw the sea so rough before as I did from my window to-day. This storm was the cause of a shocking occurrence not far from here. A Portuguese frigate, the *San Juan Prinzipe,* belonging to the squadron stationed here, was cruising as usual at the eastern entrance of the Straits. In the intense darkness the captain mistook the Rock of Gibraltar for the Punta Leona, which lies opposite, in Africa, and as he shaped his course in accordance with that mistake, the ship steered on to the shore near the Spanish Fort Barbara. The false reckoning was discovered too late, yet an effort was made to turn the ship quickly, but in vain. The keel stuck fast, and as the sails were being changed the irresistible might of the storm caught the hull, and the frigate was literally turned upside down. In the afternoon several officers of the battalion rode out to see the tragic spectacle. The tempestuous force of the sea had left but a few shapeless fragments, which lay about a pistol-shot from the shore. A few unfortunate creatures had still clung to these feeble remnants since midnight, half-benumbed with storm and wet. Some hung in the numbness of death, entangled in the sails. Numerous lookers-on stood on the shore, deeply affected. In spite of the inconsiderable distance, they were unable to carry out their longing to be of assistance, owing to the tremendous surge. At last one of the half-insensible survivors fastened himself firmly to a piece of wreckage, and cast himself on the mercy of the waves. Sometimes disappearing, sometimes lifted high, he was at least so far fortunate as to get so near the shore as to be in water only up to the waist. But being almost insensible, and only capable of the one idea of the saving qualities of the piece of wood, which had been wrenched from him by the concussion of the waves, he caught sight of another piece of wreckage floating *from* the land. Regardless of the safety he had almost attained, the senseless creature was on the point of turning back to the sea, when several of the onlookers, including Blair, the General's adjutant, a noble-hearted man, rushed into the water, and at the risk of their own lives drew the man, almost lost for the second time, on shore. Another attempt on the part of one of his fellows at the same time failed. The sea devoured him, and never rendered him again. A long stretch of the beach was strewn with crushed fragments, as well as corpses cast ashore. One of the exhausted sailors washed ashore died in the hands of those who were helping him, while several became the victims of immoderately administered and therefore fatal spirituous cordials. It was pathetic to see the two nations at war with one another, the Spanish and English, joining their efforts to save a few hundred sufferers of a third nation. In spite of the tempestuous weather, numerous residents of Gibraltar hastened to the scene of the disaster. No difficulty was made about opening the Spanish lines. The Spaniards' barracks were the nearest place of refuge. All imaginable means of help and comfort had been sent there by the magnanimous sympathy of the English. The English naval officers specially distinguished themselves, and the Brigadier O'Rell commanding in the Spanish lines vied with them. Of the frigate's crew 199 perished, and 116 were saved.

On May 30th orders unexpectedly arrived for the brigade of the Legion to hold itself in readiness to embark for England.

On June 16th the anchor was weighed in cheerful spirits, for it was known by this time that the brigade, reunited with its brethren in arms, was destined to take part in a fresh expedition to the Continent. That evening they sailed homeward bound with a brisk east wind along the African coast of the Straits, and away from Gibraltar. The last garrison orders contained the following farewell message:

The General cannot let these two battalions depart without expressing his most complete satisfaction with the conduct of both officers and men while in this fortress, as well as his confident hope that wherever they may be in the future they will earn the same distinction and win, as well as deserve, success.

CHAPTER 5

The Expedition to Denmark
1807—1809

The homeward voyage of the two Line Battalions lasted quite five weeks, and was attended by serious complaints, among which the scurvy was conspicuous. Not till July 24th did the transport-fleet cast anchor off Deal, on the south-easterly extremity of England. When they got home they found that a great proportion of their brethren in arms were not there, having been sent to the assistance of King Gustavus IV of Sweden in his expedition to Stralsund and the island of Rügen. The conclusion, however, of the Peace of Tilsit between France and Russia made the Swedish campaign abortive.

Denmark had, during the war of 1807, held constantly to the side of France, under the colour of neutrality, partly in hopes of deriving extensions of territory from the French victories, and thinking it in any case safest to be on Buonaparte's side. For this reason Denmark had, partly under compulsion and partly of its own accord, not only mobilised about 4,000 land forces, but also prepared a numerous and well-equipped fleet in its harbours.

Moreover, the English Government had ascertained that by certain secret clauses of the Treaty of Tilsit the whole Danish navy was to be put at the disposal of the French Emperor. By this the latter would not only become master of the Baltic, but would have a strong ally by his side in his formidable naval war with England. Besides which, the French generals, Bernadotte and Davoust, had already advanced to Holstein in order to close the Sound from the landward side, and to engage Sweden on the west, now engaged in a struggle with Russia in Finland.

In order to obviate the success of these plans a strong expedition was equipped in England, of which the 1st Line Battalion of the Legion was destined to form a part. These, therefore, had but five days in which to obtain provisions at Deal, and fit themselves out to take the field. During these days Christian gave Louis (now withdrawn to Bohemia, his official position in Dresden having become untenable) a fugitive sign that he was alive.

Deal, July 27th, 1807: Best of Brothers! In flying haste, in every sense, just a few lines. I had the happiness to receive your dear letters of February and March, at last here, after a year and a half. All the others must undoubtedly have got lost. If you knew how glad I am to get the ones I have received, you would be convinced that my feelings for the few with whom I am connected in this world, limited as those are to a very small number of individuals, are as fervent and hearty as they ever were, and as they will be to my end, especially now, after the stupefying effect of all I have gone through, and the bitter deprivation of news from all who are dear to me, during the weary time I was stationed at Gibraltar. If it were possible to pour out my feelings on the past, the present, and the future, it would be—extremely hard as it sounds—inadvisable to do so in a letter from me to you. I limit myself, then, to stating that I am glad to hear of your *relatively* tolerable position, that I hope for you all, because I hope as long as I live, and that, lastly, I am myself, thank God, fairly well, and leading a soldier's life. I only hope Ruggiero's saying in *Ariosto* will be fulfilled in my case: *There is no other safer road, than that in which the sword shall lead me on.*

Farewell—farewell, best of brothers! God keep you and yours, and send you such happy days as may be in such a miserable period as ours. Your Faithful Brother, *C. O.*

The destination of the fleet remained an impenetrable secret. In order to keep its fitting out and departure concealed, an embargo was ordered on the English ports so rigid that not even a fishing-boat was allowed out, wherefore, "the gourmands of London and the seaside resorts had to mourn the absence of one of the chief items in their luxurious bill of fare."

The Diary says:

Our officers on their return from London reported the most flattering observations with regard to the battalion on the part of the Duke of Cambridge. A letter I had from him at Portsmouth was conceived in an equally favourable sense. The Duke expressed a most friendly wish to see me in London. But the uncertainty about our departure made my absence to such a distance impossible.

After a tolerable passage, the fleet arrived in the Sound on August 8th, between Kronborg and Helsingborg, consisting of 14 large men-of-war, and 160 transports.

Everything had, however, a peaceful external aspect. English officers went ashore in boats to amuse themselves, "a bad example", which Christian forbade the battalion to imitate.

Diary, August 9th: The general question is, is this attack on Denmark justifiable, fair, and politic? And it can undoubtedly be looked at from very different points of view. Necessity and self-preservation are of course the most prominent reasons. Still, it is a matter of regret that this place should have been chosen for attack. A more direct blow at the universal oppressor were preferable. Forward, however!

Diary, August 12th: All reports confirm animosity of the Danes, which is not difficult to account for. If there is anything in the rumour that Prussia will march an army into Sweden in case Denmark is attacked, that is one reason more for looking on the resistance of the Danes to England, under the present circumstances of the Continental subjection to the common oppressor, as natural and justifiable. Small occasions of exasperating other nations, through want of consideration, have more effect on the feelings, alas! than is on our side desirable.

Gentz writes at the same time to Louis Ompteda, who was then in his confidence and shared his opinions:

Töplitz, August 26th, 1807: I entirely disapprove, like you, of the principle of this undertaking; it has no rational object. The destruction of Denmark can do Buonaparte no harm, and English trade no good. The way of the Sound was open already, and the Danes showed no sign of an intention of closing it, and probably would not have dared to. But if they did, there would still be time to attack them. What do they want from them more now? Their alliance? I would not give one sailor for that. And supposing it really were worth anything, people need not flatter themselves that they could overcome the Danes' fear of the French. Now they are throwing the Danes into the arms of the French, and making the already quite sufficient exasperation against the English still greater in all directions. On the one hand, the perfidious declamations of the enemy will find fresh nutriment, now that, among other privileges, he has taken possession of the monopoly of speaking on the Continent. On the other hand, as one of the main reasons for the prevalent ill-humour is the immense contrast between the unshaken firmness of England and the abjection of its contemporaries, it will be more slandered and hated the more energy and greatness it develops.

Sending a powerful fleet to the Baltic was a good and proper measure, but at that point matters should rest. It might possibly occur to Russia to attempt hostilities against England. England's war with Buonaparte must be carried on absolutely outside Europe; that is the best field for the display of England's resources and strength. Twist and turn this Danish expedition as I may, I cannot get any use out of it. I am afraid the thing is ill-considered, and will lead to no good end.

You can readily guess that, holding these views, I do not wish for any bombardment of Copenhagen. If any important interest depended on it, I would be the first to say that England should take no notice of public clamour, but go its own way. But every addition to the general exasperation which is not absolutely necessary ought to be avoided.

Christian's Diary, August 13th: It is said that the principal demand made in Denmark is the surrender of the Danish fleet until peace is established. The Danish reply is said to be that they would rather burn the fleet than surrender it.

The continuation of the journal for the next two months got lost, probably on the journey home, as we shall subsequently gather.

On August 21st the English land-forces were disembarked. In the encounters preliminary to the siege of the capital, the 1st Line Battalion was not engaged, being detached to the Castle of Sorgenfrei near Lyngby, a few hours' journey to the north of the capital, and was thereby the cause of the flight of the Royal family to Kolding, in Jutland. With it went also the Chief Lady-in-waiting to the Crown Princess, Countess Minister, born Ompteda. She was the paternal cousin of Christian and Louis, beloved by them as a sister, and widow of an elder brother of Minister the Minister. Hostile proceedings therefore against the royal family were peculiarly painful to Christian. He wrote shortly afterwards to Louis:

You will know how destiny has decreed that Amalie Münster should literally be put to flight by my personal arrival. Reality often produces complications far exceeding those of romantic fiction.

On September 1st began the bombardment which lasted three days. Large fires occurred. The Crown-Prince Regent of Denmark, who remained outside the actual theatre of war, was consequently unshaken in his determination to resist.

On September 6th, General Oxholm, commanding in Copenhagen, capitulated. The Crown Prince Regent expressed (from a distance) his extreme disapproval of this surrender. Fortunately for the town it had already been carried out. The Danish fleet, consisting of 18 ships of the line, 15 frigates, 6 brigs, and 11 gunboats, were taken to England.

On October 13th, the 1st Line Battalion embarked again on board the transport *Caesar Augustus,* Captain Jaffrey, on its way home to England. The passage was delayed by alternate storms and calms. Short notes from day to day say: "*October 26th,* calm; *27th,* moderate wind sprang up; *28th,* midnight, our ship run down by the *Inflexible* ship of the line, 64 guns. Imminent danger of sinking; masts gone; 5 officers and 165 men saved themselves by climbing on board the *Inflexible.* I remained behind." An account given by Christian, written from the Hague November 7th, speaks of this catastrophe and its results:

When the fleet and army left Copenhagen on October 21st, I was with a detachment of the 1st Line Battalion on board the transport *Caesar Augustus,* a very good vessel, on which I had previously made the voyage from Gibraltar to Copenhagen. We left the dangerous Cattegat behind in the incredibly short period of twenty hours, a distance of more than thirty German miles, so that we had already passed the Point of Skagen early in the morning of the 22nd. The wind now became less favourable. However, all proceeded as usual, until about midnight on the 27th to 28th October we were all suddenly called on deck by a noise. To our horror we became aware that the man-of-war *Inflexible,* 64, had got her bowsprit fouled in the rigging of our mainmast. The wind blew fresh, causing heavy bumping on our larboard side, which threatened continually to sink us. All our forces were applied to releasing us by cutting away the tangle, but it took us more than an hour to get free, during which time the prospect of immediate sinking was before our eyes. Our main and mizzenmasts were snapped off like hazel-sticks by the superior strength of the yards of the ship of the line. The wonder is that no one was crushed by their fall. The figure-head of the *Inflexible* made a hole in our side seven feet across, very little above the waterline. The whole quarter-gallery and part of the cabins were carried away. The two ships lay so close together that during the danger 5 officers and 165 men rescued themselves by climbing on board the man-of-war. They were quite right, and I encouraged them, though I was resolved to be the last of my command to leave the ship. At last we got free, but the sea was still too high, and the fleet too far off and scattered for it to be able to render any assistance to us in the darkness. In the morning of the 29th, we first saw the full extent of our damage, but observed also with joy that the ship's bottom had not suffered, as there was no water in the hold. The first thing now was to nail up the dangerous hole as well as possible, and erect a jury-mast. Towards midday on the 29th we passed the *Inflexible.* From a conversation I had with her captain it seemed clear that none of the men were lost of those who transferred themselves to her. For us to change ships was impossible owing to the high sea on. We were left to our own resources. The weather soon grew stormy, and during the 29th and 30th the wind blowing from the west and north-west hindered our approach to the English coast. In short, owing to the unmanageableness of the ship, we were driven towards the Dutch coast. Before daybreak on the 31st, after making futile efforts to wear the ship, we found we were driving straight ashore, and were again in danger of sinking. Happily our united efforts to cast anchor succeeded. We dragged at first, but it ultimately held, and at daybreak we found we were opposite a telegraph erected on the Dutch coast near Terheyde, a short mile southward of the Hague. With a westerly wind and rough sea there could be no thought of getting away. We showed no colours, and it was impossible for any one to approach from the land through such storm and surf. Towards midday on the 31st we saw cavalry and infantry on the shore, and at three o'clock artillery, which opened fire on us, and that with extreme accuracy, as a ball through our bulwarks testified. I agreed with our captain that we should hoist the English flag inverted, which is the *signal of distress*, under which we had already sailed, the day after our first accident with the English fleet. Until we got help it bound us to   nothing, and truly indicated our condition. They then ceased firing, but to come to us was impossible. Towards dusk the firing began again. At first we did not quite see why, but afterwards   supposed it was intended to obtain a definite sign of surrender on our part. The wind was still from the north-west, and the sea so rough that should we cut away the cable, we should infallibly be dashed ashore. Of fifteen shots which came on us one after another, two pierced the hinder part of the ship, and what we had to look forward to if the fire continued was being sunk without   resistance, having cast our own guns overboard. Under these circumstances we were under the painful necessity of striking our flag, implying that we surrendered the ship, and became ourselves prisoners of war. From that moment I felt that we were bound in honour to give up any idea of getting away in case of a change of wind. Had we been able to stick to the signal of distress, I should have had the cable out at the first favourable moment, so as to make an effort, even in the wretched condition of our ship, which was literally threatening to fall to pieces, to escape to England. But Providence interfered, for as soon as the night of the 4th to 5th November the ship went to entire smash. We had been landed on the 1st by means of Dutch boats. We cannot sufficiently praise the conduct of the Dutch officers and inhabitants, who received us with respect, sympathy, and—I may use the expression—heartiness. The Minister of War, van Hogendorp, had taken all his measures with regard to us in a similar spirit. On the 2nd, we were transported to The Hague. The men obtained capital quarters in the barracks of the Grenadier Guards, while to the officers the hotel *Au Parlement d'Angleterre* was assigned, and we were all invited to dinner by the War Minister the same day. He held out to us hopes of soon obtaining our release. The officers who shared all these events with me were Captains von Marschalk and Saffe, Lieutenants von Saffe, Goeben I,[2] Carl von Holle, Ensign von Holle, and Regimental Surgeon Kesseler, with 200 non-commissioned officers and men. On the *Inflexible* were left Captains La Roche von Starkenfels, Lieutenant and Adjutant von Ompteda, Lieutenants von Borstel Heine, and von Schlüter I. These were all well when we last saw the *Inflexible,* Their situation is in many respects more painful than ours, but I repeat that their conduct was fully justified by the circumstances, and was partly the result of my own persuasion. *Christian Ompteda.*

During this stormy weather, other portions of the Legion suffered grievous losses by drowning. The 3rd Hussars lost about 50 horses, and 25 men; one transport was lost with 40 invalids; another, that of the 7th Line Battalion, vanished with 8 officers, 172 non-commissioned officers and men, and the chaplain with his wife and children. The 2nd Line Battalion lost 9 officers, 212 men, 30 women, and 5 children. The total loss of the Legion in this brief bloodless campaign came to 1157 heads, more than a tenth of its strength! Christian writes to Louis from The Hague, November 10th:

Probably some newspaper has already informed you of the

2. It is usual in Germany to distinguish officers of the same surname by a suffixed numeral instead of initials.

annoying accident which brings it about that these lines are dated from The Hague. I have sent a full description to Frederica (brother Ferdinand's wife) of the ill-luck which has pursued me and some of my companions since the 27th ult. After all we underwent from that date to the 1st inst. we owe thanks to Providence for saving our lives, and we owe the expression of our recognition to this hostile country, in which we are prisoners of war, for our extremely liberal treatment here. For this our chief gratitude is due to one of your former diplomatic colleagues, the present War Minister here, van Hogendorp, formerly Dutch Ambassador at St. Petersburg. He has united official measures in our favour with personal courtesy. When we first met, one of his first questions was 'whether I was related to you?' It pleases me to suppose that my affirmative reply proved beneficial to myself and my companions in misfortune. If the War Minister's proposals are accepted, we may look forward to being exchanged before long. My health, thank Heaven, continues good. Since March 14th I have only had a few lines from your wife, and that at Copenhagen. And having been for so long wholly in the dark, with regard to all that concerns you and yours, and those few beloved persons my interest in whom no time or absence can weaken, I need not describe to you the bitterness and depth of that deprivation, from which I have suffered since I left Ireland, that is to say for eighteen months. Let me therefore enjoy the pleasure of an answer without delay. One thing more I will ask. For one year I have heard nothing from Regensburg (where the Reden family resided). I entreat you by your brotherly love to give me some news from there. I adjure you to hide from me *no* reason, whatever it may be, which occasions this silence. *C.*

I will let the Diary tell of the further wanderings of the shipwrecked prisoner of war:

November 5th: The *Augustus Caesar* sank last night. Baggage partly saved, partly plundered.

November 8th: Informed that the non-commissioned officers and men who are prisoners are to be moved into Fort Löwenstein to morrow, as some of them have committed excesses.

November 9th: Non-commissioned officers and men taken off to Löwenstein *via* Rotterdam. My offer to accompany them thither, on account of the bad spirit which had broken out among a considerable number, was declined by the War Minister.

November 10th: Invitation from the War Minister. Received intelligence of an order, according to which we are to go to-morrow to Gorkum (Gorinchem-on-the-Waal).

November 11th: Left the Hague in a *trekschuijt,* and travelled by Delft and Overschien to Rotterdam. A comfortable way of travelling, but put at a disadvantage to-day by the uncommonly bad and stormy weather. Arrived at 2 p.m. at Rotterdam. The President of the Municipality, Mynheer van Teijlingen, a kind, friendly old man, to whom I applied for our further directions, gave us quarters for the night.

November 12th: Went on board a yacht at 7 a.m., which was to take us to Gorkum. Did not sail till 11 a.m., with the flood-tide, owing to contrary wind. Reached Dordrecht at 4 p.m., where we remained the night.

November 13th: Left Dordrecht at 8 a.m. A gentle wind, which only permitted us to advance slowly against the current of the Maas, induced us to land near Papendracht, whence we walked along the dyke to Gorkum.

November 14th: After an interview, disagreeable, but appropriate to our condition, with Colonel Ampt, Commandant at Gorkum, I went in a boat up the Maas to Löwenstein, scarcely half-an-hour's sail. The men very glad to see me again. They were not so comfortable there as at The Hague. I saw the room in the old castle which served as a prison for Hugo Grotius. The floor has collapsed, just as his principles of international law have.

November 16th: Reply of the War Minister to my proposal concerning exchange: 'That at present it *(i.e.,* exchange), or even the sending of a *parlementaire* to England, had been declared to be impossible by the King of Holland. So our fate is decided for the present, being evidently ruled by a Power higher than any here.

November 19th: Letter from the War Minister, in which he demands our parole that our letters to Germany shall refer to *private affairs only,* so that they may be safely forwarded by the Commandant here.

November 25th: The War Minister informs us that it is the King's desire that all our letters should be inspected. In this way, the parole arrangement falls to the ground, to my great-satisfaction, for it is one which should only be made use of in cases of unconditional necessity. Numerous visits at Fort Löwenstein.

December 3rd: I now am pleased to learn from the English papers that the *Caesar Augustus* is lost, and that all are drowned.

December 5th: Three of my officers obtained leave from the new War Minister, General Janssen, to go and visit their relations in Hanover. I cannot leave my men.

December 11th: Walked by Dalem to Löwenstein in a thick snow, to see our prisoners. Many pale faces, consequence of lost liberty, damp, inferior barracks, want of occupation and exercise, neglected cleanliness, and insufficient clothing. In one word, a sad sight. I tried to console them and cheer them up, and the great majority seemed pleased at my. coming. The remains of our band sounded their instruments, which had been saved. I bade them play *God save the King,* and even under the depressing circumstances that glorious song did not fail to have its effect.

December 14th: As I came back from visiting our sick in the hospital to-day, some one told me that an *Officier des chasses de S M. le Roi de Hollaude* had been inquiring for me. At first they said 'An officer from the King, from Utrecht.' I began to form hopes of freedom, which were, however, soon brought to nought. The man re-appeared, a Mr. van Barneveldt van Norderloos, occupying a position in the hunting district here similar to that of our chief ranger. He brought me a very friendly letter from our old friend Heekeren, now *Capitaine general des chasses.* He placed the hunting here at the disposal of myself and my companions in misfortune, a friendly attention intended to make the monotony of our existence more tolerable. The Dutch Club here has also invited us in.

During this sad winter a few letters passed between Christian and his brother Louis, but not directly, as the latter, who was living in Prague, was suspected by the French police (and with reason) of the honourable offence of being an English political agent, and belonging to the same kin as *le nommé Stein*, and the *misérable scribe Gentz*.

In the *Correspondance inédite de Napoleon Bonaparte*, 7., 385-387, will be found the secret report of an M. B—— (Bourgoing, French Ambassador in Dresden), dated June 8th, 1808.

> *Sire—Il existe, en ce moment une chaîne d'intrigans dangereux, qui s'étend de Toeplitz en Bohême à Vienne, et de Vienne à Londres. A Toeplitz un chevalier de L. {de Mezay), qui a servi autrefois, dit-il, dans les mousquetaires gris et qui a le brevet de major au service de Russie, est lié avec le baron d' Ompteda, ci-devant ministre de Hanovre à Berlin et à Dresde. L'un et l'autre sont en relation avec M. Gentz qui demeure habituellement à Prague depuis que l'ambassadeur de l'Empereur l'a fait sortir de Vienne.*
>
> *On est parfaitement informé à Toeplitz de l'object de correspondance de ces intrigans avec l'Angleterre. Ils s'efforcent par leurs supports et leurs propos de semer les défiances entre la France et l'Autriche.*

The communication of the brothers' letters was undertaken by Baron Vrints in Bremen, the tried old friend of the family. But as the letters were subject to inspection, their contents were so veiled in mystic language as to be at this time nearly unintelligible, so much so, that various repeated questions imply that the brothers were frequently not sure of each other's own meaning. There are remarkable indications of, in fact, a glaring light cast on the fearful, personal, police, and financial persecution under which North Germany, and especially the *ci-devant* Electorate, suffered, really in revenge for the formation of the Legion. The financial aspect of this pressure placed the brothers in a state of serious embarrassment. Friend Vrints writes from Bremen that good exchange was was not to be had at that place, because nobody had any money. Even loans owed by otherwise safe debtors could not be realised, because the Government had imposed a forced loan on Hanover. To secure this, all private loans were suspended for a whole year, and no claims in connection with such were admitted by the courts. *Wherefore no Hanoverian has any credit.* On account of the Continental embargo there was no opening for agricultural produce, the farmers *stewed in their own juice,* and the tenants could not pay. "I have myself landed property worth 180,000 thalers, and cannot even get an advance of 2,000 to 3,000 thalers on it."

It was therefore natural that a righteous passion for vengeance and a sullen hatred of the French should arise and intensify in Christian's own smaller Fatherland. Even the following generation inherited this feeling of instinctive hatred of the traditional *hereditary enemy,* who had branded our sufferings so deeply on our hearts, never been sufficiently chastised for it, but was ready, on the other hand, to begin new mischief. Such feelings as these take their own independent course, regardless of actual political criticism.

The then much-abused Rhine-confederator is free from these memories, except in an indirect sense through his native *sovereign* princes, and not essentially responsible. In any case he could see in the collapse of the mouldering system of paltry states a kind of excuse for foreign domination.

Diary, January 1st: Beginning of another year. Hope it will be a happier one than the last. Mr. Müller. first mate of the *Caesar Augustus,* came to see me to-day, bringing two very clever drawings of the critical periods of our misadventure with that vessel as a present.

These two water-colour sketches are still in existence.

January 13th—22nd: Our Captain Jaffrey has succeeded in escaping on board an American ship to England.

January 26th: Decree of the King of Holland forbidding *all ships without distinction* (except those of the Allies, and their prizes) to enter Dutch harbours. This destroys our last hope of escape.

January 29th: The sailors of the *Caesar Augustus* imprisoned in Löwenstein made an attempt to escape in ferryboats two nights ago. Hemmed in by drifting ice, two of them ventured to cross its treacherous surface to get ashore, and were drowned. It is a characteristic feature in the surviving fugitives, that after working their way through the ice to the land with immense trouble, they went into the nearest public-house, and proceeded to drink there until re-arrested.

March 1st: The 3rd Dutch Hussars quartered here have been reduced from 1,000 to 600 men. Those withdrawn from the regiment are mainly Prussians, who, after the destruction of the Prussian army, were drafted into this and other Dutch regiments. Already a few weeks ago all the Germans were taken from the Dutch regiments which happened to be in Oldenburg, and different parts of Westphalia, and put at the disposal of the King of Westphalia. The latest thing is that all the officers here from his territory have received their discharge with two months' pay. All these sudden changes proceed from the fact that the French are taking over the Dutch service.

March 21st: An acquaintance here came to my room, and announced to me, to my great surprise, that I was—Free! He had just heard the news from Colonel Ampt. I was to be exchanged against a Dutch colonel. Much in this transaction was obscure to me, wherefore I, in executing the protocol required by Colonel Ampt, stipulated that in case the English Government did not confirm the exchange, I was to be at liberty to return to Holland as a prisoner of war.

> The correspondence between the brothers certainly proceeded during this period, but seems to have got lame in its wings. Not only does a whole month regularly elapse between the departure and receipt of a letter, but also the compulsory blankness of the contents exhausts the inclination to write at all.

Gorkum, February 14th 1808: You seldom get a letter from me, dear L. But if a person may not say what he would like, and if what he could say is not such as he would select to dwell upon, it becomes difficult for him to make up his mind to write anything. It is some trouble to break a silence, the motives of which are at the least liable to be misconstrued where complete freedom of communication could count on perfect mutual understanding. Still, I ought long since to have returned thanks for the pleasure given me by your letter of January 4th, even if I cannot mistake the leading implications in it. I quit this point, however, to mention something of a cheerful character. I unexpectedly learnt from a sure source (the Minister Münster) that our good Ferdinand is well, and will probably very shortly receive his majority. I at once forwarded this intelligence to Verden, where our poor sister-in-law had been placed in a pitiable state of apprehension by those cursed croakers, who intensify the real evils of our unfortunate country, and invent fictitious ones—in short, by the cruel sympathy of commonplace friends. Our two cousins likewise, Augustus (captain, and at the time adjutant to General the Earl of Rosslyn) and Ferdinand (who saved himself by going from the *Caesar Augustus* on board the *Inflexible),* are of good cheer. I am intensely curious to know the meaning of an expression in your last letter, where you allude to a certain *mediator.* Could you not illumine this dark saying by a single ray? Lastly, accept my thanks for the news from Regensburg. I have since also received direct information *(i.e.,* from Mrs. Van Reden herself) of the events in that part of the world.

> Louis had been complaining that the Minister Münster left him wholly without instructions or answers to his reports. Christian furnishes him with an explanation in the veiled form of diction adopted under the circumstances, as follows:

The reasons which prevented me from expecting the above most valuable information *(re* brother Ferdinand) lead me back to a point in your letter, with regard to which I should like to put your mind at rest, as I can feel only too well the necessary delicacy of your position in that quarter. It seems to me that the silence of which you complain admits of a natural explanation. Think of your respective *local positions* since 1806, and the uncertainty about your several places of residence, at a time when even *within* the same great circle (Germany) the nearest relatives and friends do not know where to find one another. You can then reckon how great must be the uncertainty with regard to similar matters on the *other* side of the big cleft (the sea). Add to this the pressing necessity of withholding everything likely to be of a compromising character, and it seems to me that sufficient reasons are furnished by all these circumstances. Yet I perceive that all this is of merely general application. Among the countless torn threads of my acquaintances and concerns is the one which constituted my (in any case lax) relations with the man we are talking about. Until two years ago I had to do with him personally and by letter, both in Germany and afterwards; and I must do him the justice to say that his friendly attitude and tone to me remained always unchanged. I should like to say also the following in his favour. With the best will in the world he might easily be in the same predicament as Archimedes, unable to find the point to serve as fulcrum to move his little world—not *out* of its polar equilibrium—that has been done already—but *back into* it, if but partly.

> Christian then touches on the unhappy lot of Field Marshal Wallmoden, "the man we last saw at Mölln." Wallmoden lived in retirement in Hanover, after 1803, suffering much under the sad responsibility with which he had been burdened by the Convention of Artlenburg, in reference to the army and country. Moreover, his property had greatly declined in value. Led on by a dubious ambition, proceeding, perhaps, from his birth, to belong to the *high* nobility, he had obtained an Imperial patent as Count, in the year 1781, and bought at far too high a price the comparatively worthless so-called county of the Empire of Gimborn in Westphalia, an artificial territorial mutilation of the Empire made for the benefit of the notorious Count Kolbe-Wartenberg. In such wise he obtained a seat among the Westphalian peers. The entire collapse of all husbandry under the French extortion had a ruinous effect on him.

How unspeakably happier had his lot been, if, at the time, he had behaved exactly contrary to the way in which he did, let the results be as unfavourable as they might! I am convinced, dear L., that you do not belong to that class in our country to whom my adherence to that opinion might seem extravagant in view of all that has since passed. No; all that we have gone through strengthens me in the unshakable persuasion that to have perished then sword in hand were salvation and deliverance, and that our real irrevocable extinction was completed by our illusory deliverance (by the Convention of Artlenburg). I say this to you in full belief that our opinions coincide in this, that the most valuable possession a nation can have is its *character*. That once sacrificed, the worth of what is left is proportionate to the depreciated worth of its owners, and tends most surely down the road that leads to ruin. I express this bitter truth without reserve, for I have never ceased to feel it deeply, in spite of my nearly five years' absence from the scene of my fatherland's desolation and woe, in spite of having been transferred to very different conditions. Perhaps I have become more sensitive to this feeling from the contrast, being no longer there where intimacy with all that morally and physically crushes mankind, and the total absence of anything to cheer the mind, leave no other impression than that of having to do without former *comforts*. It was very-pleasant to get a friendly word from S——st (Scharnhorst). If you have an opportunity, thank him for his remembrance of me, which is very precious.

On April 14th, and again on May 2nd, Christian speaks, from The Hague, of his hope of being soon once more united with *his people*.

The Hague, May 9th, 1808: At last the long-delayed moment is actually at the door. Tomorrow, Heaven permitting, I take my departure. I can tell you nothing of the circumstances which have occasioned the delay.

Christian failed to find his battalion in its old quarters at Bexhill, for it had embarked in the month of April on an expedition to Göthenburg in Sweden. Christian arrived there on June 3rd, and took the command. But the flotilla returned to England no later than July, owing to disagreements between the English Commander-in-Chief, General Moore, and Gustavus IV., the eccentric Swedish King. But it was not long permitted to him (Christian) to renew his life under the conditions which had grown dear to him. The English Government had decided to oppose the impetuous progress of Napoleon in the Pyrenean Peninsula.

On July 31st, the Legion sailed thither, with the army placed under the command of Sir Arthur Wellesley, in 168 transports.

We find the journey of this powerful fleet described in the following graphic language:

There is something magnificent in the sight of so vast a fleet of transports under full sail. In the centre are visible the bulk of the troopships; on the flanks, front and rear, are the convoying warships. The whole moves forward in the same formation, under the trustworthy command of the Commodore, with the precision of an army on a wide plain. Towards nightfall is heard the signal to assemble ships, and the slow sailors advance gradually into their allotted positions. Should a calm set in, which is not unusual at the close of a summer day, the ships rest like houses on the glittering surface of the deep. The sun sinks in majesty into the endless mirror which radiates back its image; and at the instant when the last faint rays of the life-giving sphere vanish from our sight, at the moment of most perfect peace, there breaks simultaneously from all the men-of-war the thunder of the sunset guns, and harmoniously mingled with music, vague wind-driven sounds are carried through the fleet, and close the enchanting scene.

The voyage lay first down Channel and then through the Bay of Biscay.

Here the billows towered like mountains in slow succession. The approach of such gigantic waves seemed to threaten the voyagers with instant destruction. But at the critical moment the vessel rises on the crest of the wave, and surveys all the fleet as from the battlements of a high tower. The ship then immediately descends into a fearful abyss, in which not a trace of what had just been seen was visible, but from which we again arise to repeat the former spectacle.

On August 17th the fleet assembled in Vigo Bay, somewhat to the north of the Portuguese northern frontier. From there the transports, favoured by the wind, followed the glorious Portuguese coast from Entre Douro e Minho onwards.

In the night of August 19th there was a fog, which occasioned serious inconvenience. The atmosphere grew suddenly so dense that it became necessary, in order to avoid collisions, to fix lanterns on the mizzenmasts. As even these precautions did not seem sufficient, recourse was had to horn-blowing. This melancholy music, by means of which each ship betokened its presence, was continued without interruption throughout the night. In spite of that, it was found at break of day that several ships had got their rigging mutually entangled.

On August 23rd and 24th the fleet anchored at the mouth of the small river Meceira, north of Lisbon.

The disembarkation of the troops in this bay was attended by extraordinary difficulties, and even considerable danger. The weather had grown rough, and the surf on the steep shore was of exceptional violence. A considerable number of boats were capsized during the landing, and it is only due to the courageous and untiring exertions of the seamen that such accidents were limited to so small a number. The English sailors, fired by the example of their officers, might be seen wading up to their shoulders in readiness to haul the boats up on to dry land the moment they were thrown ashore by the surf. The horses, which had been on board ship for many weeks, and were now obliged to swim ashore, only reached the land with the greatest difficulty. Some such unfortunate animal, cast on shore by a wave, and unable to stand up at the moment, would frequently be dragged back by the next wave, to be again cast on shore only to be washed back. Thus several horses were lost.

The landing of all the regiments composing the Legion was, owing to these circumstances, only accomplished by the evening of August 29th. The troops then moved towards Lisbon, and took up a position in the neighbourhood of that capital.

Christian's capacity for duty was now again brought to a standstill in a lamentable way. He had contracted the germs of a serious illness during his stay at Gorkum, an insanitary, swampy den of fevers. This led to a sad relapse to his former unfortunate mental disorder. His condition was so aggravated by the hardships of his two sea-voyages that Christian—according to the battalion journal—had to remain on board ship invalided.

he was relieved of the command of his battalion and brought back to England. His friends and comrades there, even his commander, the Duke of Cambridge, found all their various efforts of no effect on the afflicted man. There is no information about his life during the winter of 1808-9. The supreme hope rested now on the influence his so much loved and respected brother Louis might have on him. The latter, therefore, was requested, at the instigation of the Duke, to come in the early part of 1809.

1809

It was not till May that he received the sad intelligence that Christian was living in the neighbourhood of London ill, and again in a condition of severe mental affliction. Louis at once decided to go to England, and look after the sufferer himself. With this purpose was united another which cannot be wholly passed over here, in order to make Louis' own account of his own and his brother's further experiences intelligible.

Prussia was at the time waiting to see what would be the outcome of the war which had broken out in April between Austria and France. As a large proportion of Napoleon's forces was necessarily detained by the English in Spain, there was some reason to expect success on the part of Austria. In such a case heavily oppressed Prussia would have made common cause with the latter. It was therefore thought desirable to approach England, with which relations of an ostensibly hostile character still prevailed. Louis Ompteda entered into negotiations about this with the Prussian Minister, Count Goltz. Their result was the outline of a subsequent treaty of peace between Prussia and England. For the safety of the ensuing correspondence on this subject, Ompteda was entrusted, as a mark of the greatest confidence, with a Prussian cipher.

The perils and adventures of this journey of Louis' are so very characteristic of the conditions then prevailing in our enslaved Fatherland, and will display such an unfamiliar aspect to the present generation, that they may be set forth here in the words of his own description.

In order to get my passport for the French authorities whom I would be likely to meet at every step, I had to apply to the French Ambassador in Berlin, Count St. Marsan, whom I had met in society on various occasions. I received from the servant the dry reply, 'that he (the Ambassador) was very busy just now, and I had better apply to the First Secretary of Legation, M. Caillard, if I had anything to say.' In my position I had to put up with this treatment. I had myself announced to M. Caillard, and asked for a pass to travel by Hamburg to Oldenburg, where I resided. He asked me different questions about my journey, and then said he would 'place my pass before the Minister for signature.'

In the evening I met Count St. Marsan in society. He came up to me at once, and made the fullest apologies for the nature of the reception given me at my morning visit, and said it was entirely occasioned by a misapprehension, that is to say, that a M. Empeytaz, a merchant belonging to the French colony in Berlin, had been announced to him, a man who was constantly visiting him, and pestering him with his concerns. Still, I did not like it. I was not without anxiety lest M. Caillard should make secret marks of suspicion on my pass, a thing I had no fear of the Ambassador himself doing.

On May 26th I left Berlin. In order to encumber myself with as few impedimenta as possible, I took no carriage of my own, only my servant and a light portmanteau. I drove extra-post, day and night, by the Hamburg road. The second morning I reached Lenzen, and hastened on without stopping there. As I knew the route well, I soon noticed that we continually got further away from the highway, and approached the Elbe. At last the road totally disappeared, and we got into a large marsh, the postilion driving over stock and stone and through deep water-pools, so that it was surprising that the carriage did not get smashed or upset. All my cursing and scolding was thrown away. I scarcely got any reply from the phlegmatic fellow.

At length, however, we safely reached the post-station of Lübtheen in Mecklenburg. When we stopped before the post-house, the *Schwager*[3] calmly turned round and said:

---

3. Lit. *brother-in-law*. An untranslatable semi-slang expression applied to postilions, roughly analogous to the English *uncle* for *pawnbroker*.

'Well, are you satisfied now?'

'The devil a bit,' was my answer. 'That cursed route of yours has made me feel as if I had been broken on the wheel. Why on earth didn't you stick to the highroad?'

'You see, sir, you don't understand. I knew that the whole length of the road was beset with French and Dutch soldiers, who let no vehicle pass, not even the mail, without examining all the passengers very strictly.'

'Well, what's that got to do with me?' I replied in surprise.

'Well, sir,' answered he, with an arch expression, 'I thought you had a suspicious look about you, you know.'

I laughed, and gave him a liberal gratuity. And he was not acting without due cause. Schill had just then been driven back with his corps on Mecklenburg, and troops were following him with the object of cutting off his. communications and intercepting him. The cunning and patriotic postilion had taken me and my servant for disguised *Schill's men*.

When I approached the town-gates of Hamburg, I saw several hundred men at work on the ramparts to get the fortress into a state of defence against—Schill's Volunteers!

I alighted at an unpretentious inn, which I left as little as possible, in order not to attract attention in Hamburg, as I was bound to contemplate the possible danger of meeting people who knew me, who might have unintentionally compromised me.

The following day I went to the Chancery of the French Minister to get my pass *visé*. My Berlin pass was taken from me with the statement that it would be returned *visé*. This I did not like, but had to put up with. On the next day, no pass; and I awaited in vain during the day following. I now began to be uneasy. But as I wanted in any case to know what my precise position was, I went on the third day to the Chancery again, and complained with some asperity of the unheard-of proceeding of keeping me waiting so long for my pass, and so wasting my money The secretary, who happened to be present, apologised with some embarrassment for the delay, saying that the Minister, Buonaparte's well-known private secretary, M. de Bourienne, had been away in the country for a few days. When I, with an expression of righteous indignation, asked the secretary what was the charge for the *visé*, I received the very polite reply: 'Monsieur ne paye rien.'

Very glad to have got my pass, I took my leave without seeing M. de Bourienne. He never mentioned my journey in his memoirs, although he asserts that he was 'informed of *all* secret machinations.'

During the time I was in this way obliged to spend in Hamburg, I confided my two-fold purpose to a few members of the former Hanoverian Ministry, who resided at Altona as private individuals. In order not to be arrested with the Prussian cipher in my pocket, I parted with it, and it was sent in pieces, by those most peculiar means of communication then used for correspondence with England, to London, where I found it complete on my arrival.

I had in the meantime acquired the conviction that the strict French embargo made it impossible, or, at any rate, extremely dangerous, to attempt an embarkation in the Elbe, so I was obliged to roam further overland and seek salvation in the Weser.

I accordingly began by going by Harburg to Verden, where the wife of my youngest brother Ferdinand, then serving with the Legion in Sicily, resided. She recommended me to the advice and support of a man who was said to deserve the fullest confidence, who, however, at a later period brought on himself a very unhappy fate, led on by mistaken ambition and injured vanity. He was the court-assessor Palm, then second in seniority in that capacity at Verden. At that time he was undoubtedly patriotic, and meant well, and I cannot refuse to bear testimony in later clays to those qualities in him, according to my best convictions.

Palm, an extremely able man, was soon recognised and utilised by the French as such. Later on he became employed in the secret police. As soon as May 1813 he was expelled from Töplitz as a French spy. Palm's enthusiasm and personal attachment to Napoleon induced him to go back to Germany in 1815 on behalf of the latter. A criminal process and severe imprisonment were the natural consequences. The Certificate in the year 1821 must have largely contributed to the obtaining of his pardon.

Palm assured me that it would be impossible for me to take ship in the Weser, but that I must seek some other point nearer the sea where I should be less observed. To that end he gave me introductions to well-disposed persons at different places on the coast. These addresses consisted, however, only of single initials, which he wrote on loose pages of my pocket-book, informing me that I need only show them. In order to get me the more safely through Bremen, which was simply swarming with customs officials, he lent me his own carriage, which was well known there. Not far from the gates, however, I got out, and walked behind at some distance from the carriage, and passed, therefore, wholly unnoticed by the gate-watch. Palm had given me an introduction to a family in Bremen in whom he placed confidence. The lady of the house procured me a hired carriage to take me the following day to Varel, where I intended to try and embark on the Jahde. The next morning the driver did not take me by the usual way, by Delmenhorst and Oldenburg, but across country over heath and marsh, where we had to cross small but swollen streams, not without danger to our lives. In Varel I got down at the best inn, the landlord of which had been recommended to me by Palm. I at once applied to a ship-owner, likewise on Palm's recommendation, in order to obtain the means of making my voyage. He told me that a snip had started only the day before, so that probably a few days would elapse before another went, in order not to attract the attention of the *douaniers*. So I had to patiently return to my inn, deciding to leave my room as seldom as possible, as the house was always filled with *douaniers* and *gensdarmes* passing in and out.

In a few hours' time a man walked in unannounced, with a shabby grey overcoat and rather poor appearance, and addressed me abruptly:

'You want to get a ship to England?'

I replied:

'How can you ask such a question, knowing, as you must, that all communication with England is forbidden?'

The unknown persisted:

'But I know for certain that you want a passage to England.'

'That must be a mistake. I certainly want a passage, but it is to Norway, not England.'

The unknown stuck to his point:

'It is not a mistake, because I heard it myself from the shipowner you went to see;' and he mentioned the name of the man Palm had directed me to.

I now exhibited doubt and impatience, informed the unknown that he was a liar, and threatened to kick him downstairs if he did not leave my room.

'All right,' he said. 'Then you will stop here. I sail at midnight.'

With this he departed abruptly.

I could not do otherwise than ensure myself against the immediate danger of being exposed to a French spy who might be setting a trap for me.

However, the thing kept dwelling on my mind, so I sought the shipowner again. I there learnt, to my joyful surprise, that the offer of my unknown friend was perfectly genuine. I then pointed Out the great imprudence of not informing me beforehand of the step he had taken, as I could not possibly confide in a total stranger without running the greatest clanger. I then requested him to put things right for me again, which he did. At midnight I was on the shore where the ship which was to take me was at anchor.

I found my unknown on board immediately. He was no less a person than a Bremen smuggler, and owner of the cargo. I explained and apologised for my behaviour to him. There were also two young merchants from Hamburg who wished to proceed to Spain by way of England. The total ship's company consisted of the skipper, quite a common man, and a lad of sixteen or seventeen. Our captain did not seem extensively furnished with provisions, for on the following day he offered us no food whatever, not even for payment offered, and we had to fall back on some bread we happened to have with us. I had the cabin floor to sleep on, which was so narrow and short that I could not lie down at full length. My portmanteau served as a bed. The Hamburgers and my servant slept on deck.

Before daybreak, when we were hardly out of the Jahde, the ebb came on, to our great embarrassment, and we stayed as near as possible to the west bank aground on the mud-bank. Not far off, towards the east bank, we saw the French gun-sloop, on board of which was stationed the customs watch. The skipper strictly forbade us to show ourselves on deck for fear of exciting attention.

As soon as the tide came in the skipper hastened to get afloat, and as we drew very little water we fortunately got out of the Jahde before we could be overhauled. It was then that we first had time and leisure to observe the extreme fragility of the vessel to which we had entrusted our lives. But, as the weather was fine and the wind favourable, we nevertheless made very good progress. Forgetful of the past dangers we put chairs on deck to enjoy the beautiful morning, and the younger Hamburgers helped us to pass the time with some cheerful singing.

We were now in the direction of the mouth of the Weser, where the French had taken away the buoys, when our skipper, who was not at home in these waters, heaved the lead several times in succession, and declared with some anxiety that we were only in three and a half fathoms, while the vessel required at least three. My smuggler grew deathly pale, and the two Hamburgers looked uncomfortable. I, being then unacquainted with seafaring, tried to cheer them up by pointing out how the water near the ship was whirling in foaming circles, which I took to be a sign of greater depth. But the skipper explained to me that it was just that that meant we were running on a sandbank. We really did graze it several times with the keel. With some effort, however, we managed to get over it and away without disaster.

After a time, when we were approaching the estuary

of the Elbe, we heard the reports of cannon-fire, which on the sea has a peculiarly clear sound. I learned later on that it was an English frigate which had engaged some French gunboats at the mouth of the Elbe. At last, towards 3 p.m., we anchored off Heligoland. Our disembarkation did not take much time. We were recommended to have recourse provisionally to the town-house, where our passports would be examined before we were allowed to go up above on the cliff where the residence itself was. This town-house had been built on the shore below after this rocky islet was taken possession of by the English as a trading station, from which smuggling was extensively carried on with the Continent, which has given rise to a considerable traffic. Besides this there were a few other houses on the shore erected by Hamburg merchants, who had migrated with their families from that town in order to carry on business from here.

After a short time an English sergeant appeared, who seemed to perform the functions of a police agent. He first demanded the passports of the two Hamburgers, and found them correct. Then he asked for mine. I explained that I had none. He gave me a searching, thoughtful glance. When I asked for paper and pencil to write my name, and asked the man to take it to the English Vice-Consul, Mr. Nicolas, his surprise increased. That gentleman I had made acquaintance with at the headquarters of Field Marshal Wallmoden in 1803.

The sergeant then left us, after placing an English sentry with drawn side-arm in the room where we were. We were not permitted to speak with one another, or to approach the window, lest, perhaps, we might make secret signs to some one outside; we were scarcely allowed to move, so great were at that time the precautions taken about Heligoland. It was the first and last time in my life that I have been under arrest.

After a short time the sergeant returned, fairly satisfied. He very politely invited me at once to come up to the top of the cliff, where Mr. Nicolas had already got a lodging for me.

After my arrival in the fisherman's cottage, where I

had been provided with a lodging, I at once received a visit from the Vice-Consul. He asked me to dinner, which I was very thankful to accept. Another invitation, however, I was obliged to refuse, as it was some nights since I had had any proper sleep, and I felt very tired from the journey. It happened to be the 4th of June, King George III's birthday, and was to be celebrated by a ball in the evening. For that purpose a dancing-room had been arranged on the deck of a fine brig which had been stranded at the foot of the cliff. In the stern of the ship a kitchen had been partitioned off. The hold served as storeroom. I was, however, very glad, on the whole, not to have been there, for the proceedings at this festivity became rather stormy. A few of the junior officers of the English garrison had invited some pretty but perfectly respectable girls belonging to the island to the ball, and these appeared in their certainly rather rural national costumes. Upon this the elegant bourgeoisies from Hamburg refused to dance in the same set with these native girls, and on this subject a quarrel arose, in which the English officers and the Hamburg gentry came to blows, which disturbed the hilarity of the evening rather unpleasantly. On the morning following I received a visit from the local commandant, Lieutenant-Colonel von Kentzinger, an Alsatian by birth, in the English service. He besought me to extenuate and minimise this unfortunate occurrence as much as possible in London, which I undertook to do.

In the afternoon I embarked on the packet which plies regularly twice a week between England and the island.

During the journey we had an unfavourable wind which drove us perpetually northward towards the harbour of Yarmouth instead of to Harwich, our proper destination. Towards the evening of the fourth day we were not far off the locality of Aldborough, and it was impossible to reach Harwich that day. As I was specially anxious to reach London as soon as possible, I requested the captain, to whom I had been particularly recommended in Heligoland, to put me ashore before night. Pie explained to me that it was contrary to his strict instructions to land a passenger before the delivery of the mail-bag. I having expressed myself as prepared to take charge of it, the captain made signal by a cannon shot, and hoisted the mail-signal, a flag with a white horse on it. We soon perceived through a telescope a rowing-boat approach from the coast. The captain gave me the mail-bag, and particularly charged me to take *four* horses and *two* post-boys for the last stage to London, in order to enter the capital with them. I promised to do so, though I did not know why, but supposed this little comedy was pre-arranged, and had something to do with the rise and fall of the Exchange.

My arrival in England happened exactly at the time when the first intelligence of the successful battle of Aspern (May 21st and 22nd) had arrived. The general curiosity as to the further successes of the Austrians was greatly excited. I received at once a practical proof thereof, for when my boat drew near to the shore, a large number of the inhabitants of Aldborough had come down to meet me. The crowd pressed round so closely that I could scarcely find a spot to set my foot on when I jumped ashore. They overwhelmed me with questions, exhausted themselves in admiration and laudation of the Austrians, and received me as the bearer of most important news from the Continent. The whole crowd accompanied me into the town, where I first had to visit the Custom House in order to have my luggage examined, which was done with strictness, though politely, after which a new and unforeseen difficulty arose. It was not thought right for me to continue my journey, because in this little town there was no *Alien-office*, a department exercising control over foreigners who might land. In addition to this, it happened a few weeks ago that Prince Starhemberg, who wished as Austrian Ambassador to travel *incognito* to London, had also landed at Aldborough, and been allowed to pass through, which had brought down a sharp reprimand on the local officials. But this time the mail-bag helped me through. I declared that 'I would not let it leave my hands, and that if it arrived late the gentlemen at Aldborough would be responsible.' The permission to continue my journey was then accorded with a bad grace, and I started towards midnight in a post-chaise.

According to my promise I took four horses and two post-boys at the last station, and reached London about four in the afternoon of Sunday, June 11th. My postilions drove like mad, and I noticed the curiosity with which people looked at me as I rolled along the streets, and perceived that I was an object of special public attention.

I drove straight to the Foreign Office in Downing Street. Mr. Canning, the then Minister of Foreign Affairs, was absent, so Mr. Bagot, Under-Secretary of State, and a confidential friend of Canning, received the bag from me. After a preliminary conversation, he had me conducted by a Government messenger to Blake's Hotel" (now Brunswick Hotel) "in Jermyn Street.

On the following day all the papers were full of the news 'of a gentleman just arrived in London in a chaise and four, bringing great news from the Continent.' So it appeared that the comedy had obtained the intended effect.

From London Louis went to Windsor, where the Minister, Count Münster, was staying with the King. The *Memoirs* proceed:

My reception at Windsor was not pleasant, as wrong impressions arose as to the purpose of my journey.

The fact was that Count Münster did not wish for any closer personal relations to develop between the King and Ompteda, whom he honoured always with a certain amount of jealousy.

After some explanations, I explained that I should confine myself solely to the one object of my journey, to see my brother, and return with him to the Continent as soon as his condition permitted, but that I must stipulate for the right to place a written account of my negotiations in Berlin before His Majesty the King personally. The first statement proved soothing, while the second could hardly be refused.

My first care now was to obtain exact information as to the state of my brother's health. I found him in London plunged in deep melancholy.

I soon received a command to come to Windsor to be presented to the King on June 18th. I was introduced by the Minister to the Cabinet of George III, where the King received me most graciously, and asked questions about the state of things on the Continent. Then he asked:

'How did you find your brother?'

A question I found rather embarrassing, in connection with the particular personage, to answer.

The King had been mentally afflicted himself in the year 1788, but had afterwards entirely recovered. His second attack, which lasted to the end of his life, first set in in 1810.

But I thought I had better answer with as much candour as possible.

Then the King said: 'And what are you going to do with him now?'

I replied that my intention was to take him as soon as possible to Carlsbad, which had done him a great deal of good on a former occasion. For that purpose I would have asked for leave of His Majesty for my brother, had not the latter expressed the wish to leave the service of the King, on account of his scruples lest he should stop promotion in the corps for his comrades in the field while he himself was unfit for service on account of his long illness.

'I won't take his resignation,' the King quickly replied. 'Your brother is one of my best field officers[4]'

English equivalent for what are called staff officers in Germany, the word being, however, perfectly appropriate here.

'I have known him since he was a page. I will give him six months' leave to start with, and if you find your brother is not then quite recovered, I can perhaps prolong his leave further.'

The King then went into particulars as to the proper physical treatment of the patient, and asked me what were his customary favourite occupations, and said that I ought

---

4. *Field officers* in an English infantry regiment, as C. Ompteda's practically was, are those officers above the rank of captain, in contradistinction to captains and subalterns, who are called *company officers*.

to accustom him again gradually to some definite work, at first simply reading something which would not be too much strain on the mind, then easy translations from one language into another, but all with the greatest care to accustom the patient to use his intellect without excessive effort, so as to restore his lost confidence in himself.

This wise advice, which flowed from the monarch's very heart, I subsequently adopted as my rule of conduct, and it increased the deep and sincere gratitude which I already owed for numerous earlier kindnesses to George III.

July to the end of August 1809

In this way nearly two months have passed since my arrival in London. In the meantime, owing to the unfortunate result of the battle of Wagram, political conditions on the Continent have entirely changed. I saw there was nothing more to be done in pursuance of the one object of my journey, so it was the more necessary to hasten in order not to fail in the other, the bringing of my brother over to the Continent, so as to enable him to make use of the Carlsbad cure before it was too late. But continual preparation was necessary in order to the possibility of carrying out this plan, which he at first vehemently resisted.

In spite of this all was made ready for the return journey *viâ* Sweden.

On July 31st I went to Windsor to obtain leave from the King. In the Castle Count Münster and I met him (the King) unexpectedly on the stairs. His Majesty parted from me after a short conversation with most gracious expressions. In the interval between that and dinner we went for a stroll in the neighbourhood of the Castle, in which Mr. Canning, the Minister of Foreign Affairs, joined us. At parting, I informed him that I was on the point of leaving England again. Mr. Canning, through whose hands the fragments of my Prussian cipher had passed, asked me, *apropos* of that, if I had received no letters from Berlin? On my negative reply he retorted with an odd ironical expression: '*Ça valait bien la peine de vous exposer par un chiffre, pour ne pas vous écrire du-tout!*'

The greatest difficulty now was to get my brother to start. Although naturally, when in a healthy state, a singularly fearless man, and one cool in the presence of danger, his darkened imagination had conjured up the most fearful visions of what things he would meet with if he left London. He had not himself the force to shake off these phantoms, and all persuasion on my part was in vain. At last his friend, Captain Timäus of the *Legion*, succeeded in getting him into the carriage. I sat beside him, and drove (while he resisted violently) quickly through the streets of London.

As soon as we had left the town behind us, and the further we got away from it, the calmer his disturbed mind became. After giving him this first proof of the illusory nature of his forebodings I found him ready to acquiesce in all my arrangements, but I had to give him unremitting supervision.

On August 13th the travellers embarked at Harwich, and landed on the 17th at Göthenburg. Thence they proceeded by land to Carlscrona, the sea-way through the Sound being closed.

A land journey in Sweden has its peculiar difficulties, for quickly as one may drive by post, the horses must be ordered beforehand, as they are furnished by peasants ; and besides that, there was no sort of provision for the personal comfort, or even the progress of the traveller. We had to hire an open chaise and the harness in Göthenburg, to be subsequently returned from Carlscrona, and we even had to buy a few bad whips and provide ourselves with wheel-grease. Then we still had to hire a man to drive who knew the way.

On August 19th, towards evening, we started, after sending the servant of Count Ferdinand Kielmansegge, our fellow-traveller, ahead as what they call *Förbode*, to order horses all along the route. For that purpose he could only obtain at each station a two-wheeled cart, exactly like our dung-carts, and in this our boxes and portmanteaux were forwarded. And so our journey began, down the west coast of Schonen, by Warberg and Halmstad, and thence across the country by Carlshamn to Carlscrona. Our coachman drove like mad from the start. Although it is customary in Sweden to let the horses go full gallop downhill, we soon discovered that our driver was completely drunk. We looked on at this with apprehension for some time; but when it became really too bad, and talking was of no use, we had to make him, partly by force, relinquish the reins, which we confided to the peasant owner of the horses, who sat behind our carriage, while our own state-coachman had to assume that position instead.

When we looked round, after a while, in some anxiety lest he should come to grief behind, we were just in time to notice that the fellow (to whom we had paid part of his fare in advance) had jumped out of the carriage, and was staggering home to Göthenburg. We pursued, brought him none too gently back to the carriage, and put him on the box, so as to have him under observation. When he had slept there a few hours he became reasonable again, and we had no reason to make further complaints of him.

At each station we found fresh horses tethered before the post-house. The harness was transferred, and we were off again. The owner of the horses could find himself a seat somewhere on the vehicle, or hang on behind; else he must follow after to see that he got his horses back at the next station. The poor devils do not seem accustomed to receive gratuities, as they displayed so much humble gratitude and pleasure at receiving a few coppers. I had taken a supply of the latter with me, as these coins were then rarely to be met with in Sweden. One met with scarcely anything but tattered thaler-notes of the *Riks-bank,* for which it was difficult to get change.

As we reached Halmstad towards midday, in very hot weather, which is a town surrounded with bad fortifications, we saw several soldiers sleeping on their faces on the inner side of the ramparts. Their red uniforms with short tails almost led us to suppose them to be English or Hanoverians, but we soon learnt that they were part of the Danish garrison of the island of Bornholm. They had mutinied, taken possession of a ship, landed on the Swedish coast, and were now in custody here.

This trying journey lasted nearly five days. It was not till the 23rd that Carlscrona was reached. There the travellers took an English cutter, of which the duty was to cruise between the Swedish and Prussian coasts to keep up communications as much as possible, particularly with Kolberg. As this vessel was not fitted up for passengers, the invalid only got a tolerable berth, while his brother slept on planks, and instead of bedding and a pillow had a sack stuffed with flags of all nations.

During the night I heard the boatswain *(Steuermann)* come into the cabin of the officer in command, Lieutenant Nelson, to make a report. The latter at once wrapped himself in his cloak and hurried on deck, and I was immediately afterwards hunted out of my resting-place by the shout of 'Clear for action!'

Above, I found the crew busy making the sixteen guns ready, while pikes were distributed to all of us for defence against boarders. I folded my papers round a stone with the intention of dropping them into the sea in case of defeat. Just then day began to break, the sea was rough, and we saw pretty clearly a big ship under full sail, making suspicious movements. As the repeated summons to 'Lie to' through the speaking-trumpet was without result, Lieutenant Nelson sent a ball through, the rigging. That answered, and a boat set forth, which only arrived with much effort. It now appeared that the ship was only a large trading brig, which had wished to avoid inspection, but produced perfectly regular papers. So both of us got off with nothing but an alarm.

The next day the wind changed, so that a rapid alteration of the sails became necessary. The Lieutenant sent the requisite number of men twice up the rigging, and either by want of skill or ill-humour the manoeuvre was badly executed, and the movement of the vessel became more and more disagreeable. Now Nelson went aloft himself to superintend-He came down in great wrath, and desired to know the names of those who were in fault. No one wanted to give them. 'Very well,' said he, 'if nobody is to blame you are all to blame, and I'll treat you accordingly.' And he had them all on deck, one after the other, and treated each to three dozen with a rope's end. The discipline was of a pattern character thenceforward.

In one of the battalion journals the remark is found relative to the effect of this punishment:

Twelve lashes on board ship are equal to one hundred and fifty lashes in the army, on account of the thicker rope and stronger arm.

On August 25th, in the afternoon, we were in the deep water off Kolberg. We could not enter the harbour in an English ship, on account of the nominal state of war with Prussia. So we had to await a pilot, for whom secret concerted signals were made. With him I went into Kolberg, after arranging certain signals with Lieutenant Nelson so that I could find the ship again in the sea outside.

I had a private understanding with the house of Schröder in Kolberg. They used to forward then, and till 1813, my letters and couriers to and from England. In the town I made myself known, in confidence, to the Commandant, Major von Hüser, who took it very seriously, and only gave me permission to travel further when I showed him, in addition to my ostensible French passport, a private one from the Minister Count Goltz.

These matters kept me until eight o'clock in the evening. When we came down to the shore again to look for the English cutter there was not a vessel to be seen far and wide. Night was coming on. Our boatman had put up a lighted lantern on our little mast. It was already very dark when he suddenly hauled down the light and put it out. He asked me, with some anxiety, to speak as low as possible and keep very quiet, as we were in the immediate neighbourhood of a large ship, which, from its black sails, he recognised as a French privateer, which spread fear and alarm in that neighbourhood. We left our boat now entirely to the waves, only taking care not to be observed by the Frenchman. The night was very cold with a sharp breeze. To shelter myself, I lay flat down on deck, as I had neither cloak nor overcoat, expecting to have been on board again before evening. Fortunately the sea was calm. At last the wished-for day broke, and we discovered the cutter on the far-off horizon. It approached, and I got on board again. It had been chasing a ship the evening before, and so got quite out of the direction in which I was to have found it.

As we left Kolberg on August 27th, I was astonished to see the state of ruin of the very inferior fortifications, which might have been the paltry ramparts of a little free-town. It was inconceivable to me how my friend Gneisenau managed to keep up a defence behind them so long against the French. He himself gave me later on the following explanation—viz., that he had trusted little to his low ramparts, which on the other hand were permissible in such flat *terrain,* but had perpetually endeavoured by sudden sorties to keep the enemy in a disturbed state, and thus keep him from an actual assault. On my asking what was the strength of his garrison, he said: 'When I took the command I had 4,000 men; I lost 2,000, and I marched out with 6,000.' This arithmetical riddle was explained by the fact that after the disasters to the Prussian army on the other side of the Oder (1807), many men singly, or from the sea, of the scattered and broken regiments volunteered to place themselves under the banner of Kolberg's brave defender.

The brothers went by Stargard and Schwedt to the Schlippenbach estate of Schönermark in the Ukermark, where Louis' family lived. Christian soon left for Carlsbad, accompanied by the faithful Hegener, who had been up to 1803 his servant, and since then that of his brother. The sea voyage had made a wonderful improvement in his condition. But when the proposal to travel as far as Bohemia was placed before him he again resisted violently. It was only after a serious struggle for fourteen days, and by the pretence of a Royal command, that he was got to the point of departure.

CHAPTER 6

In England
1810—1812

Christian Ompteda came from Carlsbad to Berlin in October 1809, a little better, and settled down, or rather hid himself, there. Still afflicted with a violent dread of human society, he only left his hotel in the remote Konigstrasse after dark. It was there that he had sought to secrete himself far from the circles in the capital he had once frequented, and he himself named his abode *my Jew's shelter*. Louis, however, who supervised with affectionate care the most suitable treatment for the patient, could only show himself in Berlin at long intervals, knowing himself to be watched by the French secret police. He had therefore engaged the assistance of their mutual friend Scharnhorst as spiritual nurse, almost the only person the sick man would tolerate the presence of. Scharnhorst, who had been with Christian in 1794 and 1803, had in the early part of 1810 resigned his position as Minister of War, after the French Ambassador in Berlin had said that "General Scharnhorst was one of those persons who were displeasing to the Emperor, in their present position." In the *Journal de l'Empire* an article appeared, giving out that he was a partisan of England. After these compliments he remained only official chief of the Quartermaster-General's Staff, and of the Corps of Engineers. By a secret order of the Cabinet, however, General Hake, his successor, was recommended to take the advice of his predecessor on all important questions, and follow it. Externally, Scharnhorst lived in relative retirement and leisure. He undertook his friendly task with that loyalty and insight which were characteristic of him.

The friendly confidential relations existing for years between Louis Ompteda and his countryman and intellectual sympathiser, Scharnhorst, will be illustrated by the following letter from the latter, a few months after the Peace of Tilsit (July 9th, 1807):

Memel, October 25th, 1807: Not knowing what the sad and cloudy future may be, we live here with dull, cast-down feelings, and in vain flatter ourselves with hope; we see we are mistaken. We resemble some crew saved from shipwreck, who find themselves placed on a desolate island, unprovided with any necessaries. That is the way I look at our position, and have clone so since the unhappy day of Auerstädt. Perhaps I may be wrong, and in that case I will venture to hope, my most respected friend, for your kind and amiable forbearance. After so much misfortune one begins to lose what in other cases generally remains to mankind—hope. Our King and our Queen have come out infinitely greater and more lovable in their present unhappy situation than ever before. The Queen suppresses her sorrow, the King shows himself to be a true philosopher. The Minister Stein has been here for three weeks, and has taken over the Home Department, and with it the executive as well. Beyme is become President of the Supreme Court, but stays here till the King goes back to Berlin. Otherwise all our Ministers except Schrotter are dismissed, and a lot of Generals. Most of the officers are put on half-pay, and only complete regiments receive pay on the peace-footing scale; 5,000 cavalry horses are being sold now, the train and artillery horses are given to the country which is devastated, some of the villages in Prussia being so ruined that their places can only be recognised by the scattered stones of the chimneys, while the rest are half depopulated. Hunger and trouble have produced diseases of all sorts; and that is how we stand.

Hearty thanks for the kind messages from our friend in England (Christian Ompteda). Nothing could make me happier than to hear that you are both well and prosperous. I have not precisely established my children, but so far provided for them that they are not in immediate need of my help, and am myself already fairly familiarised with all that is likely to happen to me—at any rate, with a future which will not be a happy one. With hearty and sincere friendship, and respect from yours, *Scharnhorst*.

Scharnhorst always felt himself united by living bonds to his native land. His two sons, William and Augustus, were in Spain with the Legion. It was not till the mobilisation of 1813 that their father introduced them to the Prussian army.

He was very attentive to his intimate former Hanoverian comrade, and treated him quite according to the prescription of George III, seeking, in addition to his already steadily carried on course of reading, to stimulate him to personal literary effort. He particularly impelled Christian to translate into English one of his own military works; it is unfortunately no longer possible to ascertain which.

When the cure-season approached, in the early part of 1810, Louis tried to persuade the invalid to make use of Carlsbad once more. But all the repeated attempts in that sense were futile. Christian's excitement rose every day more, and it became a matter of alarm lest the little ground gained should be lost. Even the alternative, *Carlsbad or—resignation*, which his brother made use of, was without effect. So Louis found himself compelled to offer the resignation of the apparently hopelessly-unfit-for-service Christian to the Duke of Cambridge, commanding the German Legion. The latter replied, September 1810, with the most gracious and sympathetic expressions.

Singularly enough, from that time, the patient's condition began to improve, as if his soul had been freed from a heavy burden and could now wield its wings once more. Also the tendency to personal literary work again awoke, whereas a few weeks before the sufferer could only work himself up to writing a few short letters.

One of these, written between June 29th (anniversary of the beginning of his attack) and July 19th, 1810 (day of Queen Louisa's death), has been preserved—to his Brother Louis' Wife:

Hearty thanks, dear sister, for your news about the Queen. I unite my prayers with yours for the preservation of a life so precious to this country, as that of the excellent sovereign lady, with whose loss it is threatened. Although incapable of any good myself, I can recognise it, love it, and wish it for others.

To Louis, July 16th, 1810:

Thanks for your note of the 14th. The news of the victory in Spain would make me rejoice, were it not that every such thought reminds more painfully of the misery of my own condition. My wishes are for the welfare of you and yours. But I am incapable of contributing to it as I ought, and cannot express the still sadder truth which is connected with that.

Scharnhorst was careful to utilise the favourable tendency he had helped to produce, by bringing the patient, now rousing himself to fresh intellectual life, into contact with a man of similar opinions and culture—the bookseller Carl Spener, whose name the *Haude and Spener Gazette* preserved to their end. The road to this connection seems to have been opened by the insertion by Scharnhorst of some of Christian's compositions in the paper, without the author's name, and perhaps without his knowledge. Christian writes to his brother on November 14th, to the effect that he, unexpectedly and unintentionally, had assumed the, to him not wholly appropriate, functions of the *invisible girl* (a piece of acoustic ingenuity by which a voice is made to sound as from a glass bell). This course of things, once begun, developed actively in the form of articles for the paper, which were always gladly received, unless the Censorship interfered, and of correspondence which took a continually more intimate tone. And yet the writers never saw one another. Spener first learnt the name of his correspondent on March 11th, 1811, the day before the latter left Berlin. November 27th, 1810, Spener writes:

The unknown benefactor, whom I have to thank for so many learned and interesting contributions, which I, Heaven knows, gave to the public without any hesitation, unless withheld by *les gros clous de la necessity*, as Voltaire puts it—this powerful thinker and statesman will, no doubt, pardon me if for the moment, when only one form of postal communication is open to me in which to reply, I confine myself to hearty thanks. *C. Spener.*

The envelope bears the inscription *Ignoto*. The *form of postal communication* was Christian's cautious old servant.

Of the various compositions of Christian on the most different subjects, the following only, of December 25th, 1810, is inserted here, as it deals most worthily with the death of the noble Queen Louisa, and at the same time shadows forth prophetically the victories of the years 1813 to 1815. It was accompanied with the following lines to Spener:

December 27th, 1810: In the annexed I send you a few thoughts suggested by the papers of the day before yesterday.

On December 25th, 1810, the body of the Queen was transferred from the cathedral to the mausoleum of Charlottenburg.

Perhaps this subject should not be treated further, except by the revering silence of memory. You are in a better position to decide about such considerations, wherefore please deal with this enclosure with regard to publication according to your choice and conviction. The only things I should like you, in case you take the negative view, to keep by you, at any rate, are the wishes and hopes in the concluding lines, which, flowing from a sincere heart, an unknown stranger would fain treat as a forecast of better times, in which also he expresses his gratitude for the protection and external peace he has enjoyed during the past year under the Prussian sceptre.

The essay is headed *Palmam qui meruit, ferat!*

This simple and beautiful motto, once chosen by a great man gone to crown the splendour of the services of another [1] great man now also passed into eternity, is again today unwillingly revived in our memories by the moving apotheosis, through which a transfigured spirit, lately removed from here below to a better abode on high, has been enabled to appeal more impressively to the whole people as their domestic and public guardian angel. And just as everything, on this occasion, bears the stamp of the deepest and truest feeling, so it does also that of the sublimest allegorical significance. Who can approach that noble,

---

1. Pitt chose the motto for Nelson, when the latter was made a peer after the battle of Aboukir.

simple monument now enclosing the sacred remains—when on occasions, wisely made rare, the doors of the ante-chamber are open to permit the eyes their wistful glance—without remembering the palm of victory which, too soon for our world, has become the crown of every womanly, every royal virtue?

But the essence of love is a mutual giving. Wherefore that earthly palm now laid in sorrowful affection on the sarcophagus will one day be given back by the hand of her now dwelling high in glory, in exchange for the compensating deathless palm of victory in the manifold battlefields of time. And thus will love for love, in its most noble and sublime form, become through the centuries a model, encouragement, and reward for millions.

On January 15th, 1811, Christian sent Spener a paper on the extremely favourable pension regulations for British sailors and soldiers out of service, with a view to refuting the assertion of the *Menteur Universel* that they were reduced to beggary. He gives an extract from the appropriate Act of Parliament, and remarks:

This extract might perhaps have been more abbreviated. In England the statutes are made long and broad, and expressed in the singular and plural numbers, and the past, present, and future tenses. On the other hand, you can depend upon every letter and title, and are armed against all caprices of absolutism. Yet a line often stands in the way of the constitution, legislation, and institutions of thousands of years.

Spener replies:

Berlin, January 22nd, 1811: Willingly as I would accept the really interesting contribution about the pensioners of the English army, I dare not. *Closely watched as I am*, it would infallibly be treated by a certain house, Unter den Linden (the French Embassy), failing anything more important, as an Anglicism of most criminal tendency, as a recruiting drum for the German Legion, and I as a directly traitorous recruiting officer, especially as I am known already by my fruits as an anti-Gallican. From the special and tender attention which the Great Mogul devotes to daily papers, knowing them to be the levers of public opinion, from the care with which he

diminishes their number so as to make supervision easier and surer, I may be certain that the doom of mine is
already pronounced in case of an occupation here, and
the fulfilment only postponed to such an occasion, and
that the more that the *fellow-paper* (the *Vossiche Zeitung*)
takes the other side, is on particularly good terms with
the house Unter den Linden, and in the presence of the
foreign ruler is always held up to me as a pattern. But
my paper is not merely my hobby, it is the crutch of
my old age. The book-trade, which amounts to nothing
just now, never brought me in daily bread, because I, in
my amphibious way, never carried it on in a business-
like way. *C. Spener.*

About this time arose also the literary connection with
Henry von Kleist. Since the beginning of October 1810 the
Berlin Abendblätter had appeared, a journal of the most modest proportions, dedicated to instructive entertainment, a veil
under which it carried out patriotic purposes. In the very first
numbers the lonely invalid had found articles which he believed he detected, from their style and tone, to be the work
of Adam Müller. This man had already been pointed out by
Louis as a friend holding the same opinions. Christian, therefore, sent in contributions to him which were unsuitable, on
account of their tone, to the Spener *Zeitung*. When he learnt,
towards the end of October, that Kleist was the editor, there
developed an active correspondence between them. Kleist to
Christian Ompteda:

Berlin, November 24th, 1810. Mauerstrasse 53: My
Lord[2]—I send you back herewith your essay *On the latest condition of Great-Britain*, printed and struck through
by the censorship. The two strokes seem to me to be
two swords laid crosswise through our dearest and most
sacred interests. It were idle to describe to you the state
of triumphant joy and emotion in which the perusal of
this most masterly article, and especially its sublime close,
has placed me and my friends (for several impressions are
in circulation). And I would most respectfully beg you to

---

2. *Euer Hochwohlgeboren* in original, for which there is no precise English equivalent,
even as *Baron* is not precisely equivalent to *Freiherr*.

provide me an opportunity to give verbal expression to the feelings of esteem and friendship which I entertain for you, and remain, etc.

The article was directed against an unfeeling comment on the illness of George III which appeared in the same Abend-blätter. It concludes thus:

Moreover, the present seems the moment in which the sight of such a noble monarch should be deeply impressive even on neutrals, even on honourable foes; a monarch whose fullest possession of all private virtues cannot be denied; a true kingly father whom the loss of his dearly beloved youngest daughter has cast down to the awful suffering of the saddest form of affliction which can befall. This should at least impress us, who are sufficiently replete with high emotions to shed tears for King Lear on the stage as he holds his dead Cordelia in his arms.

Christian replies (to Kleist) November 28th:

Your letter has been a source of undeserved food to my pride. The value of my article consisted merely in its subject. With my actual acquaintance with the same, with my yearlong and manifold opportunities of intimacy, and my affection founded on a thousand reasons for gratitude which will only end with my life, I can scarcely say less. But indeed, the greatness and the merit of the subject demand a more complete setting forth, a more worthy encomium. It was not till after my earlier contributions that I found out your name, in No. 19, a name revered by me in earlier years as one blooming in the garden of Germany's poetical literature. A name too early fair, however beautiful and fruitful, ripened in the fields of honour of past time, and imperishably treasured in the gallery of noble Germans. The spirit which speaks with such life and force in your ode to the King proves its descent.

Finally, Christian expresses his regret "that I must unavoidably be compelled to forego for the present a meeting so infinitely precious to me."

Their personal meeting was brought about later on by Louis. Soon after that there were small misunderstandings about the manner of admitting single articles; but the connection was kept up till January 1811, when in a becoming way it quietly came to an end, *which,* writes Christian to Louis January 24th, "considering the perpetually increasing recognition of the divergence of our views, was the best thing." It appears that the attitude of the *Berlin Abendblätter* became more and more displeasing to him. From another point of view the respective ends of the two men denote from absolutely opposite sources the nature of their characters. For Kleist before the end of the year gave up his life in morbid melancholy in pursuance of an exaggerated notion of friendly duty, while Christian Ompteda, on the other hand, four years later, with no less conscious determination, sacrificed himself for duty, honour, and his country.

With the new year the letters to his brother Louis become again numerous and copious.

In December 1810 the Emperor of the French had carved out and made part of the French domain the recently constructed Kingdom of Westphalia, the Grand Duchy of Berg, the Duchy of Oldenburg, and the three Hanseatic towns. The mouths of the Weser and Elbe became thereby entirely closed to free trade. An official assurance was given that it was for the Continental welfare that the regions of the Elbe and Weser were to be protected from the pernicious commercial agitations of perfidious Albion! The brothers in this way fell into danger of having their Oldenburg feudal estate sequestrated *on account of felony.*

Berlin, January 7th, 1811: I learn to-day from a good source that the Duke of Oldenburg has had an offer (from Napoleon) of a *desired* exchange of his possessions for other lands, and that the same proposal has been insinuated at St. Petersburg. It is about the same as when a swindling horse-coper tries to pass off a knacker's horse as an equivalent in exchange for a good useful steed, of which the rider is fond, and is also beloved by. You are right. All this leads infallibly further than people perhaps imagine. (This brigandage of Oldenburg will pave the way for an essential excuse for breaking the Franco-Russian friendship of 1807.) A voice is rising quietly in Germany which very possibly may one day break into thunder. The English sometimes say in a good-humoured, half-reproachful, half-praising, jocular way—*the Germans are slow, but sure.*

That we are the former no national vanity can permit us to deny. May it prove that the English have not overdone the praise in the latter quality—a thing which, judging by their character, is not likely to have been their intention.

With reference to what I said about a public voice I would request your attention to the last numbers of the excellent *Hamburger Correspondent,* partly to the disposition of many articles, partly to the sense an educated person can find between the lines, as well as to the matter in books reviewed, and what the criticism expresses. Louder and more impressive is the tone of the *Hanover Magazine,* of which the audacity is astounding. I could say more about the Jena *Literary Gazette* than the space of a letter permits. I will only say that I could take more pleasure in the learning keenness of mind, and the persuasive faculty of Schlegel as a countryman of mine, if so much talent were not in such an unworthy way, I will not say applied, but disfigured with schoolboy tricks. At the same time a return to a better spirit cannot be ignored in the *Literary Gazette.* I find a proof of that in the list of the *personnel* of the French universities and public schools, a nomenclature which can have no interest except to set forth the *incredible* deficiencies which prevail in this principal focus of all intellectual enlightenment. Not for nothing follows the extensive vacation list of the very full half-yearly library catalogue at Jena. Not for nothing is the work mentioned among French books *for sale: Monumens inédits et l'Antiquité, expliqués par Winkelmann, gravés par David, traduits de l'Italien.*

Then immediately follows the announcement of a new German work, *On Contagious Typhus*—a bitter allusion which requires no comment. Voices of this sort I could produce several more of. But *Il y a loin de là à la trompette de Jéricho.* And wherefore all that from one transferred to a state of inactivity? What you tell me from Timäus (serving with the staff of the Legion in England) can no more concern me, as it (resignation) was, after all that has occurred, only the inevitable issue. And, as regards that, what claim could I have on that noble nation which—I being unable to serve it as I could and ought to have—has sought to ensure me against starvation? But no more of that.

There is a rumour going about here that *Sa Majesté Jérome* and *Sa Majesté Louis* are to be retired on pensions of two millions, while the rest of Westphalia is to wander in the same direction as the Hanseatic towns (be incorporated in France). All this is a proof how the most adventurous revolutions are made palatable, and that the whole people will soon learn to excuse themselves with the smart reply of that weathercock in the English Parliament, who said: 'Sir, my principles are to change.'

I wonder what the great man of the day thought of the immortal truth recently proclaimed in Parliament by Perceval (relating to the performances of the brothers in the capacity of kings):

'In appointing the functions of an office, it is a dangerous thing to arrange them according to the personal virtues of those who are to fulfil them.'

You may be sure that Buonaparte is less concerned in the exclusion of English goods than of *English truth*—i.e., the light that proceeds from the English papers, and its *plain speaking*. I am living in a state of things to which I am dead, but I cannot do without spiritual opium ! But I keep awake for the scene (the war in Portugal), where I ought to be watching at the outposts, and would willingly purchase happiness with my life.

A great part of the further letters contain continued observations on literature of the day, in newspapers, periodicals, and books. They are not introduced here, as their subjects are partly rendered obsolete by subsequent history, and partly forgotten.

Christian's morbid avoidance of human society was in the meantime overcome by yet another personality—one so winning, indeed, that the very blackest misanthropy could not withstand it. This was his brother's young step-son Count Charles zu Solms-Sonnenwalde, who, in the richest bloom of his youth, was the favourite of circles he belonged to or might enter. He served at that time in the newly raised battalion of the regiment of guards—then the only one, now the first— at Potsdam, under the command of Prince Charles of Mecklenburg-Strelitz, brother of the recently departed Queen. Already in the campaign of 1806, when he was an officer with his elder brother in the King's regiment, the striking appearance of the seventeen-year-old youth had given pause to the French dragoons at Prenzlau, who held the sabre already over his head in single combat, after the regiment had been ridden down and brought into disorder in the streets of the suburb. With the exclamation, *C'est dommage, il est trop beau!* one of them twisted the sword Solms had raised to defend himself out of his hand, and made him prisoner. But not only the attraction of congeniality and the young man's radiant amiability won the inclination of his otherwise so reserved older friend ; the latter saw in him also an officer of great promise, whose further training he felt called upon to influence. By what means and in what sense he undertook this is shown by the following two letters:

Berlin, December 21st, 1810: Dear Count Solms—The accompanying work on the *Spirit of Light Troops in the Field* seemed to interest you. Perhaps you have forgotten its actual title. Allow me, therefore, the pleasure of making it your property. May the work be of some value to you, and may you think of him who offers it to you as of one who once passionately loved this subject, and tried to practise it; one who has now nothing left but the hearty wish that it may be carried out by his friends—at least, those whom he still gladly reckons as such—with success, and that you may be one of them.

This wish the recipient of the gift fulfilled in the years 1813 and 1814. He was wounded at Gross-Görschen, and found an early grave in light-troop service on March 31st at the Barrière Pantin before Paris. He rests there in the cemetery of the Montmartre.

Berlin, January 31st, 1811: Dear Count Solms—Your letter has caused me sincere pleasure. I can only disclaim the extremely high value you set on the communication of the work on the *Spirit of Light Troops.* I took pleasure in your agreement with ideas on a subject over which I have lingered with the liveliest interest, which I still find an agreeable task in the memory and study of, and I rejoice in the sympathy of a young man whom I value, whom I see going forward in a noble path which can lead to such glorious aims, and I hope and wish With my whole heart it will lead you to them. When I had the pleasure of seeing you I had only cursorily gone through the pages, and the praise I gave it proceeded from the fact that it seemed to me the first work in which the *Spirit* of troops was exclusively dealt with, *without* which all mathematical and mechanical combinations can easily come to grief, as manifold experiences have taught, but *with* which, on the other hand, especially when not opposed by analogous elements, deeds of wonder may be achieved. Since then I have read the book at greater leisure, and found some qualifications, or rather limitations, of my praise called for. When I next have the pleasure of seeing you we can continue to entertain ourselves over these particulars. The name of the author, Perrin-Parnajon, seems to me to be assumed. The work contains several examples borrowed from the Prussian campaigns of 1792-95. No Frenchman would have known these in detail, or, if he had, would have used them as arguments.

I could go on chattering on this subject, but I am getting to the end of the paper, so there is nothing left to say but a hearty farewell. *C. O.*

Christian's supposition with regard to the nationality of the author was not confirmed. The book appeared from the house of J. C. Hinrichs in Leipzig in 1811 under the full title: *Spirit of Light Troops in the Field according to the Latest Tactical Principles; or, the Training of Rifles, Chasseurs, and Partisans. A practical text-book for officers of the light arm. With some experiences communicated by C. von Perrin-Parnajon, Imperial French Captain en réforme. Leipzig, J. C. Hinrichs, 1811.* Inquiry at the firm of Hinrichs in Leipzig has led to the following reply, for which our thanks are due:

That in the agreement of June 14th, 1810, which is written in flowing German, the author signs himself 'Imperial French Captain *en réforme* v. Perrin-Parnajon, now private man of letters in Leipzig.' Perrin lived in Weimar until 1805, where the first edition of his *Dictionary of War* appeared, and that at the author's cost. As an *honorarium* Perrin received thirty thalers, and one specie-thaler which he had borrowed from Hinrichs in the winter. The edition consisted of one thousand copies, of which in 1855 four hundred and sixty were still in stock, and were thereafter sold as waste paper. It would seem, therefore, out of the question that the author bore another name.

Anyway, Christian's mistake goes to the credit of the writer as a Frenchman.

In the spring of 1811 Christian left Berlin, and settled with his brother Louis and family in Dresden, where a spacious house in the Friedrichstadt, with a large garden, took them all in. The garden gave the invalid the opportunity, according to his inclination, to go out of doors by daylight, and he soon extended his walks into the open fields, which he could reach without much chance of being seen. He was then given the wholesome duty of looking after Louis' only son, and a son of the brother Ferdinand (now with his battalion in Sicily) of about the same age who lived in the house. The tuition of these two boys had been undertaken by Deacon Trautschold, of the Friedrichstadt Church, who soon became an intimate friend of the family. All these reasons, together with his regular attendance at church (which soon began), helped to bring the spiritually afflicted man who needed religious sustenance into friendly relationship with the mild and circumspect pastor. This acquaintance was one of the first which broke down Christian's dread of strangers. Later on he came to associate more intimately with one or another of the other frequenters of the family circle, though as yet his feelings had not risen to the pitch of entering any society outside.

Christian still worked in Dresden at the before-mentioned translation of Scharnhorst's military work. Under the date of May 21st he writes from Dresden to Scharnhorst:

I will ask your consent to a few notes I have added for the benefit of English readers, who are not so familiar as we are with the Seven Years' War, likewise to a couple of observations on the English army, which my inmost convictions will not allow me to suppress, which, moreover, in no way contradict any statements of yours. Your views on the Russian army are as instructive as they are interesting.

The author of *Scharnhorst*, Professor Max Lehmann, remarks concerning this in his Supplement 9: *Lost Memoirs of Scharnhorst of July 1811* (2., p. 655):

What can have become of this manuscript? For whom was the English translation intended? Can Ompteda have taken it with him when he went over to England by Kolberg in 1811?

The latter question might be answered in the negative, even if there were any question of a *manuscript*. For one thing, from the circumstances under which—as we shall hear—Christian made the journey. Further, because the translation, begun in the winter of 1809-10 appears, together with Christian's above letters to Scharnhorst, to have been finished in May 1811. Wherefore the subject of Christian's translation must have been an older work of Scharnhorst. In any case, it could not have been dated from July 1811.

The whole political world was at this time in a state of suspense over a question, the issue of which, it was generally felt, would decide the next development of the fate of Europe, whether Napoleon would now bring matters to a breach with Russia. Louis Ompteda received orders from London to repair to Berlin in order to influence as much as possible the attitude of Prussia at this important crisis.

There he entered into secret negotiations with the Chancellor Hardenberg. The latter was strongly desirous to get trustworthy information as to whether, and to what extent, Prussia, in the event of her resisting Napoleon, could depend upon English assistance, particularly in the matter of supplying arms. Written correspondence with London was impossible on such a subject. Ompteda, therefore, proposed to send a person of confidence and acquainted with the matter to England to obtain verbal information.

In the meantime, Christian's recovery was making surprising progress under the favourable influence of his domestic life. He associated with different acquaintances who were passing through, and particularly embraced the society of Carl Solms, who was in Dresden on long leave, so much so that the excitable invalid took the young man's direct contradiction quite calmly. So Louis thought he might safely propose his brother to go over on this mission. He invited him to Potsdam, to meet young Solms. That Christian should agree while there to stay in the house of a friend, the rich manufacturer, Hesse, was a

decided sign of improvement. He accepted his brother's proposition eagerly, and both secretly and with great caution entered
Berlin at night-time. Hardenberg, in order that the sending of
the envoy to the coast might not proceed directly from the
Government, had handed over the details to Gneisenau, who at
the time under the title of State Councillor was beginning what
he two years later helped to carry out as Blücher's Chief of the
General Staff. What passed between these three men we may
learn from *Gneisenau's Life*, by Pertz, Part 2., pp. 167—178:

> The Minister Münster had sent a trusted envoy to
> Berlin to consult with Gneisenau. This was the Baron
> von Ompteda, a man of absolutely trustworthy charac-
> ter, noble mind, and warm patriotism, who had done
> essential service in those troubled times, who lived af-
> ter the war many a year as Hanoverian Ambassador in
> Berlin with his family in friendship with Gneisenau,
> and after the departure of Count Münster (1831) was
> Hanoverian Cabinet Minister in London at the Court
> of King William IV. There he did much to bring about
> and strengthen relations of mutual benefit between the
> King and country by means of the State fundamental
> law; and on the change of Government in 1837, unlike
> his colleagues, true to the memory of the deceased King
> and his oath to the fundamental law, retired from public
> affairs, and spent the last years of his life, respected by the
> best in the land, in Celle (Died 1854.)
>
> On September 10th the negotiations (between
> Gneisenau and Louis Ompteda) came to a conclusion.
> It was agreed what demands should be placed before
> the English Government. Ompteda arranged them in a
> letter for Count Münster, and proposed that it should be
> conveyed by his eldest brother, the lieutenant-colonel,
> whom he brought in secretly from Potsdam, and intro-
> duced to Gneisenau at his house, Unter den Linden, in
> the night of September 12th. Gneisenau devoted several
> hours of conversation to explaining to him the secrets
> which could not be trusted to paper, and gave him a note
> in which he had set forth his proposed plan of campaign,
> and besought immediate help.

In the meantime Louis had got a chaise ready, with the assistance of Gneisenau's confidant, Colonel Chazot. So Christian at once began. . . .

. . . . the journey by Kolberg to Sweden and England. The admiration he felt for the distinguished man, whose personality fully justified previous descriptions, and the memory of that unique night were expressed for years afterwards in Ompteda's letters. He arrived safely in England, brought the papers entrusted to him, and remained in that country long enough to meet Gneisenau there again in 1812.

Louis provided his brother with a letter of recommendation to the English Admiral, Sir James de Saumarez, who was stationed with his fleet off the Swedish coast, near Göthenburg. The journey so far was not without difficulty. Christian was obliged to creep through Sweden overland, under an assumed name, and provided with an insufficient passport. In Wingo-Sund he reached the fleet, where the admiral gave him a very good reception, and sent him in a special frigate to England, where he arrived on October 5th, and his communications were extremely welcome to the English Government.

1812

Christian spent the winter of 1811-12 in London. We know next to nothing of his external and internal occupations. Public correspondence was only possible by special couriers (with the Continent). Much was lost or intercepted. On February 1st, 1812, Louis Ompteda writes to the Minister Münster:

> Gneisenau himself has specially cautioned me not to trust the Prussian post-office, as Herr von Segebarth, who presides over the secret-opening department, is much interested in keeping up peace with France, so as not to lose his very profitable place here, and is therefore very attentive to all correspondence dealing with politics in any way.

Therefore the correspondence of the two brothers during the winter appears to have been mainly confined to a few brief notes regarding one another's health and doings, forwarded, as opportunity might serve, through the Hanoverian Chancery. Even this form of communication seldom occurred. Louis received from the Minister, who did not attach much importance to regularity, only one short reply during the whole year 1812. He himself had no safe opportunity to write to London between June 26th and August 16th, and then to November 16th.

It was not till May 21st that Christian found an opportunity to communicate, and that took three months before it reached his brother's hands. The latter had complained of Münster's total silence. Christian, who had read his brother's reports, says:

I have shared with persons of the greatest consequence here the impression of the gravity of your despatches. I could prove to you from the marginal notes I found on them that they had received the attention they deserved. But there are utterances I must withhold, the non-expression of which you must put down to his (Münster's) natural cold reserve, in order not to draw any unsatisfactory conclusion therefrom. Mere general views as to the state of affairs are ill adapted for this form of communication. Moreover, Münster has had the gout very badly since February. He is getting better now, but is very much pulled down. With Castlereagh he is, outwardly, on a good footing. Decken (!) is working into that statesman like a mole. Decken and Münster are in open antagonism. About myself I have nothing to say. The most exalted individuals are displaying the most benevolent views towards me, but only circumstances can decide and end my present state of inactivity. I have *inter pares* occupied too distinguished a post to easily get into it again without beginning lower down. Besides, I will never purchase this by servility to inferiors.

On August 20th, 1812, Gneisenau came to London. He had, like Scharnhorst, sent in his resignation early in the year, when Prussia found herself compelled to ally herself with Napoleon against Russia. Both of them had opposed this step to the extreme of their power, in close alliance with Louis Ompteda. The latter had not only a large English consignment of arms ready and afloat in the Baltic, but also placed the English fleet at the King's disposal as a last refuge in case of extremity. Gneisenau had done more work in the direction of war in Russia and Sweden. He worked out general plans for the liberation of Eu-

rope, for the Prince Regent in London. With Christian Ompteda, whom he met again, he soon struck up an intimate friendship. When Ompteda found him one day working at the above
plans, he sent him a note in the afternoon to this effect:

Could you make use of the following theme as a section of the
important work I found you at this morning? *That the division of
Germany and Italy into small states has always been the true reason of
French supremacy.* Wherefore, let every nerve be stretched to reunite
each of these countries into one strong independent kingdom! Pardon the interruption—you are already working for that!

The calm now set in before the great Russian snowstorm.
While awaiting the approach of this powerful ally, and the decision of the English Government, Gneisenau went to the baths
of Buxton, southward of Manchester. While there he proposed
to Ompteda a tour in the north of England, but the latter was
just then detained by matters connected with his re-appointment. He wrote to his friend at Buxton on October 15th:

Since yesterday I have both your letters of the 11th and 15th
inst. Most precious to me they were. Anything that brings you
nearer to me or me to you is infinitely grateful to my heart. Apart
from a few noble friendships which my lucky star has allotted to
my share both in the Fatherland and under far-off skies, being
now really isolated almost, in one of the thickest human throngs
on the surface of the earth, it is a singular favour of Heaven
which brings me one of the most distinguished and worthiest of
men as a friend, at a period of my life when I could not easily be
more sensible of such a privilege. Good! Since I was so fortunate
in the first memorable hour of our acquaintance to comprehend
you in *one* respect, and work according to *your* intentions, may
that be a surety to both of us, that we shall understand each
other in the main, in heart, mind, and feelings; even though we
may differ on matters of detail, and may this agreement be the
watchword of our future relationship. I am heartily glad to hear
that you are well, also that you have a more favourable aspect to
judge the character of this nation from than that presented by
the movable or immovable stoniness of the capital. What you
say of the attractive qualities of your acquaintances there, brings

back to me agreeable recollections of similar favourable experiences which I was once fortunate enough to have in some of the southern provinces. But long ago I used to hear of the wonderful (human) thaw in this country, which takes place the further north you advance. I am more pleased to hear your acquaintance has advanced from a trio to a quartet than if it had become a duet You can laugh. I did not acquire the advantage of this view of things without a reason. Prince Reuss (64, Köstritz, Major in 2nd Light Battalion of the Legion) went on Tuesday to Colchester, accompanying Warthelm (Louis Wallmoden). He has come back, and I mentioned your kind suggestion (about the tour) to him. He would like it very much, but seems decided to leave England in eight days. He sends you hearty greetings. *C. O.*

On October 19th Christian agreed to Gneisenau's proposed tour, and added:

Today's post will .bring you a document in the public papers which in spirit, language, and circumstance belongs by right to the sublime class. I mean the proclamation of the Russians in reference to the destruction of Moscow. I wondered if perhaps Herr von Stein were the author. It is quite worthy of him. Your prophecy is, God willing, being fulfilled. Stormed at by a moral hurricane, which this appeal will stir in the hearts of the people of the north, who are energetic, despite their despotic form of government, threatened by the daily increasing storm-cloud under Kutusoff in the south-west, between Tula and Caluga, which hangs over that head so heavy with guilt, you give us hope that we may yet share the common satisfaction with you, and may I be more than a passive spectator! Have you read the *Times* of the 12th? If not, try and get it. It contains a worthy tribute to your friend, Tiedemann, which I read with some satisfaction, thinking of you. Goodbye. I am yours, *Ompteda.*

As Christian's fervent desire for immediate participation in the great struggle was fulfilled by his nomination as commander of the 1st Light Battalion of the Legion, on November 3rd, 1812, he adds to the gazette of his re-appointment, November 3rd, as he renounces the project of the tour:

A union might yet be possible between us even now, for a still higher purpose, even if you, yielding to pressing necessity, would consent to modify your excellent proposition so far as to defy the storms and pathless season of the frozen north in order to bring the flame of genius to enliven the strong but tough elements on the Neva and Volga. Such a union as will be when exiled Germans from the south meet exiled Germans from the north of Europe with arms in their hands, and work together from a common patriotic centre to meet at last and join hands in the heart of Germany! I am beginning to gush. Goodbye. *Ompteda.*

Yet again on board ship bound for Portugal, Christian calls to Gneisenau:

My dear friend! One hearty word of farewell. You no doubt had a letter of the 3rd from me to Buxton, which crossed yours of the 1st. I can say nothing of the latter, except that your friendly opinion tended to set up an ideal for me, to attain which your eloquent style will serve me as a spur, were your example, and our common views of our times, and the demands made on us not more impressively eloquent than even your magnificent language.

I hear you are going to Russia. May you get there in time to complete the great work *there,* and begin a *greater* in the Fatherland. Although travelling in a different direction, I do not despair to see the faithful little band of Germans in South Europe march on the soil of home once more. Besides, is not the whole European struggle *one* work ? From this point of view I beg you to continue our correspondence. Remember that communications from *you* may be of importance in the Peninsula, not to *me* only. . . . Greet your friend Chazot. And now may God and His providence defend us! Your friend, *C. v. Ompteda.*

Pertz writes:

This forecast (of a victorious meeting) *did not err,* but was only fulfilled on the day of Ompteda's death. Three years and a half after this parting the two noble warriors in the same cause met on the same battlefield. In the evening hours of the 18th June, 1815, Colonel Ompteda lay, at the head of his brigade of the German Legion, under the hoofs of the French cuirassiers, while his friend advanced with the Prussian army to exact a fearful vengeance, and to seal for ever on the same field the victory of the cause for which they had both lived.

Two years later Gneisenau concludes a letter to Louis Ompteda (Erdmannsdorf, March 3rd, 1817) with the reminiscence:"I often remember and lament my friend, your glorious brother."

CHAPTER 7

The Peninsula Campaign
1813—1814

In October 1812 the English–German army had had to raise the siege of Burgos, after several sanguinary attempts to storm it. From thence a retreat, in which much loss occurred, was carried out, by Ciudad Rodrigo, to the strong positions in Portugal. Here the troops took up winter quarters unharmed by the enemy. In the month of January 1813 Christian Ompteda met his comrades, and took command of the 1st Light Battalion, then stationed at Villar Secco in the north-cast of the country.

During the winter repose, the Commander-in-Chief, the Marquis of Wellington, had busied himself exclusively in raising the strength and fighting capacity of the army, and in completing its internal organisation. Large numbers of fresh men, and particularly officers, came out from England to fill the attenuated ranks. A sufficient provision of pontoons was established, while smaller field-kettles and tents were distributed to the troops. Moreover, the *chenilles* which had served hitherto, were put out of use, and woollen blankets introduced, which in case of necessity might serve for tents. The 2nd Light Battalion of the Legion formed with the 3rd a brigade under Colonel Colin Halkett, in the First Division of Infantry of General Sir Thomas Graham.

When Christian landed in Lisbon he found his own battalion at some distance, near the Douro, and the Spanish frontier. For the transport of baggage for this long march he had, in addition to his three horses, to buy two mules, and that at the *enormous* price of 1,600 marks.

The financial pressure on these men, so full of sacrifices, is made evident by the following letter, at a later date, to Louis, on whom Christian had, in his brotherly confidence, drawn a bill for the above amount.

You can imagine that getting a fresh outfit in November 1812, in London, with an entirely different uniform from the old, as well as three capital horses and their trappings, has pretty well exhausted my means.

The line wore red, and the light battalions green uniforms.

However, I was fortunate enough to be able to cover nearly all my necessary outlay without borrowing, and still to have a decent sum over for necessaries on the journey, and arrival at Lisbon. But at the latter place the aspect of things changed. The enormous rise of prices melted away my cash. The method of calculation, which was not sufficiently known to me in England, made vain my expectations of supplies there, which I found entirely missing.

This discreet hint is explained in a paper of *Gneisenau* (2., 698) of March 26th, 1813:

A donation of £100,000 to £200,000 sterling the English Government will very likely give, but favourably as they are inclined towards Prussia, I doubt if they will enter on a treaty of subsidy with Prussia. *They have left their own army in Spain for five months without pay!*

Wellington opened the campaign in the month of April. The relative strength of the armies opposed to one another had considerably changed since the previous year, to the advantage of the allied English, Portuguese, and Spanish, owing to the sending away of French reinforcements to Germany. The Allies advanced with nearly 200,000 men, whom the French could not oppose with more than 130,000.

The general plan was to invade Spain northward from the Douro, and move forwards as near the coast as possible, in order to ensure the needful supplies by keeping in communication with the seaports. General Graham's division formed the extreme left wing. Before starting Christian gave his brother Louis a sign of vitality:

Villar Secco, May 2nd, 1813: Dear Brother—A countryman of ours, Captain Ernst Düring, *aide-de-camp* of Lieutenant-General Stewart (English military *attaché* to the allied headquarters), has perhaps already had the pleasure of meeting you, or you will probably hear from him. This supposition is my motive for enclosing these lines in a letter for which I am indebted to Düring. I will not say a word about the times and our conditions and feeling in and towards them. There is no way of expressing the inexhaustible.

God grant that you are well, and have found, and will go on finding a safe shelter from the storms, and that the same is the case with all yours, and that you have exchanged the favourite Dresden refuge in good time for a (lately) less disturbed one in the Bohemian forests. Give your dear lady a thousand kind remembrances from me, and embrace your boys in my name. A thousand greetings to all friends, particularly Gneisenau and Scharnhorst, should you have an opportunity to see those excellent men. My impatience for news from you, having heard nothing at all of you since your letter of January 10th, I do not need to describe.

My health is good, thank Heaven. God keep you, dear brother, and send us the longed-for success of our wishes and efforts. Your faithful brother, *C. O.*

Napoleon had recommended King Joseph to collect his troops in readiness in good time. This advice, however, remained unattended to, by virtue of that monarch's petty desire for independence. The French army lay scattered about far and wide, and the king, like his generals, was in complete darkness as to the movements of the Allies and the presumable intentions of their leader.

Graham's Division had a difficult task. The Portuguese province of Tras os Montes had hitherto been considered impassable, even for small detachments. And now an army of 40,000 men of all arms, impeded by a heavy pontoon train, had to get over the mountains. But all these obstacles were overcome, and on May 30th the rapid, greatly swollen Esla was crossed. The march now proceeded perpetually to the front. The French evacuated the fortress of Burgos without a struggle.

On June 18th the armies of the Allies stood ready on the left bank of the Ebro, and moved on Vittoria, where the French army had taken up a strong position. Sir Thomas Graham advanced from the north along the Bilbao road. The general attack ensued on June 21st. On the share in this action of the 1st Light Battalion Beamish says: "Hereupon Sir Thomas Graham issued orders for the First Division to attack the village of Abechuco. The light brigade of the Legion, under Colonel Colin Halkett, pressed boldly on this village under fire from two batteries. The 1st Light Battalion was the first across the river (Zadorra), and as it pressed impetuously into the place, the enemy were seized with a panic, and left four guns and a howitzer in the hands of the battalion."

This movement of Graham cut the great military route to France by San Sebastian, and limited the enemy's retreat to Pamplona and the defile of Roncesvalles. The haste with which this (retreat) was undertaken was so great, that the French left all their artillery and baggage on the field. A hundred and fifty guns, four hundred ammunition-wagons, and a rich treasure-chest, fell into the hands of the victors. The losses of the Allies amounted to not more than 5,000 men, while that of the enemy was, moderately reckoned, 6,000, excluding prisoners.

Christian, in the triumph of success at last, after so many years of grievous disappointment, writes the day after the battle to Louis:

Bivouac of Cerio, one League to the front of Vittoria, towards Pampeluna, June 22nd, 1813: Best of Brothers!—Providence sent us all and me as well a most happy day yesterday, of which I must leave it to our great leader to set more fully before you the theme of *veni, vidi, vici.* In my small sphere I have looked on and co-operated as much as was possible, and it happened that the two Light Battalions of the K. G. L. had an interesting part in the great heroic drama. I am well and sound, and the losses of the battalion which I command are relatively insignificant.

I hope this blow will electrify afresh there where the lamp unfortunately seemed to be sinking, so clear have the big fires blazed. Since January I have heard nothing of you—and at what a period! Still, I heard through Münster of your journey (to the opening of the campaign in Silesia and Bohemia), and that was consoling. Oh, but that nice quiet house in the Friedrichstadt! I hope your people are all right. But Bautzen!! I know next to nothing of that except the place of the great struggle. Remember me to all, *all*. I am *in a hurry* to get on the march again. Please write to me as explicitly as possible. A thousand greetings to my Nicodemus friend (Gneisenau, thus jocularly referred to because his real sympathies displayed themselves in a secret nocturnal interview). He shall hear from me fully in my next. Greet also heartily him for whom I did the translation (Scharnhorst), and assure him of my hope that his accident, of which I read in the papers, will not have any dangerous consequences. Embrace all yours, as you are embraced by your faithful brother, *C. Ompteda.*

Louis was, unfortunately, unable to convey his brother's greetings to their much-honoured friend Scharnhorst. The latter was wounded on May 2nd at Gross-Görschen, and went back to Dresden. There Louis Ompteda saw him, as he has mentioned in his reminiscences:

A few days later (May 7th), I went to see General Scharnhorst, who had received a bullet-wound in the right leg at the battle of Görschen, which at first was not at all serious. I found him fully dressed, and lying on the sofa wrapped in his mantle. He told me he had sent out officers in different directions to gather more exact tidings of the advance of the enemy, but he assured me at the same time that Dresden was quite safe for the moment.

On May 8th Scharnhorst started for Vienna, turned back at Znaim much worse, and arrived May 31st at Prague. There, on June 3rd, Louis Ompteda again sat by his friend's sick-bed. He reports of it to Count Münster from Reichenbach, June 12th, 1813:

It was found necessary to perform a second operation on General Scharnhorst, as inflammation had set in in the wound. He got fever, which assumed a nervous character, and weakened him to such an extent that he had to keep his bed, and could only carry on conversation with General Radetzki and the officers who were sent to him with the greatest effort.

An apparent improvement followed, so that the sick man was able, on June 18th, to write reassuringly to his daughter:

I hope to be among the first combatants as soon as the war breaks out again, and will devote all means in my power to that end.

Then he suddenly became worse. His eyes and mind became obscured, and on June 28th. his heart ceased to beat. Christian's greeting from Vittoria of June 22nd was not able to be told in the spiritual ear of the father of the general armament of the people, who was not permitted to see the completion of the great work which was the occupation of his lifetime.

For the battle of Vittoria Christian received the great golden Vittoria medal, which is preserved as a sacred relic in his family. Alongside it lies a cross of the Legion of Honour, which he, according to the then custom of war, had taken from a French officer whom he took prisoner with his own hand.

The beaten French army took to flight, after one of the completest defeats they had yet suffered, towards the fortress of Pamplona, in confusion, One corps, under General Foy, had not taken part in the battle, but nevertheless also retreated in the direction of Tolosa. Graham got orders on June 23rd to intercept it. His vanguard was formed by the Light Battalions of the Legion under Colonel Halkett. The enemy, about 5,000 strong, had taken up a position behind a wall on the other side of a stream near the small town of Villafranca. The 1st Light Battalion attacked the enemy forthwith, supported by Portuguese troops, and took the bridge, while the 2nd crossed the stream higher up. But the French, disinclined to endanger their safety by a stand-up fight, retired through Villafranca, covered by the fire of their skirmishers. Major Prince Reuss (64, Köstritz) of the 2nd Battalion was wounded by a bullet in the left arm on this occasion, while Christian Ompteda had his horse shot under him.

Supported by cavalry, a detachment of the enemy held out for a short time in a toll-house. When they ultimately withdrew it was to an accompaniment of loud ironical cheers. When the Germans rushed into the house they found an unhappy Spaniard hung up with his own sash to the roof. The corpse was still warm. The French fled in the greatest haste through Villafranca, leaving their haversacks, knapsacks, and even portions of their clothing which might impede their flight, behind them. They were not pursued.

This was only a preliminary combat to the attack on the little fortified town of Tolosa, which barred the road to San Sebastian and the passage of the Bidassoa. The attack on Tolosa was so arranged that a Spanish detachment was to go round the town and attack from a superior height, which was to be the signal for a general advance. Beamish reports as follows:

> The advanced guard of the Legion under Colonel Ompteda therefore halted about six hundred paces from Tolosa, under protection of a curve in the road, to give the Spaniards time to carry out their orders. But as the latter did not proceed with that rapidity which Sir Thomas Graham thought necessary, the General turned to Colonel Ompteda, after the advanced guard had been waiting nearly a quarter of an hour, with the words: 'You see, Colonel, the Spaniards are not going to the front as they should. Your battalion must go instead. Go on!'
>
> Colonel Ompteda at once set forward, sending two companies in advance under Captain C. Wyneken. This first line had covered no great distance before they found themselves exposed to the fire of the town. The gate was barricaded, and the defences of the town seemed, on closer inspection, to be much more formidable than had been originally expected. The town was not only completely enclosed, but both gates, the Vittoria and the Pamplona, were also carefully barricaded, and flanked by convents and other large buildings occupied in force by the enemy. In order not to be needlessly exposed to fire from the gate defences during the advance, Wyneken made his companies jump over a low wall on the left of the road, along which they advanced under cover through a vineyard close up to the town. But finding their way suddenly stopped by a high convent wall they had to climb into the road again, which, owing to the deeper level of the garden, and the steep scarp of the road wall, was no easy matter.

As soon as the brave *Jägers* had climbed into the road

they rushed courageously to storm the Vittoria gate. Success was here impossible, owing to the strong defensive works, so they at once took shelter in the courtyard of a neighbouring convent on the left, where they were soon joined by the rest of the battalion and its commander.

The Vittoria gate was defended by strong palisades, behind which thick planks had been set up to cover the defenders. Over the gate a wall-gun was put in position, crenellated blockhouses stood on each flank of the narrow front of the town to which the road led. To the left of the town was a deep and dirty canal, which connected with the river or ground in the possession of the French. Not far from this junction a little drawbridge, also defended by a blockhouse, crossed the river to a side gate of the town.

It was not fair to expect infantry without guns to overcome obstacles of this strength. But Ompteda, being a capable soldier, and repelled by no difficulties, led out three companies from the convent yard all the same, with bold determination against the place.[1] These had scarcely shown themselves when a destructive fire came from the gate and blockhouses, and did much lamentable damage in the ranks. The troops were put into open order, and sought such cover as they could get against the enemy's fire. Some jumped into the canal, and others hastened to a house on the left. Eighteen men and Lieutenants von Vincke and C. Heise found shelter in the canal. The position of these small detachments was highly dangerous, for they were fired at in front by one blockhouse, and in the rear by the other, while the fire from the town reached them on their right, and that of the advancing Spaniards (who took them for French) on their left. The natural consequence was that scarcely a man escaped death or wounds.

In the meantime, the skirmishers of the line battalions had driven back the enemy along the Pamplona

1. It is perhaps not without psychological interest that the thus described old soldier once said in the family circle, the conversation being on *cannon fever*: "I know it quite well. Every time I come under cannon fire again after an interval, a nervous shiver affects me, which only goes off after I have got used to the hum of the balls."

road and from the surrounding heights, and were pressing on the town from that side. The enemy made a stand
on the bridge, but soon fell back into the town. Here
they opened a murderous fire on the Germans from a
convent alongside the gate. The Germans lost several officers and men, and as they had no means of forcing the
gate, they took temporary shelter behind some houses
outside. In the meantime, the 2nd Light had advanced
against the Vittoria gate with a 9-pounder, and the gate
was burst open with a couple of close shots. As soon as
that entrance was forced the defence at the Pamplona
gate began to slacken, and so the pioneers of the line
battalions succeeded in making an entry for the troops
there.

The French then hurried out of the town. But it was
already late, and the darkness made it impossible to distinguish troops of different nationalities, so the enemy
came off with less loss than he ought under more favourable conditions to have suffered.

The losses of the Legion in this attack were considerable. The 1st Light Battalion lost most—5 officers, and
31 non-commissioned officers and men. The total loss
of the five weak battalions before Tolosa was 14 officers,
and 156 men, a sacrifice which might have been much
lessened by a more calculating conduct of the attack.

The Battalion Journal reports:

The enemy might have been compelled to retreat by
simply surrounding the place. General Graham had it
stormed unnecessarily.

Gneisenau says, in reference to events of this description:

The English army is the best in the world, and the
worst led.

Christian mentions this action himself in a letter to the
Minister Münster:

Camp at Ernani, in Guipuzcoa, July 3rd, 1813: My dear Count—
A request on the part of Prince Reuss gives me occasion to mo-
lest you once more. He has had the ill-luck to be wounded on

the 24th inst. in a successful fight near Villafranca (on the main road from Vittoria to Bayonne). The bullet spared the bone of the right arm, and it is to be hoped that the flesh-wound will be healed again soon. But in the meantime he cannot use his right hand, and requires some one else's arm to get on his horse (he has not left us), and some one else's hand to write for him. The envelope, which contains other letters to his parents, and is addressed by him with his left hand, just to show he is alive, he has handed to me, desiring me to send to you with the urgent request that you would forward them.

Since the great day of Vittoria, our brigade, which has for some time occupied the honourable post of advanced guard to the 1st Division under Sir Thomas Graham, has had two lively engagements—on the 24th at Villafranca, and on the 25th at Tolosa. Driving back the enemy, capture of both places, and ultimate retreat beyond the frontier of the French corps under General Foy, which, coming from Bilbao, did *not* take part in the battle of Vittoria, were the happy results. They were not purchased cheaply, as the battalion which 1 have the honour to command counts since the 21st inst. some eighty killed and wounded. Personally, I have been very fortunate, for the loss of my best horse, which I lost by a shot at Villafranca, is a small sacrifice for two honourable and victorious days.

I give you these details in the persuasion that you will accept them with your old friendly goodwill, for otherwise I should have to apprehend lest they should seem to you *like staking shillings where there is a continual run of millions.*

You will derive information about our large operations from the fountain-head. In the army itself one naturally learns little that is trustworthy about corps at a distance. One thing we are sure of, that everything is going on as well as possible.

In Bayonne great consternation is said to have set in, and the inhabitants taken to flight. We are stationed here only three or four leagues from the French frontier, and two from San Sebastian, which is already strongly invested, and after the arrival of our heavy artillery, which is already being disembarked at Delia, the serious attack will probably be made.

Summa: All is well, and Heaven seems to bless the sublime plans (though simple, like all that is truly great) of our glorious leader with success throughout.

May you experience similar successes in the north. To that wish I have nothing to add except the assurance of my unchangeable and respectful attachment. *C. Ompteda.*

At the siege of San Sebastian, which was terminated in September by a storm, after two months' bombardment, the 1st Light Battalion was only occupied in the lines of circumvallation, with the exception of bold Captain Christian Wyneken's company, which took part in the second and successful storm.

The Battalion Journal of September 29th reports: "Our commander, Lieutenant-Colonel Ompteda, was nominated Colonel of the 5th Line in place of its Colonel-Commandant, who died August 4th before San Sebastian." Christian immediately took over his new battalion, which had already earned in the army the honourable nickname of the *fighting battalion*, which it preserved under its new chief until and through his death.

On October 7th Sir Thomas Graham crossed the French frontier river, the Bidassoa. Beamish writes:

> The passage of an army over the Bidassoa, by means of fords, in sight of the enemy, presents unusual difficulties. The tide rises sixteen feet in this river. The smallest accident or delay therefore not only makes the whole undertaking futile, but involves extremely dangerous consequences. The enterprise demands on that account the greatest punctuality in the carrying out, and the strictest exactitude in planning.

In the above case, the calculated movements of the different columns to that end were crowned with the most complete success. The ascent of a rocket gave the signal to start at the ebb, and the different columns were at once set in motion over the intervening sandy plains towards the river. The First Division formed two columns in the centre, the light battalions of the Legion at the head. Wading up to the waist in water, these lost several men in crossing, who, being wounded, were carried away by the stream; but the arrangements had been so carefully made, that the heads of the columns were halfway across the river before they were discovered or harassed at all by the enemy. As soon as the light troops had reached the other side, they immediately attacked the hostile piquets with vehemence, and drove them out of the natural shelters behind which they had posted themselves. The main columns followed in the best of order, and at once formed for attack. For the passage of the guns a bridge of boats was made, and the movement covered by a battery on the rising ground of the left bank.

The Allies were victorious at all their points of attack. In November the enemy was forced back from his fortified positions on the Nivelle and Nive, after a continuous series of successful actions lasting five days. The upshot was that the French army was driven back on Bayonne, and there surrounded in a semi-circle.

In the evening of November 10th the, regiments *Frankfurt* and *Nassau-Usingen*, of the Rhine Confederation, under Colonel von Kruse, crossed over to the Allies with bands playing, and united themselves with the liberators of their Fatherland.

Christian Ompteda had several opportunities of distinguishing himself in this five-days' struggle, which received subsequent recognition in the shape of a gold clasp to the Vittoria medal, with the inscription: *Battle of Nive*.

The brave defence of Marshal Soult cost the Allies 302 officers, and 4,727 non-commissioned officers and men. The infantry of the Legion got cantonments round St. Jean de Luiz, close to the sea-coast, between Fuenterrabia and Biarritz, where were also the headquarters of Lord Wellington, who was glad to see the vigilant Germans in his neighbourhood.

1814

The short interval of quiet which now ensued was utilised in strengthening the condition of the army. The whole force was apportioned into three divisions. The infantry of the Legion belonged to the third, the left wing under General Sir John Hope. Its Line brigade was commanded by Major-General von Hinüber.

It seems worthy of mention that, at this time, the horses of the Legion, corn and hay being wholly deficient, were fed on turnips and prickle-broom *(Ulex Europœus)*. The latter, pounded fine and then crushed, formed a nourishing fodder, which was generally used in French Navarre, and also for cattle. The condition of the German cavalry provoked astonishment among the English Generals, the secret of it being that the German troopers shared their own rations of bread with their animals.

The troops were prevented by the violent wintry weather from getting into a state of activity until February 15th. Then occurred a series of movements and combats by means of which the left wing occupied the district between Bayonne and the sea, and finally crossed the Adour below the town. A singular occurrence at this time took place, which is mentioned in the recollections of that distinguished artillerist General Sir Julius von Hartmann.

A detachment which had been the first to cross the river, had to halt there some time. The French drew near the little band, with full confidence in their numerical superiority, to a distance of three to four hundred paces. Then the rocket-guns, which had taken up a position in front of the line, discharged their destructive projectiles into the dense columns with such striking effect, that the enemy at once retreated in great confusion. The rocket-guns went after the enemy, and there was now beheld the extraordinary spectacle of strong masses of war-hardened infantry giving way without resistance to a dozen opponents. So deep, indeed, was the feeling of dread created, by this new and alarming weapon, that the columns could not be brought to a stand till they had reached the citadel. Five-and-twenty men, mostly badly wounded, fell into the hands of the British.

A prominent exploit in this series of actions was the storming of the entrenched heights of St. Etienne, which to a certain extent command the town of Bayonne, performed by the 1st and 5th Line Battalions on February 27th. This success brought the Allies so close to the citadel that their distance from its works was scarcely two hundred paces. Here they were exposed to a murderous cannon-fire, and Beamish says:

> Towards five in the afternoon a strong hostile column was seen issuing from the citadel and advancing rapidly to drive the Allies out of the position they had won. The skirmishers of the 1st and 2nd Line with a detachment of the 5th and 2nd, under Colonel Ompteda, and the Light

Brigade under Lieutenant-Colonel L. Bussche, at once fell on the enemy's masses with the bayonet, and put them to flight. Not being willing to resign so important a position, the enemy re-formed, and returned after the lapse of half an hour to the attack a second time. But the same troops again advanced to meet him, and threw themselves on him with such irresistible impetuosity, that the enemy was once more obliged to seek safety in flight. The losses of the Legion in this hot engagement were extremely serious. The officers all went in front of the troops for a most heroic example, and the high degree of resolution and contempt of death they displayed assured them a most just claim to honourable mention in the official records of this action.

The Battalion Journal says :

General Hinüber and the two Brigadiers, Ompteda and Bussche,' rushed' the outer town at the head of their men. The 5th Line lost six officers. The total loss of the five battalions of infantry of the Legion amounted to 328 officers and men. General Hinüber himself got a contusion.

This completed the enclosure of Bayonne, and the siege now began, under the command of Lieutenant-Colonel Hartmann of the Artillery of the Legion.

The duties of the troops engaged in the siege were extremely difficult and exhausting. The weather became immoderately rough and stormy, and the work in the trenches was so highly dangerous that it could only be carried on at night-time. To this was added the danger of nocturnal attacks, and the insecurity of the bridge of boats over the Adour, which it lay in the enemy's power to destroy, in which case the Allies would have had their main communication severed. In fact, the dangers to which the troops were exposed were so numerous, and the necessity of extraordinary vigilance so peremptory, that they were not even allowed to change their clothes during the siege. Moreover, a great scarcity of provisions prevailed in the camp. The price of provisions rose to an abnormal height, and it was only gradually that the country people became accustomed to bring their produce to the troops. Later on a lively market set itself up in the village of Boucant, but the prices were always at least three times the real worth of the things.

During the month of March the siege continued. Soult, leaving Bayonne to itself, withdrew eastward, and Wellington followed after him, until there came on the 11th and 12th of April the victorious but sanguinary battle of Toulouse. It cost the Allies 6,500 men, and was *wholly unnecessary,* for the couriers from Paris bringing news of the suspension of hostilities arrived at headquarters on the evening of April 12th, having been delayed by accidental circumstances.

The official news of this only reached Bayonne on April 27th, wherefore there was also a purposeless shedding of heroic blood there in a *sortie* of April 14th. The English, careless as they often were, let themselves be taken by surprise, and the fortune of the day had to be restored by the re-occupation by storm of St. Etienne by the three line battalions of the Legion. The German infantry lost 14 officers, and 180 non-commissioned officers and men. General Flay, who was to blame for the surprise, was killed, while General Hope, in supreme command, was taken prisoner, badly wounded.

On April 28th, the white flag at last was displayed on the citadel of Bayonne, and a salute of three hundred guns announced the Restoration of the Bourbons.

The relative quiet which preceded the last sanguinary storm gave Christian an opportunity to write a longer letter to his brother:

Petit Marquit, Paroisse of Tarnos, with the investing Corps of the Citadel of Bayonne, April 6th, 1814: Dear Brother—I have had the great pleasure of receiving your letter of November 5th last duly from Prague. But I perceive from it that I was unfortunately not so lucky with regard to your reply to my letter of June 22nd last. And now there occur to me, as I look through your other one dated 'Reichenbach, July 18th, 1813,' the circumstances under which you mention the loss of my No. 17, which I wrote you from Villar Cecco in Portugal, March 14th, 1813. The non-arrival of that particular letter is the more annoying to me, inasmuch as it contained the announcement of a money transaction, in which I drew a bill on you of six hundred thalers. As this proceeding must have amazed you in the absence of the lost explanation, this new proof of your brotherly kindness is all the more striking on account of the way you have taken this incident.

After a long explanation about matters of business, the letter proceeds:

But where are you living? It is owing to a mixture of peculiarities, partly to the happy changes in the greater conditions of the times which have occurred to our advantage, even to the partial difficulties Blucher and Gneisenau have had to combat, and owing to the dissimilar mixture of satisfactory impressions, that a mist enshrouds the personal circumstances of friends concerned in those matters which is difficult to penetrate. You announced to me from Prague the intention of following the Prussian headquarters into the Rhineland. If this intention was carried out, you are very probably now somewhere in the interior of France. I hope you are now officially accredited again as before, and invested with all the attributes of the post you never gave up for so long, and amid so much danger in the *ecclesia pressa*. In spite of the restoration of free communication between England and Hanover, it is incredible how little news reaches us all from thence. It is just as if the people there looked on us as belonging to another world. Should you meet countrymen who are friends of mine, whom I do not need to particularly name, do your best to recall me to their memories. I especially wish that may be the case with regard to Gneisenau, to whom I should like to renew the assurance of my hearty esteem and warm attachment, with the request not to misinterpret a silence on my part which I hope one day to explain and make up for.

Christian's wish for his brother was fulfilled. Louis had followed the great Prussian headquarters from Prague to Frankfurt-on-the-Main, and then to Basle, and was in the meantime re-appointed Ambassador to the Court at Berlin. He writes of it himself:

I announced my arrival at once in Basle to Minister Baron Hardenberg, and received forthwith an invitation to have audience with the King. But I had first another embarrassment to remove with the Minister. I had not received my new credentials with the nomination, as they had been given to Lord Burgersh, who was proceeding to the Continent with a mission. Baron Hardenberg accordingly informed his monarch of this. The King replied that I required no credentials, as His Majesty regarded all that had occurred between Prussia and Hanover as *non avenu*, and would gladly receive me without credentials.

Louis followed the King to Langres. When the Minister Münster himself arrived, the ambassador went back to Germany on a special errand.

In the meantime the victorious Allies were stationed together with the former French garrison in Bayonne. Thereby happened many occasions for disturbance and friction. The wounded pride of the French officers led them to frequently insult their former enemies, so that duels were the order of the day. Among the personal feuds there was one, in which Lieutenant von During of the 5th Line Battalion took part, which made some noise at the time. The French officer, his opponent, had invited several ladies to this encounter, *that they might be witnesses of how he could shoot a British officer*—only the French pistol flashed in the pan, while Düring shot this swaggerer dead, so that the ladies had only assembled to see the unseemly arrogance of their countryman chastised. The wholesome effects of this tragic issue reached further still, and set a limit to the rude behaviour of the officers of the garrison of Bayonne. To do strict justice to the officers of the French army as a whole, so concludes this anecdote, it should be remarked that a large number of those in Bayonne had only recently been promoted from the ranks.

The infantry of the Legion embarked in the middle of July at Paulliac, on the Gironde below Bordeaux, for Portsmouth. In Bordeaux—states the Battalion Journal—an advance of a month's pay was distributed. There were plenty of provisions there at moderate prices, "*for the English do not live like the French, at other people's expense.* The 5th Line was sent to Hastings, and then Christian again found leisure to write a long communication to his brother Louis.

London, August 19th, 1814: Dear Brother—You will not be surprised at receiving this letter dated from here. You are probably aware, through the public papers or some other channel, that the K. G. L., or at any rate that part of it belonging to the Duke of Wellington's army, has come back to England from the Gironde, except the cavalry, which marched overland through France straight to Brabant and Flanders. And so I landed with my battalion at Portsmouth at the end of last month, and got leave, and came here after I had conducted the battalion to Hastings. I was very glad to receive assurances of your prosperity from Friend Best (an official in the German Chancery), and to see a proof of it in the shape of your own letter from Dresden of the 21st ult, from which I learn that you have been for some time re-established in your old post. Satisfactory as all this is, I still long infinitely, dear brother, for personal news from you, for since your letter of November 5th, 1813, from Prague, I have not had the happiness to see a line from you. Probably some letters are lost, as I have unfortunately been certainly convinced is the case with certain letters of mine to other correspondents here, which is extremely annoying. I should just like to know whether the letters I wrote you November 17th, 1813, and January 9th, 1814, from the district between St. Jean de Luiz and Bayonne met with the same fate, as well as one on April 6th from the investing corps of the citadel of the latter fortress. The first letter a Prince Reuss (Henry LXIV, born 1787, died 1856), undertook the charge of, whom you no doubt saw or heard of, but of whom I have not had the slightest direct news since we parted, though I have repeatedly written to him. In times like ours, when months bring about secular changes, such blanks in our mutual relationship are thrice and a thousand times more exasperating, especially when one learns of the most important events in the most cold-blooded way long after they have happened. That is how I feel with reference to the loss, which your dear wife and all who knew him have sustained, in that hopeful

268

young man who has sacrificed his life with so many other brave ones as a contribution to the price we have had to pay for the change of things we have brought to pass. I add nothing further on this sad event, which we both look on with one feeling, except that I do not write to your poor wife, in order to avoid giving fresh stimulation to a sorrow now mitigated, I hope, by time which soothes all sadnesses.

Louis Ompteda has left in his *Recollections of My Life* the following account of the warlike experiences and heroic death of that fine, amiable and brave young officer:

My second step-son, Carl Solms, commanded a company, as First Lieutenant, in one of the battalions of the 1st Prussian Regiment of Guards, at the battle of Bautzen (May 21st, 1813). This battalion had occupied the skirt of a small wood. Opposite to it lay another small wood, on the edge of which were posted Wurtemberg light infantry. The two positions were only separated by a narrow piece of meadowland, but neither detachment ventured to attack the other, although a small-arm fire was kept up continually on both sides. As the position was a very warm corner, orders were given to the Prussian battalion that the companies should relieve one another two at a time, every half hour. My stepson was relieved once without mishap, but when he came up again with his company for the second turn, a bullet hit him and stuck in his right shoulder. He retired, had the bullet excised behind a neighbouring barn, and the wound bandaged, and came back to his post. He had scarcely got there when a second bullet took him in the right arm and shoulder. Fortunately it was only a flesh wound, but the bullets had taken such extraordinary directions that he got five wounds from the two shots. He had to be taken to the rear faint from loss of blood. When he visited me at Reichenbach, during the armistice, a good while later, his wounds were not yet healed, though he had already returned to duty.

On my journey back from Langres to Frankfurt-on-the Main, I had the great pleasure of again seeing my second step-son, Carl Solms, at Troyes. He was stationed in the neighbourhood, bivouacking on the snowy ground. I revived him forthwith by means of a good breakfast. He was delighted to be able to change his clothes, and my hosts were kind enough to have something a little better than usual prepared for him. During the meal he was in unusually good spirits. He charmed the whole family by the sunshine of his amiability, and amused us by singing Provençal songs which he had learnt in France. Suddenly a man came in with a disturbed expression of countenance, who was the gardener from a garden in the suburbs belonging to a sister (not present) of my hostess. He brought the intelligence that a few Cossacks were plundering, and had threatened to set the place on fire. Scarcely had Solms heard that when he jumped up from table, had his horse brought, and galloped off. We learned subsequently that he had driven the Cossacks out of the suburb, sword in hand. Since then I never saw him again.

In the early part of the month of April we received the news of the taking of Paris, at Frankfurt-on-the-Main. Our great joy at this was darkened by the news at the same time of the grievous loss this victory had caused us to sustain. Carl Solms had become the victim of his own fiery audacity in an attack by the Prussian Guards on the Barrière Pantin. When volunteers from his company were called for to drive out the French sharpshooters he offered to lead them. Although the colonel refused this proposal, as Solms had to remain at the head of his company, he repeatedly went forward to give better guidance to the volunteers. As he was looking round the corner of a wall to get a better reconnaissance of the French *tirailleurs'* position, a musket-ball hit him on the head, and after a few hours he expired. His enthusiastic nature, his winning, affectionate character, and fine external appearance made him infinitely dear to us, and a favourite with all who knew him. Many a time he has given me most affectionate proofs of his love and attachment. He rests in the cemetery on the heights of Montmartre,

Carl's unhappy mother relapsed into a long and deadly illness after the loss of her above-all-beloved child. Christian's letter proceeds:

Timäus got a letter, a few days ago, from our good Ferdinand (the youngest brother, Lieutenant-Colonel of the 6th Line Battalion) from Genoa, dated July 23rd, according to which he was about to travel, in company with some other officers, through the Tyrol by Augsburg to Verden to his family, on four months' leave. I hope he has got there by this time. I am delighted to see the disappointment of not seeing his people for eight years brought to an end in this way at last. His two eldest sons (Christian and Louis) are now, at my suggestion, attached for duty for a time to my battalion. They have very good certificates. Count Münster is just going by Paris to Vienna, where he expects to arrive on September 9th. A few days ago the Prince Regent did him the honour to dine with him. There were, except General Turner, only Hanoverians present, among whom I was received with special grace by the Prince as an unexpected and startling arrival, there having been no *levee* since I was here. What an endless quantity of things you and I have to tell and hear! But it is a matter of despair even to exhaust the most necessary topics. So for to-day only this, that I expect every minute orders to embark with my battalion, and the others that have come back, for Ostend, where we are destined to serve for a while in the Netherlands under the command of the Hereditary Prince of Orange. As you probably have old acquaintances on the general staff of this, to me, extremely welcome commander (whose personal acquaintance I made last year in the Pyrenees), I beg of you urgently to write to me by some channel or other. God bless and keep you! You will not regret that you are not to go to Vienna. May *that result in no Babel-tower building!*

Shortly before embarkation Christian wrote to his brother Ferdinand, who was trying in Verden to restore his health, much shattered, it was supposed, by a heart complaint, during his eight years' campaigning in the South:

London, August 26th, 1814: Dear Ferdinand—I am utilising the departure of Lieutenant-Colonel Gerber to beg you to accept the accompanying little brotherly keepsake from me. For two years I carried it about on my watch-chain, in hopes of being able to hand it to you personally, as all means of communication were at that time so uncertain. I am sure that circumstance will make it no less welcome to you.

This was a small gold seal-ring with a cornelian, and on it the family crest, two black flying eagles with a green trefoil between them, and the motto underneath, *Einig*. Brother Louis received a similar one, which his successors inherited.

I have often regretted that it has not been customary among our German families to have mottoes on their coats of arms, as it is here in England. You must have often admired the glorious meaning of most *family mottoes*, and that, according to my firm conviction, has been a powerful means of keeping up a noble and excellent family spirit. But it must possess, like the symbol of the coat itself, the sanction of centuries. So I came to have made three little seals, all exactly alike, with only the *family crest* as they call it here, and to ask you and Louis each to accept one, not out of a yearning after mock-mediaevalism, but as a symbol in one word of *our* relationship. They are distinguished by the marks of family precedence according to the rules of heraldry. The eldest is betokened by the figure in the seal with which I seal this parcel (a sun), the second by a waxing half-moon, the third by a *star*.

I hope the latter, which happens to be yours, will be a happy omen for you and yours. But may the motto *Einig* express not only our personal relationship, but be also a watchword and sign of union for all ours when we are no more, so that at least one condition of happiness may be attained for the family.

Farewell, best Ferdinand! Shortly you will hear further from your faithful brother, *C. Ompteda*.

Christian's spiritual legacy has hitherto been inviolably preserved by the successors of the brothers.

In the beginning of September, the 5th Line Battalion crossed over, with all its fellows, to Flanders, and was quartered there most of the winter in Tournay, the old station known in 1793. From there Christian writes to his brother Louis on the birthday of the latter:

Tournay, November 17th, 1814: Dear Brother—I cannot let this day pass in silence. It is true that my wishes for your happiness remain unalterably the same through all epochs of life. But old custom, the memory of similar days gone by, the assurance of more definite mutual recollections, the drawing closer of the ties which bind us—all these things make the family anniversaries suitable occasions for calling to mind all that happy bond which cannot be dissolved or weakened in affection even by long separations, or the geometrical progression with which their life-paths diverge (as I might put it, did I not fear to seem peculiar, which I do not in the least wish), or the graver developments of increasing years. Accept, therefore, my first and best friend, your brother's hearty congratulations on this day. May happiness and content fill the intervals between a long series of such successive anniversaries. Without those primary blessings no other conditions can suffice *us*. You see I am building still on the unchangeable similarity of our frames of mind.

It's really so long since I heard from you, I have had no letter since that of *last November* from Prague. We must save recapitulations till we meet again—but when?

But a few short lines about yourself and yours, and your latest conditions, would be infinitely welcome to me, who feel every day more isolated and cut off from all who are dear to me. I learn from the papers your present destination, and on the strength of that address this direct to Vienna.

> This authority was wrong, as usual; Louis had really exchanged with his cousin Frederick Ompteda, subsequently Hanoverian Ambassador to Rome.

It was from a thousand points of view unsuitable to write to you about the business *there* (the Congress) and what the result may be. I like to flatter myself with the thought that Vienna presents you with copious materials, in addition to those you have already, for the *Histoire de mon temps*. For Germany nothing will come out of it all except writing, afterwards as before.

> The letter here breaks off, and was only despatched months later. Christian applied the winter leisure to the scientific

training of his two nephews Christian and Louis (sixteen and fourteen years old), who were serving with his battalion. On December 27th the re-assembled Hanoverian Deputies presented an address, expressing their admiration for and gratitude to the Legion, and to the *Stadthalter* (Regent), the Duke of Cambridge. The commander of the brigade, General von Hinüber, acknowledged this in a document which proceeded from Christian Ompteda's pen:

> *Tournay, January 15th, 1815: Most Serene Duke, Most Gracious Prince and Lord*—Your Royal Highness has been graciously pleased to have the resolution arrived at by the deputies of the States of the Kingdom of Hanover assembled in the General Landtag on December 27th last communicated to the infantry of the Royal British German Legion now stationed in the Netherlands. Your Royal Highness' orders have been obeyed.
>
> To express the united feelings of this corps, on receiving the most honouring approval of the exalted Assembly of Representatives of the Fatherland, in a way proportionate to their dignity and our sentiments, were a duty as difficult as sacred, had we not ventured to entertain the hope that we should recognise the executor of our obligations in the same Royal Chief through whom such a rare reward was conferred on us. Your Royal Highness knows us. May it please you to speak for us, and we may then rest assured that the high Assembly you address will recognise our earnest efforts to express our gratitude for the honourable distinction conferred on us in a way becoming to their dignity.
>
> May it please Your Royal Highness to testify that we are far from founding claims on the exertions and sacrifices which, under the first commanders of the age and the colours of the British army, are at present easy, and find a sufficient reward in being remembered.
>
> We place our pride in this, that during a separation of more than eleven years, we have never lost sight, in our mind's eye, of our country; that we have never enjoyed the various benefits which have been our portion both in Britain's happy isles, or in the midst of Britain's vic-

torious army in the furthest districts of Europe, without a bitter flavour of memory of the fate of our country; that we find our liveliest joy in the tokens that the better spirit of our Fatherland has survived all oppression, till at last the heavy chains of years have been burst by the united strength of all Germans, among whom it was our happy lot to be the first who helped to set our country free, though far away from it.

May then our opinions warrant the sympathy with which we have recognised the beneficent measures of the glorious Regent of the Guelphic states, through which their extensive future welfare has been anticipated in the summoning of that Assembly in which the voice of the people can be raised in orderly freedom.

May we not err in finding a happy portent in a solemn expression of the noble President of that Assembly, that from the throne which rules a realm in which the features of the old German Constitution are respected with the surest predilection, the 'sacred fire' (quotation from the address) will spread over the whole German nation.

May a time approach in which our nation, happily great and independently safe, will be able to develop every now restricted disposition and force, being in intimate State connection with the great German family, ruled by such Regents as those under whose century of government the British realm has been exalted to the most glorious and the happiest on earth.

With the deepest respect, Your Royal Highness,
(Signed) *Hinüber*, Major-General.

Thus spake Christian Ompteda's official testament of his political conviction and patriotic aspirations. His personal *expectations* he confided to Louis, in a very desponding mood, at the end of the above letter.

CHAPTER 8

The Waterloo Campaign
March 1st to June 18th, 1815

The year opened peacefully. The Legion was expecting to be dissolved and re-constituted as part of the Hanoverian army, for the term of engagement of the men—up to six months after the conclusion of peace—had lapsed. Then there landed at Cannes on March 1st the ill-guarded prisoner from Elba, and on March 20th the Emperor Napoleon re-entered the Tuileries.

Armaments against the peace-destroyer began at once. The English army in the Netherlands was as speedily as possible strengthened, and the Legion offered its services for a further six months, an offer which the British Government accepted in March.

The following figures may serve to explain how the strength of the Legion was maintained and raised, in spite of its heavy losses:

		Men	Officers
1.	Recruited in the 11½ years from November 1803 to June 1815	29,350	1,350
	Among these, German prisoners and deserters from the French service in the Peninsula	4,150	
	German Prisoners in England	2,000	
2.	The Legion lost through death in the 11½ years	5,850	250
	Consequent condition at time of dissolution	23,500	1,100
3.	Losses of the Legion in the actions from June 16th to 18th 1815	1,687	129

The corps was formed afresh, and mainly united, with the

newly raised Hanoverian troops, to the Third Division under Charles Alten, as part of the army-corps of the Hereditary Prince of Orange. Christian Ompteda received the first brigade in Alten's Division, consisting of the 1st and 2nd Light the 5th (his own), and the 8th Line Battalions. Lieutenant-Colonel Louis von dem Busche commanded the 1st Light, Major Baring the 2nd; the 5th Line, Lieutenant-Colonel von Linsingen, and the 8th, Lieutenant-Colonel von Schröder.

The total strength of the army again placed under the supreme command of its renowned old leader the Duke of Wellington, amounted to about 70,000 men, composed as follows:—

1.	Native Englishmen		35,000
2.	Hanoverians		
	(a) The Legion (a considerable part of it being away in North Germany and Italy)	7,000	
	(b) New auxiliary corps in English pay	14,000	
	(c) Reserve from the Lanwehr	9,000	
			30,000
	Brunswickers, Dutch and Nassau		5,000
	Total		70,000

It may therefore be regarded as a historic fact that the Battle of Waterloo was fought by Englishmen and Hanoverians in approximately equal strength.

Napoleon had advanced 127,000 men by June 14th to the .French-Flemish frontier. Opposed to him stood, as yet somewhat widely scattered, 217,000 men, of whom the Prussian army of about 142,000 furnished the largest part.

Neither the design of this work nor the calling of the author is suited to undertake a description of the great battle drama of June 16th to the 18th. We will therefore limit ourselves to the Army-Corps of the Hereditary Prince of Orange, and in it to Alten's Division, and particularly to Ompteda's brigade, and accompany it on its last road to death and victory.

The right wing of the English-Hanoverian army was, at the beginning of the month of June, round about Soignies and Braine-le-Comte, between Mons and Brussels. Ompteda's brigade lay somewhat further to the south at Escaussines-Lalaing. Here Christian met with a heavy blow, the news of the sudden death of his brother Ferdinand. While his battalion was marching northwards on the way back from Sicily, he had been able to spend the winter 1814-15, on account of his shattered health, among his relations in his old home at Verden. In apparent good health, he went out for a ride in the neighbourhood, never came back, and was found out of doors dead alongside his horse. Some labourers had noticed him riding, and saw him suddenly sink out of the saddle.

So, therefore, the War of Liberation had up to now demanded four victims from this small family:

The cousin, Ferdinand Ompteda, Captain and Brigade Adjutant, had rested since November 4th, 1809, in the churchyard of Egham, near Windsor, whither he had been brought back very ill from Portugal, to die on October 31st. His brother Augustus, also Captain and Brigade Adjutant, had found his last resting-place with many comrades at Elvas, in Portugal, April 21st, 1811. Carl Solms had lain now for a year at Montmartre.

And now the beloved brother Ferdinand had joined the series. Only one of them was sped by the enemy's bullet in the tempest of victorious battle; the others had to seal their fidelity with their lives on the shady side of their calling.

The poet's words applied to them:

As for us, we have no share in the blazing renown and the glory;
We have only to bear the labour, the pain, and the sorrow;
Only upheld by our pride in the praise that our own hearts
  will give us.

Deep, true pain and sorrow for the bereaved awoke in Christian the longing which had slept for months, for written communication with his brother Louis:

Escaussines-Lalaing, not far from Soignies and Braine-le-Comte, June 8th, 1815: Dear Brother—I am just on the point of taking up our long-interrupted correspondence again, prompted by the saddest and most unexpected of motives, when I received yesterday your infinitely precious letter of May 20th. All it says of our bitter loss is what I from my soul might have written. Always in agreement over the more important events of life it constitutes a sad but consoling blending of similar minds to contemplate together as we do this irreparable loss. The particulars you recall to mind of the rare character of our excellent Ferdinand are the most expressive memorial of his worth. They are most appropriate to his unassuming merits. To honour his memory thus is a fresh bond of our brotherly love.

Yes, my dear Louis, half a century now the trefoil has held together. Ferdinand's calm disposition, your tender treatment of depressed states of mind, fortune, and too ill-balanced set of emotions, combined to produce in me without my state of mind ever being prejudicial to either of you,—we may say we have kept up our mutual relationship, intact and uninjured, to an extraordinary degree. He has been taken from us, let therefore the ties of our union be the closer and firmer. Let the autumn of life not rob the un-fallen leaves of our family symbol of its living freshness. So will it be if there be question of the oneness of our two souls. But even as I write this, I feel that the contemplation of that symbol (the trefoil) will be an everlasting reminder of our loss.

Frederica is in a state which the mind does not care to dwell on. Two letters I had from her, as those addressed to her sons give extremely painful details. She seemed to wish that we should undertake the joint guardianship of the children, and if I lived in Germany I would willingly accept that sad duty. But my being far away out of reach, and my duties in a foreign service, make it impossible for me to give the necessary attention to the particulars of such an undertaking. I think that as Frederica looked after the bringing up of the children with real maternal care during the prolonged absence of our departed brother, she had better undertake the guardianship herself, in case distance should be an obstacle to your doing so. Otherwise your experienced assistance and co-operation would be most desirable, for Frederica, for the children, and for our common interest. As the widow of an English Lieutenant-Colonel, Frederica gets £50 a year, and for every child unprovided for, £9. The Hanoverian Major's widow's pension amounts to 200 thalers, I believe. All these details, though they suggest sources of help, are but a sign of the ruin of a singularly beautiful state of family happiness.

You will be aware that the two eldest sons are here tempo-
rarily attached to my battalion, although they actually belong to
the 6th, which was in Sicily, and is now probably in Italy. They
are good, willing boys, but too young, especially the youngest (then fifteen); their military advancement at so early an age,
though otherwise advantageous, has been prejudicial to their
pursuit of most necessary studies. I have tried to make up for
that to a certain extent during the winter at Tournay, by lessons
on all kinds of subjects, but there are still great *lacunæ* which
only a fresh regular course of proper instruction can fill. These
views had doubly increased my wish to send them back for a
time to their paternal roof, in expectation of their soon joining
their father's battalion again. But this is now impossible, and
they must share the fate of the army here. It is one consolation
that in the lifetime of our departed brother, both these boys'
parents had expressed their satisfaction at that prospect, and were
fully resigned to whatever might befall their children in the future. I have given them your letters, which have produced the
impression they were intended to. If I do not send the answers
with this, you must consider the distance of their cantonment,
for I have not got the battalion with me here.

I say nothing of the recollections awakened by your letter with
regard to the sorrowful main subject. You may easily conceive the
impression produced on me by all these losses in our family.

From the beginning of a letter destined for you on a day
when my thoughts were naturally principally occupied with
you (the fragment of November 17th, 1814) you will perceive
that I thought you were summoned to the Congress of Vienna.
I suppose you will not *now* regret that that assumption was un-
confirmed. Kindly accept that aged fragment and excuse its having no conclusion. You know how the best of intentions do not
always get carried out.

In my next letter—for you will soon hear from me again—I
will tell you all about my present position, with which I have
every reason to be satisfied. Fate has brought me together again
with my old friend Charles Alten, who, as Lieutenant-General,
commands the division in which I have a brigade of four battal-

ions of the K. G. L. This connection with Alten is most desirable, for to him the fine saying applies in its fullest sense—*Palmam qui meruit, ferat!* Your faithful brother, *C. Ompteda.*

Once again Christian takes to his heart in loving wistfulness and thoughtful care all those who are so dear to him. He expresses his esteem for his distinguished comrade by a classic phrase, which was very shortly to be fully justified afresh by both of them. His promise, "you will soon hear from (or of) me again," was speedily fulfilled, but the above was the last written of him by his own hand. The next news of him reached his brother in the form of the imperishable testimony of honour written in the history of war, which was conferred on his faithful soldier by Christian's renowned leader; that was the palm laid by Wellington on the hero's grave of his Colonel Ompteda.

It must be remembered that on June 15th and 16th, the Duke of Wellington advanced his army from Brussels southwards along the road to Charleroi, while the greater part of the Prussian army lay to the south-east by Ligny. After a struggle, in which a great deal of loss was incurred, the latter fell back northwards on Wavre, where they reformed on June 17th. The Hereditary Prince of Orange advanced his troops from Nivelles south-eastwards towards Quatre Bras, a farm at the meeting of the Brussels-Charleroi and Nivelles-Namur roads. In this engagement, so rich in losses, which resulted in the repulse of Marshal Ney's attack, and involved the death of the brave Duke Frederick William of Brunswick, only a part of Alten's 3rd division was present. Ompteda's German brigade only arrived in the night of June 16-17th, and halted on the road from Nivelles to Mons.

The following events are set forth in as exact as possible correspondence with the almost simultaneous observations of a series of officers in Ompteda's brigade. They were later partly delivered personally to his brother Louis and partly otherwise published. To them is added, in conclusion, the service-journal of the 5th Line Battalion.

The reports give an immediate impression of unforgettable actual experience, while at the same time there are reflected in them the personal opinions of his subordinate comrades on their leader.

These sources of information on Christian Ompteda's last hours combine to the following effect:

The brigade commanded by Colonel Ompteda consisted of the 1st and 2nd Light, and the 5th and 8th Line Battalions of the King's German Legion. It belonged to General Charles Alten's division in the Army Corps of the Prince of Orange. Captain von Einem was Brigade Adjutant and First Lieutenant von Brandis personal *aide-de-camp* (last Hanoverian War Minister in 1866).

Immediately before the opening of the campaign of 1815 the battalions of the brigade were cantoned in different localities between Braine-le-Comte and Escaussines. The brigade staff was at Escaussines-Lalaing.

On June 15th the battalions of the brigade got orders to make haste with the cooking and giving the men their pay and to march to Escaussines, where the brigade was to concentrate. This was done towards 11 p.m., and the troops spent the night in a friendly wood near Escaussines.

The active spirit and zeal of the Colonel got the brigade on the march towards Nivelles with the first dawn of morning of June 16th. We reached that place about 10 a.m., and halted on the road in expectation of further orders. These soon arrived, and the brigade resumed its march towards Quatre Bras. Here, near the point where the roads cross, the colonel halted us, and made the men pile arms and rest. There were no other troops visible except a few Dutch cavalry and single officers of the general staff. It is therefore probable that Ompteda's brigade was the first formed body of English troops to make its appearance on the battlefield of Quatre Bras. But our brigade did not have the honour of taking part in that day's struggle. The Duke of Wellington had received information that Ney intended detaching a corps to turn our right flank, and so gain the road by Nivelles to Brussels. He therefore ordered the necessary counter movements to paralyse this plan. To that end, Ompteda's brigade, the first to hand was ordered to go back part of the way they had just come. On the march they met a Highland regiment and the Brunswick corps, who advanced in our place, and experienced severe losses as is well known.

A short distance beyond Nivelles (near the village of Arguennes, on the road to Mons) the brigade turned to the left from the main road, and took up a position before a cleft in the line of heights separating us from the enemy. At this point the first cannon shots announced the beginning of the battle of Quatre Bras. A division of Dutch troops marched in rear of the brigade, and formed the second line of our detached corps.

The afternoon passed, and the thunder pealed in our rear, but the expected enemy never appeared. Probably he had been convinced of the sufficiency of Wellington's precautionary measures, and withdrawn to his main body. This has furnished a motive for the reproaches of subsequent French writers against Marshal Ney, 'that he weakened his army at Quatre Bras by sending out useless detachments, and wasted time in useless marching backwards and forwards.' These gentlemen either ignored or suppressed the fact that a considerable part of Wellington's army was also detached by the prescribed counter-manoeuvre, so as to be unable to take actual part in the combat.

As it became evident towards evening that the enemy had given up his turning plan, our brigade marched back to Quatre Bras, arrived about ten as the last cannon shots were sounding and encamped for the night with their weary comrades on the battlefield.

On June 17th the Duke retired the whole army northwards to the position before the village of Waterloo, including the Hereditary Prince of Orange's corps which came by Genappe. General Alten's Division marched on a side-road which, skirting Sart-a-Mavelines and Bezy, joins the main road near Genappe. In the retreat which began towards midday Colonel Ompteda had the honourable task of forming a detached part of the rearguard with his brigade, destined to cover the right flank of the retiring army, as well as for the ordinary purposes of a rearguard. A byway which formed a chord to the curve described by the road from Quatre Bras to Genappe, and might have been extremely damaging to the retreat if in possession of the pursuing army, was confided to their care and courage.

The army had been already some time in retreat, and the enemy's advanced guard in sight before Ompteda's chivalrous temperament permitted him to withdraw his brigade. Its retreat then took place in perfect order and quietness, but in the full expectation of being shortly attacked by the enemy. To our surprise, however, only one cavalry detachment followed us with a couple of light guns, which saluted us from time to time with a few harmless shots. About parallel with Genappe the brigade entered a village (Bezy). This was occupied for an hour with the design of ensuring the main body of the army time to leave the defiles of the Genappe road behind them, before it would be possible for the enemy to press along our shorter route.

During the time we spent in this village, Ompteda's sense of righteousness was shown in his treatment of a little raid the soldiers made on the poultry of the inhabitants who had taken to flight. He at once put a stop to this very severely, with the explanation that the property of the subjects of a friendly country must, under all circumstances, be held sacred by the honest soldier, and this principle was not to be assailed with the excuse that 'the enemy would take it if we didn't'

The brigade was not, however, seriously attacked here, and ultimately continued its retreat. In the meantime, after a hot, close forenoon, the tremendous storm of rain, which has become historic, fell, and so softened the roads and fields that the men sank up to their shins, and the march was seriously impeded. This unexpected incident might have resulted unpleasantly for the brigade. When they reached the place where the bye-way again joins the main road close behind Genappe, a French Lancer regiment advanced out of that place. The English 7th Hussars tried to repel the Lancers, but without success. At this critical moment, when the brigade was in the greatest danger of being cut off, Ompteda displayed the most complete presence of mind and calmness in the dispositions he made. Now, however, the English Horse Guards flung themselves in an irresistible attack against the Lancers, scattered them like spray, and pursued them through Genappe. The brigade then obtained time to reach the end of the road, and unharmed and in good order to rejoin the main body of the rear-guard.

The position which the Duke of Wellington had chosen for the final determining struggle was on a gently rising ground extending east and west, and south of the little village of Mont St. Jean. Here the two roads, going northwards from Genappe and Nivelles, unite with the main road to Brussels. On a similar, parallel, and somewhat lower line of rising ground, about a cannon shot (of that period) further south, the French army advanced.

The depression between the two heights varied in depth. The road from Genappe crossed the middle of the heights. There it was cut across by a hollow way coming from Wavre in the south-east and going to Braine-la-Leud. The right wing of the Anglo-German line of battle lay east of the Nivelles Road, *appuyé* on the farm of Hougomont, the left by Papelotte southward of the road from Wavre, the centre on the intersection of the above-mentioned roads—Genappe, Mont St. Jean, and Wavre-Braine-la-Leud. The intersection itself was occupied by Ompteda's brigade as left wing of Alten's Division, north of the Wavre-Braine road, while on its right, in the direction of Braine lay the Hanoverian brigade of Kielmansegge. In the hollow along which the road runs, and to the south of the latter, stands on the Genappe road the farm of La Haye Sainte. The yard of it was protected with walls and hedges, with hedged gardens to the north and south. Along the northern garden hedge, in a cutting, ran a steeply scarped pathway eastwards to Papelotte. The farm of La Haye Sainte was occupied, as an important advance post, by the 2nd Light Battalion of the Legion (belonging to Ompteda's brigade), under the command of Major Baring. Near it, on the road, was the 1st Light Battalion. The whole was under the immediate command of the Hereditary Prince of Orange (the latter had accompanied Wellington's army during the last part of the war in Spain and the south of France, but without any command in it). The Prince was born on December 6th, 1792, and was therefore at the time a young gentleman of twenty-two, to whom the present formal command had had to be given, as he was the son of an English ally. He was an inexperienced apprentice in the school of war, but in other respects a young officer of great personal courage, coupled however with a naive princely sense of importance natural at the time, but serious for his subordinates.

The evening passed in comparative quiet, its silence interrupted only by a few cannon shots. The rain continued with trifling breaks throughout the night. It was, therefore, difficult to keep up the watch-fires, and the ground was trodden into deep mire, and most of the regiments had had little or no food since June 15th. The men and horses were provided with such nutriment as was possible; but what could be furnished was unfortunately by no means sufficient. Until break of day most of the troops remained in bivouac, numbed with cold and wet, and in a comfortless condition. Colonel Ompteda had been for some time at La Haye Sainte. Not satisfied with the means of defence which had been authorised by the commander of the corps, which he found insufficient, especially on account of the absence of artillery, he spent the night, wrapped only in his blue cloak, by the staff watch-fire of his own (the 5th Line) battalion.

"I would have willingly," writes a friend, "thrown a woollen blanket round his shoulders as a more efficient protection from the perpetual rain, were I not convinced beforehand that he would refuse it, as the men by superior orders, had not been allowed their blankets that night."

Probably on account of an expected surprise.

The Colonel sat silently, plunged in serious and profound reflection, like one of Ossian's heroes whose spirits-see the events of the coming day pass in cloudy procession.

This simple but graphic representation of the last night-watch of Christian Ompteda has been happily reproduced, as a perpetual memorial for the family, in a striking oil-painting by the talented and unfortunately too soon deceased painter, George Bergmann, of Hildesheim.

The morning and early forenoon of June 18th were spent by both sides in reconnaissances and preparation for the conflict. The Battalion Journal says:

At daybreak we got under arms. As the rain fell in streams, both armies remained quiet till midday, and our cooking proceeded. Reconnaissances were carried out on both sides, and we could distinguish Napoleon on his grey horse.

The total of the Duke of Wellington's troops was 55,088 men, with 116 guns. The rest of his army, about 15,000 men, were placed in the rear for the protection of Brussels. Only the English and the Legion could be reckoned on as trained and war-experienced soldiers, and they amounted to about 32,000 men. Opposed to them stood Napoleon's war-hardened veterans, 75,000 combatants, with 240 guns. For the rest the young Hanoverian troops maintained the fame of their colours with trifling exceptions, and the Dutch showed themselves no less capable in a general way, except one brigade, which left the field without serious resistance at the very commencement of the fight.

Towards half-past eleven the enemy began to move. The first attack was directed on the Anglo-German right wing, on the chateau of Hougomont. After that had failed, the enemy flung themselves on the centre, then La Haye Sainte, which was the position of Ompteda's brigade. The infantry pressed in such strong masses, a complete division, on the gardens and buildings of the farm, that the two Light battalions of the brigade were not sufficient alone to withstand such an attack. On that account, the 8th Line, stationed just in rear of this point on the left wing of the brigade, was sent to the front by the colonel to attack with the bayonet. The enemy's infantry gave way. But a mass of cavalry advanced, wholly hidden hitherto behind some rising ground, and fell on the men of the two battalions placed behind trees and hedges, and treated them to a sanguinary encounter, in which the 8th lost its commander, Lieutenant-Colonel von Schröder, 7 officers, and nearly no men. "The battalion lost its colours, and was so roughly handled that it could not be advanced during the rest of the day, but remained in square" (Battalion Journal). Nevertheless, this second attack of the enemy was victoriously repulsed with the help of Lord Uxbridge's heavy cavalry, brigade, the Life Guards.

Colonel Ompteda advanced the 5th Line in support of the 8th, and in this wild struggle his horse was shot under him. His aide-de-camp undertook the duty of bringing a fresh horse from the reserve.

During the second attack which now took place on Hougomont, the centre was left in peace. But when this was for the second time repulsed, the storm broke out again on the centre. Ompteda's brigade had to sustain a more than furious attack of cavalry, but the steadiness of the German battalions remained unshaken. Trusting to their invincible formation, they reserved their fire until the cavalry were close upon them, then rained in bullets which brought about confusion and destruction in the ranks.

A detachment of cuirassiers had already made four attacks on the 5th Battalion formed in square, and withdrawn to a safe hollow after each ineffectual charge. But the officer commanding those cavalry remained going up and down with the greatest coolness, *en vedette,* on a little piece of rising ground, looking out for a favourable moment to renew the attack. Colonel Ompteda, who was in the square, called on several men to set the square free from the observation of this Frenchman, but all the shots missed him, and the charge was repeated a fifth time. At last a sharp-shooter of the 1st Light Battalion, who had been brought wounded inside the square offered to make the attempt, and desired to be brought to the front for the purpose. His leg was smashed, and the great loss of blood had weakened him ; but the brave fellow took his faithful musket in hand, and *dropped* the courageous officer from his horse at the first shot.

The invincible squares withstood all attacks, and Baring's resolute sharpshooters were still maintaining their position in the farm of La Haye Sainte. Napoleon, grasping that all attacks on the English centre were fruitless unless he was in possession of this place, decided on a second more forcible attack. It was five o'clock, when three entire divisions advanced against the farm.

At this time the 5th Line received orders through an English *aide-de-camp* to advance against the enemy's infantry. The officer in command, Lieutenant-Colonel von Linsingen, at once deployed the square and went to the front. But the battalion had scarcely crossed the space between it and the hollow leading to the farm, and was about to ascend it, when the enemy's cavalry, behind the same height on the other side, broke on the right wing of the battalion, which must undoubtedly have been doubled up had not the English Life Guards from the rear charged and cut the enemy's cavalry to pieces.

Soon after this, Colonel Ompteda, still unmounted, came into the freshly formed square of his battalion, in its old position, and took the command. An *aide-de-camp* again galloped up from the direction of La Haye Sainte, and called out at some distance in English:

"Fifth battalion, deploy and advance!"

The colonel went out of the square to him, and said, also in English, and in a friendly manner:

"Would it not be advisable to advance in square, and not form line till close to the enemy's infantry?"

But when, after the complete justification for the suggestion furnished by the recent event, he received the abrupt reply: "God damn it! my order is to order you to deploy immediately!" Ompteda faced about and ordered the battalion to deploy and advance.

His anticipations were at once fulfilled. The battalion had barely deployed and got in motion when it was attacked by cavalry, concealed behind the rising ground. A new Hanoverian cavalry regiment which ought to have covered the advance had—the only one to do so on that day—unhappily left its place. This time, however, the square was fortunately re-formed before the enemy came within striking distance.

Battalion Journal:

The enemy made many cavalry attacks on the position of our Division, wherefore the battalions were formed in square. Only the 5th, owing to the nature of the ground, had to be always on the move, and alternately deploy and form square owing to its exposure to both arms. The battalion beat off three cavalry attacks, in one of which the square was not quite formed when the enemy was eight (sic) paces off. Our Brigadier and Battalion Commander, Colonel von Ompteda, seeing the critical nature of our position, did not leave us any more.

The pressure on La Haye Sainte increased. The farm was so closely surrounded on all sides that every bullet of the Jägers bored an enemy through. But the Frenchmen were not to be shaken. They stormed unceasingly against the gateway of the yard, which it had not been possible to close. Man by man they were bayoneted by the Hanoverians in the gateway, till a heap of slain assailants made a breastwork for the defenders.

But now the inspection of the ammunition store resulted in the discovery that it was already half expended. Baring therefore sent to the Brigadier for a fresh supply to be sent as quickly as possible. But it was impossible to provide this. The Jägers were armed with carbines, and there were no cartridges at hand to fit them. The wagons laden with them had got pushed back along the Brussels road in the confusion there prevailing, and never came on to the field, wherefore this demand, like a second which followed it, remained unsatisfied. In the meantime, the supply of ammunition had come down to three or four rounds per man!

In this extremity Colonel Ompteda sent the skirmishing company of the 5th Line to the front, to La Haye Sainte. He did so with a heavy heart. The battalion had already, the day before, had to give up its Grenadier company to keep communications open on the Brussels road. Now he was losing the second flank company as well. The two now left were thus reduced to a little band of *scarce two hundred*. (Battalion Journal, 227.)

The company sent to La Haye Sainte lost on the way, by cannon fire, at that moment raging furiously on the centre, its captain, von Wurmb, and 14 men. A passing ball came into the middle of the Duke of Wellington's staff, which was halted at this dangerous place, and took one of his officers off his horse. The Duke cast a brief glance down at him, and calmly put his Dollond (field-glass) again to his eye.

Baring had in the meantime got from Ompteda another reinforcement of 200 Nassauers. But all this could not replace the lacking ammunition, and La Haye Sainte had to be evacuated. The defenders withdrew from the yard to the northward garden, and thence to the 1st Light Battalion in the hollow. The French pressed after them, and the struggle began afresh. The 1st Light lost thirteen officers and the 2nd eleven.

The rising ground immediately to the south of La Haye Sainte was occupied by French horse-artillery only, for Napoleon was determined to break the centre at any price. The hollow between La Haye Sainte and Hougomont was wholly in the possession of Napoleon, and full of his cuirassiers. Infantry and cavalry columns made attacks in force alternately, supported by their artillery, which were repulsed, but not without enormous loss to the Allies, who had *no artillery* to oppose with here.

From this time forward Ompteda's brigade had to suffer severely from cannon and small-arm fire, which proceeded continuously from La Haye Sainte. The 5th Line lost its adjutant, Lieutenant Schuck. The colonel mounted his horse, as his *aide-de-camp* was still hunting about among the reserve horses, and halted close to the battalion of which he had given the command again to Lieutenant-Colonel Linsingen, for the square of this weakened band had so shrunk that there was no room inside it.

It was about six in the evening when there appeared on the ascent in the left rear of La Haye Sainte a fresh large body of infantry, estimated at about one thousand men. This was Napoleon's last general attack, the last throw of the desperate gamester, for Bülow's troops, pressing in from the east, had already taken Planchenoit, and were threatening the French line of retreat to Genappe.

The adjutant of the Prince of Orange, Lord Somerset, came galloping to Colonel Ompteda with orders to repel this body of infantry. The colonel replied that it was "impossible, because the English Cavalry of the Guard, hitherto in the rear of the battalion, had been ordered to the left wing, so that the French cuirassiers, whose helmets could be plainly discerned in the low ground, would attack the battalion as soon as it deployed and moved from its present secure position." The adjutant rode back. Soon after, the Hereditary Prince of Orange appeared with General von Alten. Alten repeated the order, and Ompteda his opinion: "In any case we ought to be supported by cavalry" (Battalion Journal). The Hereditary Prince explained: "The cavalry visible behind the rising ground were Dutch." When the young commander had been finally convinced of the injustice and impossibility of his view, he said in a sharp, peremptory manner, with the fatal self-sufficiency of military ignorance: "I must still repeat my order to attack in line with the bayonet, and I will listen to no further arguments." The colonel merely replied in a loud voice: "Well, I will," drew his sword, and, contrary to his own better conviction, and knowing that he led his men to certain and useless destruction, ordered the battalion to form line. Then he said to Lieutenant-Colonel Linsingen: "Try and save my two nephews," and rode forth alone in front of his battalion.

The little band of 200 rapidly climbed the further side of the hollow. There they were received with a murderous fire of musketry. Ompteda called out: "Follow me, brave comrades!" and galloped into the midst of the foe, who, in all arms, filled the level ground between the hollow way and the northern garden hedge. But the battalion could only follow its colonel a little way. With a "Hurrah!" they forced the enemy back, but the cuirassiers were already on them from the right, in flank and rear. The line was doubled up, broken, and cut to pieces. Lieutenant-Colonel Linsingen lay for a short time under his wounded horse. When he could rise, he saw that his battalion was annihilated. Close to him stood the colonel's two nephews, Christian and Louis. He seized both boys by the arms, and sprang back into the hollow with them in spite of their struggles, so that the colonel's last request was faithfully carried out. Around him collected six officers of his battalion and *eighteen* unwounded men. The Brigade Adjutant, von Einem, four officers, and a *hundred and thirty* non-commissioned officers and men remained dead, or severely wounded, on the blood-stained field. The few others were missing, quarter being neither given nor taken.

The Battalion Journal describes the entire loss: "12 officers, 12 sergeants, 1 drummer, 128 men."

In the meantime, one of the captains, Captain Berger, saw the colonel ride alone into the mass of the enemy.

"I hastened," he says, "to follow him as quickly as the miry state of the ground permitted. I kept my eyes on him and on the enemy. I saw that the French had their muskets pointed at the colonel, but did not fire. The officers struck the men's barrels up with their swords. They seemed astonished at the extraordinary calm approach of the solitary horseman, whose white plume showed him to be an officer of high rank. He soon reached the enemy's line of infantry before the garden hedge. He jumped in, and I clearly saw how his sword-strokes smote the shakos off. The nearest French officer looked on with admiration without attempting to check the attack. When I looked round for my company I found I was alone. Turning my eyes again to the enemy. I saw *Colonel Ompteda, in the mid-most throng of the enemy's infantry and cavalry, sink from his horse and vanish!*

So died he—a man of noble soul, distinguished in mind and character, fitted to render his Fatherland further high services—a hero's death!

Whether he, perhaps, sought it, excited by the fate of his battalion, wounded by the obstinate and offensive behaviour of his young commander, who can tell?

His corpse was found by his *aide-de-camp*, von Brandis, hard by the garden hedge, in the late evening of this glorious but awful day. It was plundered, but fully clothed. The singed appearance of the bullet-hole in the collar of his coat showed that the fatal ball had been fired into his neck close to him in the last desperate struggle amid the masses of the foe.

Next morning Christian Ompteda's mortal remains were buried with those of ten other officers of his brigade in a common grave, hard by. the road opposite the gate of La Haye Sainte, where he has won himself a place for ever. Honour to his memory, and peace to his ashes!

Here end the reports of his surviving comrades.

A stone monument now covers the grave. It bears the inscription:

To the memory of their comrades who died a hero's death here in the ever memorable battle of June 18th, 1815.

At their head stands the name, Colonel and Brigadier Christian von Ompteda. His name may be similarly read by posterity on the Waterloo memorial of his own town of Hanover. Christian's great leader has also erected a monument to the fallen hero for the world and history, more durable than stone or brass.

In his first report of the battle, dated Waterloo, June 19th, 1815, the Duke of Wellington writes to the Duke of York:

I must, however, particularly mention for His Royal Highness' approbation: Lieutenant-General Charles Baron Alten, Colonel Baron Ompteda, Major-General Lord E. Somerset, Major-General Sir W. Ponsonby.

And his honoured friend, Lieutenant-General Charles Alten, further adds in his report from Brussels to the Duke of Cambridge, June 20th 1815:

These two days have certainly cost us dearly, and it is with hearty regret that I have to inform your Royal Highness that the greater part of our most distinguished officers have fallen. Among these I specially mention Colonels von Ompteda and du Plat. It is, however, a consolation to know that they have covered their graves with renown.

Fifty years later, a German poet (C. F. Scherenberg) sang of Waterloo. With him also Christian Ompteda found a place among the highest. The Duke of Wellington is supposed to be riding over the field the following day, and says:

But what,
Man of the Legion, art thou digging there
With love's own fury from the miry ground?

The Soldier. A treasure, my commander, that I seek,
The body of my Colonel, Ompteda.
They ordered him to march to certain death.
He marched to death because they ordered him.
See there his head! A regiment of horse
Rode over him, and yet the brave old face
Looks just as if still smiting at his foes—
Where he is now.

The Duke. And well he may! For he did conquer death,
And not death him. I too must bend before
The silent laurel crown by duty earned.
Let him lie still where he met his dire death,
No sand were lighter.

Christian Ompteda, with his serious sense of duty, would surely have repudiated this sonorous glorification. He himself would have chosen no other inscription than the simple words of Blücher's first report to his wife:

Battlefield of Belle-Alliance—
What I promised I have kept.

It was not his destiny to share the blessed hero's death within sight of complete victory before his closing eyes, like his friend Scharnhorst. His noble soul, on which the glorious sun of full success had seldom smiled, departed under the cloud of fully supposed failure, in the righteous wrath of a tried warrior at the insulting and silly treatment he had received, in the angry despair of a faithful and experienced leader who had to lead his little band into sheer, purposeless destruction as a sacrifice to ignorant youthful presumption. A hero in the deed, and a greater one in his obedient self-control. Faithful unto death.

Palmam qui meruit, ferat!

LEONAUR

ALSO FROM LEONAUR

AVAILABLE IN SOFTCOVER OR HARDCOVER WITH DUST JACKET

CAPTAIN OF THE 95th (Rifles) *by Jonathan Leach*—An officer of Wellington's Sharpshooters during the Peninsular, South of France and Waterloo Campaigns of the Napoleonic Wars.

BUGLER AND OFFICER OF THE RIFLES *by William Green & Harry Smith* With the 95th (Rifles) during the Peninsular & Waterloo Campaigns of the Napoleonic Wars

BAYONETS, BUGLES AND BONNETS by *James 'Thomas' Todd*—Experiences of hard soldiering with the 71st Foot - the Highland Light Infantry - through many battles of the Napoleonic wars including the Peninsular & Waterloo Campaigns

THE ADVENTURES OF A LIGHT DRAGOON *by George Farmer & G.R. Gleig*—A cavalryman during the Peninsular & Waterloo Campaigns, in captivity & at the siege of Bhurtpore, India

THE COMPLEAT RIFLEMAN HARRIS *by Benjamin Harris as told to & transcribed by Captain Henry Curling*—The adventures of a soldier of the 95th (Rifles) during the Peninsular Campaign of the Napoleonic Wars

WITH WELLINGTON'S LIGHT CAVALRY *by William Tomkinson*—The Experiences of an officer of the 16th Light Dragoons in the Peninsular and Waterloo campaigns of the Napoleonic Wars.

SURTEES OF THE RIFLES by *William Surtees*—A Soldier of the 95th (Rifles) in the Peninsular campaign of the Napoleonic Wars.

ENSIGN BELL IN THE PENINSULAR WAR *by George Bell*—The Experiences of a young British Soldier of the 34th Regiment 'The Cumberland Gentlemen' in the Napoleonic wars.

WITH THE LIGHT DIVISION *by John H. Cooke*—The Experiences of an Officer of the 43rd Light Infantry in the Peninsula and South of France During the Napoleonic Wars

NAPOLEON'S IMPERIAL GUARD: FROM MARENGO TO WATERLOO by *J. T. Headley*—This is the story of Napoleon's Imperial Guard from the bearskin caps of the grenadiers to the flamboyance of their mounted chasseurs, their principal characters and the men who commanded them.

BATTLES & SIEGES OF THE PENINSULAR WAR by *W. H. Fitchett*—Corunna, Busaco, Albuera, Ciudad Rodrigo, Badajos, Salamanca, San Sebastian & Others

LEONAUR

ALSO FROM LEONAUR

AVAILABLE IN SOFTCOVER OR HARDCOVER WITH DUST JACKET

WELLINGTON AND THE PYRENEES CAMPAIGN VOLUME I: FROM VITORIA TO THE BIDASSOA *by F. C. Beatson*—The final phase of the campaign in the Iberian Peninsula.

WELLINGTON AND THE INVASION OF FRANCE VOLUME II: THE BIDASSOA TO THE BATTLE OF THE NIVELLE *by F. C. Beatson*—The second of Beatson's series on the fall of Revolutionary France published by Leonaur, the reader is once again taken into the centre of Wellington's strategic and tactical genius.

WELLINGTON AND THE FALL OF FRANCE VOLUME III: THE GAVES AND THE BATTLE OF ORTHEZ *by F. C. Beatson*—This final chapter of F. C. Beatson's brilliant trilogy shows the 'captain of the age' at his most inspired and makes all three books essential additions to any Peninsular War library.

NAVAL BATTLES OF THE NAPOLEONIC WARS *by W. H. Fitchett*—Cape St. Vincent, the Nile, Cadiz, Copenhagen, Trafalgar & Others

SERGEANT GUILLEMARD: THE MAN WHO SHOT NELSON? *by Robert Guillemard*—A Soldier of the Infantry of the French Army of Napoleon on Campaign Throughout Europe

WITH THE GUARDS ACROSS THE PYRENEES *by Robert Batty*—The Experiences of a British Officer of Wellington's Army During the Battles for the Fall of Napoleonic France, 1813.

A STAFF OFFICER IN THE PENINSULA *by E. W. Buckham*—An Officer of the British Staff Corps Cavalry During the Peninsula Campaign of the Napoleonic Wars

THE LEIPZIG CAMPAIGN: 1813—NAPOLEON AND THE "BATTLE OF THE NATIONS" *by F. N. Maude*—Colonel Maude's analysis of Napoleon's campaign of 1813.

BUGEAUD: A PACK WITH A BATON *by Thomas Robert Bugeaud*—The Early Campaigns of a Soldier of Napoleon's Army Who Would Become a Marshal of France.

TWO LEONAUR ORIGINALS

SERGEANT NICOL *by Daniel Nicol*—The Experiences of a Gordon Highlander During the Napoleonic Wars in Egypt, the Peninsula and France.

WATERLOO RECOLLECTIONS *by Frederick Llewellyn*—Rare First Hand Accounts, Letters, Reports and Retellings from the Campaign of 1815.

LEONAUR

ALSO FROM LEONAUR

AVAILABLE IN SOFTCOVER OR HARDCOVER WITH DUST JACKET

THE JENA CAMPAIGN: 1806 *by F. N. Maude*—The Twin Battles of Jena & Auerstadt Between Napoleon's French and the Prussian Army.

PRIVATE O'NEIL *by Charles O'Neil*—The recollections of an Irish Rogue of H. M. 28th Regt.—The Slashers— during the Peninsula & Waterloo campaigns of the Napoleonic wars.

ROYAL HIGHLANDER by *James Anton*—A soldier of H.M 42nd (Royal) Highlanders during the Peninsular, South of France & Waterloo Campaigns of the Napoleonic Wars.

CAPTAIN BLAZE *by Elzéar Blaze*—Elzéar Blaze recounts his life and experiences in Napoleon's army in a well written, articulate and companionable style.

LEJEUNE VOLUME 1 by *Louis-François Lejeune*—The Napoleonic Wars through the Experiences of an Officer on Berthier's Staff.

LEJEUNE VOLUME 2 by *Louis-François Lejeune*—The Napoleonic Wars through the Experiences of an Officer on Berthier's Staff.

FUSILIER COOPER *by John S. Cooper*—Experiences in the 7th (Royal) Fusiliers During the Peninsular Campaign of the Napoleonic Wars and the American Campaign to New Orleans.

CAPTAIN COIGNET *by Jean-Roch Coignet*—A Soldier of Napoleon's Imperial Guard from the Italian Campaign to Russia and Waterloo.

FIGHTING NAPOLEON'S EMPIRE by *Joseph Anderson*—The Campaigns of a British Infantryman in Italy, Egypt, the Peninsular & the West Indies During the Napoleonic Wars.

CHASSEUR BARRES *by Jean-Baptiste Barres*—The experiences of a French Infantryman of the Imperial Guard at Austerlitz, Jena, Eylau, Friedland, in the Peninsular, Lutzen, Bautzen, Zinnwald and Hanau during the Napoleonic Wars.

MARINES TO 95TH (RIFLES) by *Thomas Fernyhough*—The military experiences of Robert Fernyhough during the Napoleonic Wars.

HUSSAR ROCCA by *Albert Jean Michel de Rocca*—A French cavalry officer's experiences of the Napoleonic Wars and his views on the Peninsular Campaigns against the Spanish, British And Guerilla Armies.

SERGEANT BOURGOGNE by *Adrien Bourgogne*—With Napoleon's Imperial Guard in the Russian Campaign and on the Retreat from Moscow 1812 - 13.

9 781846 774188